The EVERYTHING®
Freemasons Book

Dear Reader,

To anyone who knows me, it comes as no surprise that I remain intrigued by all things mysterious. Add in a bit of history and controversy and I'm all over it. It should be said up front that I'm not a member of any Masonic organization, and therefore have no bias toward the Masons or to any historical, anti-Masonic, or conspiratorial information. I'm simply a career journalist and writer who on any given day is caught between Spock-like logic and Emily Dickinson perceptions. In this case, that served me well.

A study of Freemasonry is right up my alley and, as it turns out, it is an alley that has splintered into many more alleys filled with ritual, allegory, symbolism, history, and controversy. No matter your opinions on Freemasonry, you can't help but admire a group that has managed to cultivate so many strong and motivated individuals while at the same time enduring a load of adversity. My sincerest hope is that you'll find this subject, as I did, to be utterly engaging, from its rich history to its alleged conspiracies, and that in doing so you gain a much better understanding of the fascinating world of Freemasonry.

Barb Karg and
John K. Young, Ph.D.

The EVERYTHING® Series

Editorial

Publishing Director	Gary M. Krebs
Associate Managing Editor	Laura M. Daly
Associate Copy Chief	Brett Palana-Shanahan
Acquisitions Editor	Paula Munier
Development Editor	Rachel Engelson
Associate Production Editor	Casey Ebert

Production

Director of Manufacturing	Susan Beale
Associate Director of Production	Michelle Roy Kelly
Cover Design	Paul Beatrice Matt LeBlanc Erick DaCosta
Design and Layout	Colleen Cunningham Holly Curtis Sorae Lee
Series Cover Artist	Barry Littmann

Visit the entire Everything® Series at *www.everything.com*

THE
EVERYTHING®
FREEMASONS
BOOK

Unlock the secrets of this ancient and mysterious society

John K. Young, Ph.D., and Barb Karg

Adams Media
Avon, Massachusetts

For my touchstones—
Ma, Pop, Chrissy, the Blonde Bombshell, Jeans, and especially Rick.
And to all Freemasons who strive to make themselves
and the world a better place.—B.K.

An Everything® Series Book.
Everything® and everything.com® are registered trademarks of F+W Publications, Inc.

Published by Adams Media, an F+W Publications Company
57 Littlefield Street, Avon, MA 02322 U.S.A.
www.adamsmedia.com

ISBN: 1-59869-059-0
Printed in the United States of America.

J   I   H   G   F   E   D   C   B   A

Library of Congress Cataloging-in-Publication Data
available from the publisher.

This book is available at quantity discounts for bulk purchases.
For information, please call 1-800-872-5627.

Contents

Acknowledgments

Many stellar individuals contributed to the making of this book. I'd like to thank the consummate professionals at Adams Media, Inc., especially Acquisitions Editor Paula Munier whom I adore, and Development Editor Rachel Engelson who was seriously on the ball. You gals are the bomb! I'd also like to thank Laura Daly, Brett Palana-Shanahan, Sue Beale, Kate Powers, Andrea Norville, and Holly Curtis. Thanks as well to John Young for his contributions to the book.

I'd also like to thank George and Trudi Karg and my sister Chrissy for their support, Jeans for all her help, Ellen and Jim, Dale, Anne and Terry, Kathy, Jim S., Jim K., Jim V., Karla, and my beloved Scribe Tribe. I love y'all way more than chocolate.

Most especially, I'd like to express my thanks and love to my better half, Rick Sutherland, who, two hours after this book was completed and sent, survived a horrific car accident. The research he did for the book, especially Chapter 16, was nothing short of astounding. And also to my dear Pop who in the same week survived his own harrowing medical ordeal. Amazing men, both of you.

—Barb Karg

Top Ten Things You'll Learn about Freemasons
Through Reading This Book

1. Freemasonry is the largest and oldest fraternal organization in the world and has many famous members.

2. The true origins of Freemasonry are a mystery. Are they evolved from Solomon's Temple, the Knights Templar, or Medieval Masonic Guilds?

3. Freemasonry isn't just for men; thousands of women and young adults belong to Masonic organizations.

4. During World War II Freemasons all over Europe were persecuted and killed, their Temples pillaged, and their fraternal order banished.

5. Anti-Masons speculate that Freemasons are Satanists and Luciferians, but that has now been disproven.

6. The Masonic family of organizations give over two million dollars a day to charities all over the world.

7. Freemasonry is not a religion or a religious cult, but their common belief in a Supreme Being has bound brothers together for centuries.

8. Many Freemasons took part in the American Revolution, including patriots, statesmen, and founding fathers.

9. The eye and the broken pyramid on the American dollar bill are not related to Masonry, but the Brotherhood is replete with all kinds of symbols, including many tools of the ancient stonemasons.

10. Many of the practices that Masons have been accused of are the result of misinterpretations.

Foreword

▶ Being a Freemason is an honor, not only because it's the world's oldest and largest fraternal organization—one that has for centuries attracted many famous members—but because it helps individuals grow by seeking knowledge, personal fulfillment, and spiritual enlightenment. Masons are individuals from all walks of life who are devoted to their families and communities and dedicated to the Craft they spend their lifetime studying.

According to its classic definition, Masonry is a "system of morality, veiled in allegory, and illustrated by symbols." To non-Masons that may sound confusing, but in reality it translates to a group of benevolent individuals who get together for social and charitable events while at the same time learning about the true spirit and history of the fraternity.

Contrary to popular belief, Masonry is not a religion or a cult, though one of the Brotherhood's primary requirements is a belief in a Supreme Being. The Craft is nonsectarian and open to all individuals who wish to learn more about themselves and others, and work to make the world a better place for themselves, their families, and society as a whole. Masons are seekers of knowledge who study the history of the Craft and rise to various levels by taking part in historic rites and rituals. In truth, there's nothing mysterious about Freemasonry, which has for centuries been burdened with the dubious title "secret society." Save for a few modes of distinction among Brothers, most everything there is to know about the Craft can be found in books and on the Internet.

What most people don't realize is that Masonry, despite all the various appendant and concordant bodies that are open to men, also includes many organizations that are open to women, young adults, and children, including Order of the Eastern Star, Daughters of the Nile, Order of the Rainbow Girls, Job's Daughters, and the Order of the DeMolay.

All of the organizations—both national and international—that comprise the Masonic family are dedicated to charitable causes, whether they are local or global. Some groups, like the Ancient Arabic Order of the Nobles of the Mystic Shrine, commonly known as Shriners, are highly revered for their tireless charitable contributions. Every day millions of dollars are given to charity by various Masonic organizations in the hope of making life easier for those in need.

The study of Freemasonry is a fascinating journey through history from the construction of King Solomon's Temple to the Legend of Hiram Abiff, and the eloquent Knights Templar. Our rituals and initiation rites are replete with symbolism that pays homage to our antiquity and the hardworking masons of the Medieval Age. But as anyone who is part of the Craft can attest, the basis for Masonry is friendship that endures no matter the circumstances or surroundings. That, coupled with the fact that the Brotherhood is enveloped in history, and perhaps a touch of mystery, makes the Masonic journey an enlightening experience that is shared by all who choose to join.

Introduction

▶ What do you think of when you hear the word *Freemason*? Does religion or a religious cult come to mind? Or do you think of mystery, secrecy, conspiracies, and blood oaths? Perhaps you shiver at thoughts of Satanism, Lucifer worship, and Jack the Ripper? If you do, then this book will permanently alleviate your fears and perhaps shed new light on a subject that bears close examination, not only for its historical triumphs and tragedies, but for its modern-day survival and tenacity.

Those who are unfamiliar with Freemasonry may well conjure up images of a secret society whose devoted followers worship Pagan Gods, hold whispered gatherings behind locked doors, and communicate using passwords and secret gestures. But they would be wrong. There is nothing cultish, evil, conspiratorial, or Satanic about the Freemasons.

Freemasons are the oldest fraternal organization in the world, a charitable group of knowledge seekers who strive to enlighten themselves morally and spiritually while making the world a better place for their families and communities. They are not a religion or a cult or a shady group of men plotting world domination. They are a nonsectarian group of brothers bound together by friendship and common goals and beliefs. They are men who honor their families, God, country, duty, and each other, and they have done so for centuries.

The term *secret society* is often used to describe the Brotherhood, but that's a misnomer. As compared to most organizations they're about as secretive as your local bank. A more apt description of the fraternity would be using the term *private* or perhaps a society with secrets much the same as any college fraternity. It's true that their lodge meetings are held in private, but what roundtable of corporate officers doesn't shut the door when having a meeting?

This book examines all aspects of the Brotherhood, from its alleged origins to its structure, history, membership, symbolism, legends, conspiracies, and everything in between. The history of the Craft is a fascinating study that, depending on your opinion of their origin, dates back to the wondrous construction of the Temple of Solomon, the valiant Knights Templar of the Crusades, or the industrious Medieval Age of stonemasons. No matter what the true origin of Masonry, the theories and speculation surrounding its history are a grand enticement.

The same holds true for the Masonic rituals, degree ceremonies, and teachings, which form a richly painted masterpiece of allegory, legend, and symbolism that is woven into the canvas of the Craft. In many ways, the Masons are an educational institution, its members learning about themselves and mankind, and imparting that wisdom to those in need. This is quite obvious when you realize how many organizations are part of the Masonic family, and the millions of men, women, and young adults who are part of Masonry.

What is perhaps most surprising in one respect is how much the Masons have been persecuted over the centuries, especially during times of war. Much of that information is left out of studies of the history of Freemasonry it seems, especially for an organization based in antiquity. But there again, it might well be expected when one is burdened with the moniker of "secret society." In this book, however, their history is detailed throughout—from ancient to modern times—as well it should be for a group that has survived eras both good and tumultuous and continues to flourish.

The Masonic legacy is one that includes many famous individuals and freethinkers who ran with the notion that the world and everyone in it are capable of great endeavors without limitations. That speaks volumes about the Brotherhood, no matter how many conspiracies beam down from the sky. History is told by those who survive and those who find their tales captivating and inspirational. And it sure doesn't hurt if there's a touch of Masonic mystery along for the ride.

chapter 1

Who Are the Freemasons?

Freemasonry is the oldest and largest fraternal organization in the world. It is a social and educational group well known for its philanthropic work with numerous charities. Often called a "secret society," the fraternity, arguably more misunderstood than elusive, has attracted and nurtured thousands of individuals and communities over the centuries. Despite all the speculation and conspiracies surrounding the Brotherhood, or perhaps because of them, the bond between Freemasons has endured and flourished.

Veil of Secrecy

Everyone loves a good secret, especially when they're on the receiving end of it. If you don't happen to be "in the know," however, the mere mention of the word *secret* begins gnawing away at the psyche, winding its way through indifference and frenzy until it reaches full paranoid maturity. Freemasons have lived with the moniker "secret society" for a very long time, and while during ancient and Medieval eras it can be argued that they were more secretive, it doesn't necessarily apply to the modern age. Or does it?

FACT

The classic definition of Freemasonry is that it's a "system of morality, veiled in allegory, and illustrated by symbols."

It's fair to say that most individuals don't really know much about Freemasonry, which has undoubtedly led to its mysterious reputation. What Freemasonry isn't, however, can be stated easily enough. It's not a religion or a religious cult. Its members are not Satanists or Luciferians. Its rituals are not bloody oaths to the death. The brethren has no connection to the Holy Grail or to the Knights Templar of the Crusades. They're not a political organization, and above all, they're not a secret group of powerful men hell bent on achieving world domination.

What Freemasonry is all about is much easier to convey. At its simplest definition, Freemasons are a benevolent, social, charitable organization whose members seek to learn more about themselves in order to benefit their families and communities. Masons are knowledge seekers, their fraternal education focusing on lessons that help them on a journey to achieve moral and spiritual enlightenment. They are nonsectarian, and while their membership must profess a belief in a *Supreme Being*, it can be any Deity. Individuals of all faiths are welcome to join.

So what's all the hoopla about? Why is so little known about such a historic organization? Why so much controversy? In truth, there is plenty of information on Freemasonry both in print and on the Web, but more often than not it's a bit confusing and often limited to a specific opinion or theory. At the root of the problem is, perhaps, their alleged secrecy, but in reality all Masons are free to acknowledge their membership, and their rules, constitutions, rituals, and ceremonies have all been written about publicly. It stands to reason that if the Masons were indeed a secret society, none of this information would even be known.

Freemasonry is often referred to as *Masonry,* the *Brotherhood,* or the *Craft.* Their members are called *brothers,* and the membership within a lodge is referred to as *brethren.*

Steeped in History

In reading these pages, one will see that there are no definitive answers when it comes to the origin of Freemasonry. Despite the astounding amount of information available on the Brotherhood including literature, historical records, documentaries, archives, Web sites, legends, expert commentary, anti-Masonic conjecture, and conspiratorial speculation, there remain many diverse opinions in regard to who they really are, what they do, and how they evolved.

From Solomon to the New World

Historians, scholars, writers, and researchers have dedicated an impressive amount of ink and energy in attempting to discover the true origin of Freemasonry. It's a subject that to this day remains a constant source of debate. One theory goes back as far as the construction of King Solomon's Temple in Jerusalem during the eighth century B.C. One of the legends that permeates Masonic rituals and teachings revolves around King Solomon's Master Mason Hiram Abiff. His story and tragic death play a great role in Freemasonry.

Many individuals have speculated that Freemasons are somehow linked to the valiant Knights Templar, an order of warrior monks who fought during the Crusades. Though no proven links have been established, there has been much written about the Masons and their possible connection to the Templars and by association to such legendary artifacts as the Holy Grail and the Ark of the Covenant.

Another school of thought is that Freemasons evolved from Medieval Masonic Guilds, but the generally accepted beginning of organized Masonry is the formation of the Grand Lodge of England in 1717.

A Controversial Fraternity

There have definitely been times in Masonic history when controversy has plagued the Brotherhood, and it was those early controversies that led to a new breed of critic called an anti-Mason. Anti-Masons have proven to be a constant, and sometimes deadly, force to be reckoned with.

In the past, there has been no shortage of theories when it comes to the writings and ritual practices of the Brotherhood. In regard to the latter, much has been made of the alleged "blood oaths" initiates are made to endure, which in reality are strictly symbolic and relate to the Legend of Hiram Abiff.

FACT

Famous anti-Masons include Adolf Hitler, Benito Mussolini, Millard Fillmore, Pope Pius IX, Edgar Allan Poe, Hermann Göring, General Francisco Franco, and Pat Robertson.

In relation to Masonic writings, conspiracists and religious groups have had a field day, choosing to analyze and ultimately misinterpret Masonic literature and even portray the Brotherhood as Satanists and Lucifer worshippers. Unfortunately, these misunderstandings are clearly the result of allegory and semantics taken out of context.

Principles of Freemasonry

Freemasons strive to help make the world a better place for themselves, their families, and their communities. In order to do that, they subscribe to certain principles and virtues which give them strength as individuals while at the same time solidifying their bond as brothers. Masons are independent men who work toward peace, love, and fraternity, and who shun all forms of ignorance and tyranny. They believe very strongly in family, country, and God, and take very seriously their moral and spiritual values, the first of which are brotherly love, relief, and truth.

Brotherly Love, Relief, and Truth

There are three great tenets, or principles, of Freemasonry—brotherly love, relief, and truth. Brotherly love embraces the concept of equality among men, especially in an organization where men of all statures, professions, and faiths bind together in tolerance and respect for their fellow man. That show of fraternal love is especially strong in regard to religion, as each member privately practices his own faith, yet is bound to his brethren by their unified belief in a Supreme Being.

Fraternal bonds are further strengthened by the concept of relief, with brothers working together to help those in distress. It is, in fact, the duty of all Masons to show compassion, sympathy, and aid to all who suffer, no matter the cause. This applies not only to fellow brethren, but to all individuals who require assistance in troubled times.

Brotherly love, relief, and truth are highly symbolic. Brotherly love represents a column of strength that seeks to bind the brethren to one another as one big family. Relief is emblematic of a column of beauty, its ornaments symbolic of joyful tears or prayers of gratitude. The column of wisdom represents truth, which permeates the sanctity of the lodge.

Truth is, perhaps, the touchstone of the three great tenets, as it philosophically pervades all aspects of Freemasonry. As a tenet it signifies the foundation of all virtue, and that a man must be sincere, honest, and straightforward in his expression. To Masons, truth is a Divine attribute that drives each man's conduct. To be true to oneself, to one's family, to mankind, and to God, moves one closer to the truth of pure spirit. The pursuit of wisdom, understanding, and ultimately, knowledge cannot be obtained without truth.

The Three Virtues

Masons are driven by many different virtues, but three of the most important are faith, hope, and charity. Masonic teachings of these virtues begin at a candidate's first initiation ceremony, with the Rite of Destitution (see Chapter 5). During the ritual lecture he learns of Jacob's ladder and its three rounds: "the greatest of these is charity; for faith is lost in sight, hope ends in fruition, but charity extends beyond the grave, through the boundless realms of eternity."

FACT

In ancient times a nymph or maiden grasping a bouquet of blossoming flowers was a symbol of hope. In modern Masonry, hope is symbolically represented by a virgin leaning against an anchor.

For an initiate, faith is synonymous with trust and confidence, especially in God. The description of faith being "lost in sight" refers to the fact that faith isn't seen, but can be demonstrated. Once an individual has established faith in God, he attains hope, which in this scenario represents immortality. Charity as a Masonic virtue is an extension of grace, a gift that brothers freely give to all who require support. Masons firmly believe in these virtues and the practice of them toward achieving a higher moral standard.

The Supreme Being

One of the main requirements an individual must have in order to join the Freemasons is a belief in a Supreme Being and immortality of the soul. The term Supreme Being refers to Deity, and being that Masonry is nonsectarian and individuals of all religions are welcome, each Mason's Supreme Being is different. The more commonly used term among the brethren is *Grand*

Architect of the Universe. The only individuals who aren't eligible to apply to the Craft are atheists.

QUESTION?

What does the letter "G" stand for?
One of the most visible Masonic symbols is a square and compass with the letter "G" in the middle. The "G" originally stood for geometry, but it later came to signify God. It also stands for Grand or Great Architect of the Universe.

Masonry is not a religion and it doesn't offer salvation, but its members do have faith. One of the overriding rules of the Craft is that the brethren may never discuss religion or politics in a lodge. Masons believe that how an individual chooses to worship is private and done of his own accord. They encourage members to pursue their faith, but they never interfere in anyone's religious undertakings. Inside every lodge is a Volume of the Sacred Law. In the United States, this is typically the Holy Bible, but the sacred text varies depending on a lodge's membership. During initiation rites, a man can have any sacred text he chooses laid open on the altar or table.

Landmarks of Freemasonry

Like many mainstream organizations, Freemasons have landmarks that define Masonry and serve to guide the brethren in their fraternal pursuits. The first list of General Regulations was compiled in 1720 by the Grand Master of England and approved by the Grand Lodge three years later. In those regulations, however, the landmarks were not clearly defined.

In 1858, revered Masonic writer Albert Gallatin Mackey outlined twenty-five landmarks which he later published in *Text Book of Masonic Jurisprudence.* Many of his landmarks were generally accepted and adopted by various lodges, but have since been adapted. As a benchmark, most lodges and Grand Lodges agree on seven of Mackey's landmarks:

1. Monotheism is the sole dogma of Freemasonry.

2. The ultimate lesson of Masonic philosophy is immortality of the soul.
3. The Volume of the Sacred Law is indispensable in a lodge.
4. An integral part of Craft Masonry is the legend of the third degree, which tells of the construction of Solomon's Temple.
5. Masonic modes of recognition are to be kept inviolate.
6. Symbolism derived from the operative art of Masonry, or tools of the trade, are to remain intact.
7. A Mason must be an adult male who is born free.

Landmarks by definition are historic and unchangeable precepts, but given that Masonic lodges are self-governed, these precepts can vary.

Why Join a "Secret" Fraternity?

Individuals who join the Freemasons are amid impressive company. Over the centuries, thousands of individuals from all over the world and from all walks of life have taken part in the Craft. Its historic membership is replete with royalty, aristocrats, presidents, politicians, scientists, adventurers, inventors, entertainers, writers, philosophers, revolutionaries, and pioneers. Many of these Masons changed history; others changed the lives of their communities, their governments, and even their social systems.

But that's not the main reason for joining the Masons. In truth, many individuals join the fraternity or one of their appendant bodies, such as the Shriners or the Daughters of the Eastern Star, for social and charitable reasons. The Masonic family is enormous, with organizations established all over the world. The lives of thousands of men, women, and young adults have been enriched by their association with Masonry, and regardless of their undertaking, they have made a difference and continue to do so to this day.

The two patron saints of Freemasonry are St. John the Evangelist and St. John the Baptist. Masons conduct an annual festival to celebrate their patrons. The celebration for John the Baptist is in June, and the gathering for John the Evangelist is in December.

Freemasonry is also an avenue by which individuals can focus on personal growth. Much like other membership-based organizations, the Craft seeks to teach good men to become better men so that they can use their skills to benefit themselves, their families, and the world in general. The way an individual does that is by ascending various levels of the fraternal structure.

Degrees

Upon entering the Brotherhood an initiate begins his journey by earning a degree, or level. There are three basic degrees in Freemasonry, Entered Apprentice, Fellowcraft, and Master Mason. These are commonly referred to as the three degrees of Freemasonry or Ancient Craft Masonry, or in the United States, blue lodge Masonry. When an individual completes all three degrees he is considered to be an official Freemason.

QUESTION?

Is a thirty-third degree Mason more important than other Masons?
A Mason who has earned the thirty-third degree has completed additional degrees in the Scottish Rite and is now a Scottish Rite Mason. He is not more important than any individual who has become a Master Mason, which is considered by many to be the highest level of Masonry.

The degree ceremonies contain rituals that are highly allegorical and symbolic. Each degree serves to spiritually and morally educate an initiate and further his knowledge and history of the Craft. There are many lessons, or lectures, associated with each level. Throughout most of the degrees of Freemasonry there is a central ritual that symbolically focuses on the building of the Temple of Solomon and the events surrounding Master architect and Mason Hiram Abiff.

Once an individual has become a Master Mason he can either stay at that level, or choose to enter one of Freemasonry's two main concordant bodies—the Ancient and Accepted Scottish Rite or the York Rite, both of which confer additional degrees. Or he can enter one of the Masonic social groups, like the Ancient Arabic Order of the Nobles of the Mystic Shrine, or Shriners.

Masonic Symbolism

Freemasonry is enveloped in allegory, ritual, and especially symbolism. Many of the symbols the Craft uses pay homage to Medieval stonemasons and include the tools of their trade. Each symbol is endowed with a certain meaning. Highly revered symbols include the:

- Square
- Compass
- Plumb
- Level
- Gavel
- Trowel
- Gauge
- Apron

These and other symbols represent many of the scientific and artistic aspects of the trade like geometry, mathematics, and architecture which are all interwoven into the fabric of Masonic teachings (see Chapter 14 for more information on Masonic symbols).

FACT

Freemasonry is not governed by a single entity. All Masonic lodges are overseen by Grand Lodges, but each assumes its own authority. All Grand Lodges are equal.

It's fair to say that Freemasonry, for the most part, is generally misunderstood, its intentions, rituals, tenets, and actions often manipulated to fit a particular theory or conspiracy. The term *secret society* is perhaps better suited to the description private society, or a society with secrets, as the only things they truly keep secret are certain teachings, and their modes of recognizing one another.

chapter 2

History or Hearsay?

History is often written by those in power, and when it comes to ancient history it's often difficult and controversial to determine the true origin and timeline of events. The origin of Freemasonry has been debated for centuries, with plausible arguments made regarding various theories and legends. Whether Freemasons evolved from the great builders of Solomon's Temple, the brave monastic order of the Knights Templar, or hard-working Medieval Guilds will perhaps never be revealed, but regardless of that fact, Masons have indeed secured an intriguing place in history.

The Origin of Freemasonry

The origin of Freemasonry is a subject that has sparked inspired debate over the centuries. Not only is it argued among historians, scholars, and conspiracy theorists, but it is also argued among Freemasons themselves. With the dubious title of "secret society" it is no wonder that the complex history of Freemasonry consistently provides inspiration for tales and theories running the gamut from the epic to the absurd.

That said, it's difficult to pin down the true history of Freemasonry. Wrapped in a blanket of legend, ritual, and symbolism, the Brotherhood becomes everything from warrior monks to political assassins to guys wearing funny hats at charity barbecues. Only one thing is certain—Freemasonry is never boring, and no matter the theory or historical facts to which one subscribes, the very essence of this philosophical group of men is an intriguing study.

There are myriad origins associated with the Brotherhood and the Craft, ranging from the legendary Temple of Solomon and the Knights Templar to the astronomical aspects of megalithic times. Hundreds of books and articles have been written on these and other theories, and while some have been dismissed for sheer lack of evidence or as perhaps wishful thinking, others have made sound arguments to the contrary. Whether a proposed Freemasonry origin is true or false will perhaps never be proven, but the legends and symbolism that permeate the Brotherhood most assuredly takes their lead from historical events.

The Temple of Solomon

One of Freemasonry's alleged origins dates back to the building of Solomon's Temple in Jerusalem from 970 to 931 B.C. Considered by both the Bible and the Torah as the first official temple in the Holy City, it was a massive undertaking that required thousands of men, enormous resources, and the skills of many master craftsmen.

It is said that King Solomon, son of David and Bathsheba, was in dire need of a master artisan and consulted one of his friends, Hiram, the king of Tyre, to see if he could offer such a man to work on the great temple. Eager to help build a house of God, the Tyrian king dispatched his master workman, a skilled artist named Hiram Abiff (alternately spelled Abif).

FACT

Solomon's Temple was destroyed by the Babylonians in 586 B.C. It was rebuilt seventy years later only to be destroyed by the Romans as punishment when the Jews rebelled against them.

Both the Temple of Solomon and the legend surrounding Hiram Abiff play a significant role in the rituals, legends, and rhetoric of Freemasonry. A temple constructed by stonemasons of the era seems a logical step in the evolutionary history of Freemasonry, but as with most theories involving Masonic origin, connections to the temple builders and to the tale of Hiram and his fate remain entrenched in speculation.

The Legend of Hiram Abiff

The character of Hiram Abiff and his connection to Solomon's Temple is perhaps one of the greatest legends surrounding Freemasonry. There is little in the Bible that confirms his true identity, but the mention of him is enough to elicit much debate over his role in the building of the grand temple.

Hiram's work and his subsequent fate is deeply embedded in Masonic ritual. His story is often referred to in Masonic texts, rituals, and ceremonies, and even takes center stage in conspiracy theories such as those surrounding the hideous crimes of nineteenth century serial killer Jack the Ripper.

According to legend, Hiram was the son of a widow who was skilled in working with gold and silver, a craft that would prove useful in the making of various objects housed within the sacred temple. Hiram was also skilled in stone work, and allegedly knew valuable secrets of Master Masonry. In the authoritative position of supervisor for the construction of the temple, Hiram had the power to elevate individuals to higher ranks of skill and *divine understanding* of the masonry craft—from Apprentice to Fellowcraftsman and to Master Mason.

A Murderous Trio

It is said that Hiram's demise came at the hands of three fellow craftsmen—Jubela, Jubelo, and Jubelum—whose aim it was to learn of Hiram's secrets and advance themselves to Master Masons. During a daily prayer session, Hiram was approached by the three men who demanded to be promoted. When Hiram refused to reveal anything to the men, Jubelo attacked him with an architect's square, Jubela slashed his throat with a measuring gauge, and Jubelum used a gavel which eventually killed Hiram.

QUESTION?

What do the slayers of Hiram Abiff have to do with Jack the Ripper?
Those who subscribe to the so-called royal conspiracy theory which asserts the Ripper was a Freemason claim a link to the three ruffians, Jubela, Jubelo, and Jubelum, due to a message scrawled on a wall at the fourth crime scene. The message referred to "Juwes."

After burying Hiram in the dark of night, the three conspirators attempted to escape, only to be captured and returned to King Solomon, where they confessed to the murder and were summarily executed (for more on their executions see Chapter 13). Hiram's body was eventually recovered and laid to rest at the temple where a shrine was built in his honor.

Divine Truth and Light

The legend of Hiram Abiff figures prominently in the initiation rite of a third degree Mason, or Master Mason (see Chapter 5). The ritual is heavily linked to the Hiramic legend with the three ruffians serving as symbols of ignorance, in contrast to the Divine Truth that was known only to King Solomon, the Tyrian king, and to Hiram Abiff.

Freemasons, in their quest for knowledge, "light," and Divine truths, symbolically link Hiram's violent death to a great loss, a resurrection, and ultimately a state of immortality. As such, it's easy to see why the Temple of Solomon, with its glorious architecture and the legendary artisan associated with it, are so heavily featured in Masonic history and traditions.

Knights Templar

When one thinks of the Knights Templar, one is often given to thoughts of legendary wars and the brave men who, atop their massive steeds, looked larger than life. Of course, imagination, aided by books and film, has a way of making all things historical appear glamorous while minimizing the realistic struggle and brutality of men in battle. These knights did indeed exist and while their legend can easily be romanticized, their purpose was far more focused. While the Knights were known for their ferocity in battle, especially during the Crusades, they were equally renowned for their banking skills and business acumen.

Knights Templar were warrior monks, a military and religious order of men founded in 1118 by French Knight Hughes de Payens. From their inception until they were almost entirely wiped out in 1307, the Templars served as protectors of pilgrims traveling from Europe to the Kingdom of Jerusalem. Taking their name from their headquarters next to the legendary Temple of Solomon, the "Poor Knights of Christ and the Temple of Solomon" were a monastic order that enjoyed enormous wealth and power.

ALERT!

One of the great historical controversies involves the location of the Holy Grail. The Knights Templar have been deeply entrenched in that mystery, with many theories surrounding them as alleged protectors of the Grail and its possible location beneath the Rosslyn Temple in Scotland.

Though their history is spread across two centuries, the Knights Templar are perhaps best known for their participation in the Crusades, for arguably creating the first formal banking system, and for the mystery surrounding their involvement with the Holy Grail and the Ark of the Covenant. To understand their rise to power and fall from grace, and their possible connection to Freemasons, it's important to examine the role they played in the Crusades from the eleventh to the thirteenth centuries.

The Crusades

In its most simplistic form, the Crusades were a series of military campaigns sanctioned by the Catholic Church to recover the Holy Land and Jerusalem from the hands of the Muslims. This series of expeditions took place from 1096 to 1291, with each Crusade focusing on a different goal. The origin of the Crusades came as a result of Pope Urban II and a speech he delivered at a church council in Clermont in 1095. At that time, the spread of Islam was proving to be a possible threat to the Byzantine Empire and accounts of Christian mistreatment at the hand of Muslims did nothing to dispel that threat.

The response to Pope Urban's request that the Holy City of Jerusalem be liberated was overwhelming, as Crusaders quickly showed their solidarity by sewing red crosses to their clothing. The true motivation for the pope's inciting the Crusades is unknown, but speculation points to religious reasons or a possible common goal to help unite any warring factions within Europe.

After successfully taking the Holy City in 1099, Godfrei de Bouillon became the first ruler of the newly created Kingdom of Jerusalem. In 1100, the rule was passed to Godfrei's brother Baldwin I, who proclaimed himself the first king of Jerusalem. When he passed away, the crown fell to his cousin Baldwin II. In 1118, nine knights approached Baldwin II seeking approval to found a new order whose mission it would be to protect individuals during their pilgrimage to the Holy Land. It was then that the Knights Templar were born, a strict order of men who took a vow of poverty, chastity, and obedience.

FACT

Any individual who joined the Knights Templar had to adhere to stringent rules. In addition to their vows, they slept on straw mattresses, were forbidden to cut their beards, and were only allowed to consume meat three times each week.

In 1128 at the Council of Troyes, the Knights Templar were given sanction by the church with the assistance of St. Bernard of Clairvaux, who helped establish the rules of the Order. Fifty years later, over three hundred knights proudly wore the traditional white mantle that denoted a Templar. The combined wealth of the order amassed as a result of donations of both property and monetary funds given over to the Order when wealthy members took their vows of poverty.

Banking on Success

By 1135, the Knights began a policy of lending money to those making the Holy Land pilgrimage. Money that was kept in temples along the route was well guarded and travelers could safely deposit funds in exchange for written receipts, and then retrieve those funds at another temple further along the route. In essence, a rudimentary banking system was begun. This system, in addition to donations, gave the monastic order a significant boost of power. By 1239, the Templars owned nine thousand castles and manors and were richer than any other continental government. In addition, their numbers had grown to over fifteen thousand.

Groups possessing such wealth and perceived power, as history can attest, often become the target of those who wish to usurp and attain control of that power. The Knights Templar were, unfortunately, victim to such persecution, not surprisingly at the hands of their very creators, the church and crown.

Templar Persecution

French King Philip IV, also known as Philip the Fair, proved to be the undoing of the Knights Templar, and the end of the Order succumbed to a lurid mix of heretical accusations and torture. A royal who lavishly squandered funds, Philip found himself in serious conflict with the Catholic Church in 1296, when he began taxing the church's holdings to replenish his own coffers. When Pope Boniface VIII threatened to excommunicate the French, King Philip ordered him kidnapped, only to have the pontiff expire after a short captivity.

It is said that the unscrupulous king then applied to become a Knight Templar and was summarily refused entrance into the Order. He subsequently set about manipulating the election of the next pope, Clement V, who then moved the papacy from Italy to France. It is unknown why these two men set out to destroy the Knights Templar, but speculation ranges from envy of the Knights' wealth and power to the king himself either borrowing money from the Templars or trying to escape the debts he owed to the Order. Whatever the reason, the fall of the Knights Templar started with a summons issued to Templar Grand Master Jacques de Molay.

Jacques de Molay

Twenty-one-year-old Jacques de Molay had become a Templar in 1265. An ambitious Frenchman, he moved up the ranks and eventually became Grand Master of the Order. Having replaced the Order's previous Grand Master Theobald Gaudin, de Molay took up residence at the Templar headquarters in Cyprus. In 1307, de Molay received word that he was to return to France on order of King Philip and Pope Clement, presumably under the guise of launching another Crusade.

De Molay obeyed the summons and returned to France unaware of the horrible fate that would soon befall him and his kinsmen. On what would prove an ironic date, October 13, 1307, Knights Templar all over France were seized and arrested. What followed was a distasteful routine of torture, where the knights were forced to either confess to their alleged misconduct including Christian heresy, idol worship, sexual perversions, and satanic worship; or face death.

FACT

It is said that the modern-day superstition of Friday the Thirteenth makes reference to the fateful day in 1307 when the Knights Templar were arrested and summarily tortured and killed.

Under extreme duress, de Molay offered a confession that he would later recant, and as a result, he and a fellow Templar were burned alive in 1312 within view of Notre Dame. Many legends revolve around the Knights Templar, and one is that just before de Molay died, he issued a prophecy that both King Philip and Pope Clement would die within a year's time. As it turned out, both men did die within the following year, but the pope just prior to his death dealt a fatal blow to the Templars with a final order that stated that any individual joining the order would be excommunicated from the church as a heretic.

Scottish Exodus

There is no agreed-upon consensus of what became of the Templars after their persecution by King Philip IV. One of the more prevalent views is that a number of Templars who escaped arrest and execution made their way to Scotland in search of a safe haven. Being that Scotland's king, Robert Bruce, had already been excommunicated from the Church, it stands to reason that the Templars would do well to fight with the Scots who were in great need of supplementing their fighting contingent.

After a successful battle against the English, it is said that the Templars were given refuge on a Scottish isle where they remained for the next eighty years. Certain theorists and historians contend that these rogue Templars eventually became a more permanent brotherhood known as Freemasons.

Masonic Connections

The connection between the Knights Templar and Freemasons is a subject that is still vehemently debated, with many significant points brought to light on all sides. Many feel that the Templars who ended up in Scotland gave birth to the Scottish Rite, one of the two major branches of Freemasonry. Other historians argue that the Masons simply elected to adopt the romantic and chivalrous history of the Knights Templar, one that would provide infinitely more backbone and drama to their history.

Given the climate of the era, one can also theorize that a persecuted monastic order, such as the Templars, would naturally gravitate toward a secret fraternal organization in its infancy. Whatever the case may be, there is no definitive proof of a Masonic connection to the Knights Templar of legend, but there are plenty of facts and myths that make the Order a very attractive relative.

The Scottish Rite

Once an individual has passed through the main three degrees, or levels, of Freemasonry—Entered Apprentice, Fellowcraft, and Master Mason (see Chapter 5)—he can continue his education with other branches of Freemasonry. The Brotherhood consists of two main branches, one of which is the York Rite, and the other is the Ancient and Accepted Scottish Rite, or Scottish Rite as it is commonly called. The Scottish Rite consists of thirty-three degrees, each serving to extend a Mason's knowledge of the Craft.

An individual wishing to become a thirty-third degree Mason of the Scottish Rite cannot apply for the degree. Masons who show exemplary community leadership and who exemplify the principles of the Brotherhood must be elected by a unanimous vote.

The origin of the Scottish Rite appears to be lost in antiquity, but one school of thought suggests its roots are with the Knights Templar who lived in exile in Scotland after their Order was banished. It is also said that the rite originated with expatriate Scotsmen, who created a lodge in France. Records show that it wasn't until 1804 that the name Ancient and Accepted Scottish Rite appeared in documents between the Grand Orient of France and the Supreme Council of France. In the United States, the Scottish Rite is divided into Northern and Southern Jurisdictions that are governed by Supreme Councils.

The Halliwell Manuscript

Considered to be one of the oldest and perhaps most significant documents of Freemasonry is the Halliwell Manuscript, or Regius poem. Discovered in the King's Library of the British Museum in 1839, the poem contained 794 lines of English verse that were then published by James O. Halliwell in 1840. According to experts, the document likely dates back to around 1390; however, the poem cites historic events long before that time.

The Halliwell Manuscript is significant in terms of Masonic history and the legends associated with that history. It also contains governmental regulations of the Craft. Perhaps the most important aspect of the poem is its telling of the introduction of Masonry in 924 by King Athelstan of England. Inclusion of this information in the manuscript gives the York Rite branch of Freemasonry an impressive and legendary lineage from which to draw.

King Athelstan

Considered to be the first king of all England, Athelstan ruled from 925 to 939 A.D. Grandson to Alfred the Great, Athelstan had a strong admiration for the art of masonry and the subject of geometry. With his patronage many castles, fortresses, monasteries, and abbeys were built. In an effort to further continue the trade, a charter was issued by Athelstan so that masons would hold an annual assembly in the city of York.

Grand Lodge at York

The first Grand Lodge meeting was held in 926 A.D., with King Athelstan's brother, Prince Edwin, serving as Grand Master. The legend as written in the Halliwell Manuscript relates that it was at that Grand Lodge that the constitutions of English Freemasonry were established based on old Greek and Latin documents. The fact that the King and his brother were so deeply involved suggests they were two of the first speculative, or non-masons, introduced to the Brotherhood.

Over the next few millennia, many individuals of royal blood would become Masons, and some speculate that Athelstan's patronage and involvement set that precedent.

The York Rite

The York Rite, which derives its name from the city of York in the North of England, constitutes the second concordant body of Freemasonry. There are three bodies within the York Rite, including Royal Arch Masonry, Cryptic Masonry, and Knights Templar. These groups confer additional degrees for Masons interested in further enlightenment and study of the Brother-hood (see Chapter 7).

As one can imagine given the Halliwell Manuscript and Athelstan's legend, the origin of the York Rite has been a fascinating source of study and debate for historians, scholars, and Freemasons themselves. Degrees conferred upon Masons through the York Rite and its associated bodies are understandably steeped in history and lore and represent a great source of pride throughout the Brotherhood.

chapter 3

A Fraternity Is Born

Prior to the formation of organized Freemasonry, stonemasons of the Medieval Age were making their mark all over Europe, and the splendor and artistry of their work is highly revered by modern Masons. Those times were not without strife, however, as Masonry endured setbacks as a result of the Protestant Reformation. But like a phoenix, it was resurrected to new heights and notoriety to form what is now a Brotherhood of legend.

Breaking New Ground

It's no secret that the origins of Freemasonry are a great source of debate. While some scholars, historians, and Masons believe the Craft is based in antiquity as far back as Solomon's Temple, others contend that Freemasons are evolved from Medieval Masonic Guilds. However, even this is a contested assertion, with some speculating that trade masons of the day had no need for secrecy as they were always traveling wherever work was available.

From the megalithic era to Medieval times and the New World, stonemasons honed their skills and combined their artistry and passion for building to create a legacy of form and structure. Using the tools of their trade they were the hands-on craftsmen who built and rebuilt as far back as ancient Egypt.

Master Builders of the Day

Masons of the trade built a variety of impressive monuments and buildings over the millennia. The splendor, magic, and artistic quality of these sites can still be seen in cities and nations all over the world, ranging from the English landscape of Stonehenge to grand European castles and the United States presidential residence, the White House. Arguably one of the most famous mason-built structures is the London Bridge, which connects two sides of London over the Thames River.

FACT

The popular song "London Bridge Is Falling Down" was conceived during the construction of the London Bridge. The local populace sang this to the masons working on the endeavor. Two of the lines find their root in Masonry: "Build it up with stone so strong," and "Stone so strong will last so long."

London Bridge had many incarnations, beginning with a wooden bridge built by the Romans in 46 A.D. After the Romans departed, the bridge fell into disrepair and was rebuilt a number of times. It wasn't until 1176 that the masons took on the enormous task of building a more permanent structure during the reign of King Henry II. England's first incarnation of the stone-built London Bridge was completed in 1209 and took thirty-three years to construct.

Cathedrals and Grandeur

During the Middle Ages, masons throughout Europe, and especially in Britain, France, and Germany, were thriving and further enhancing their faith by using their building skills to create amazing icons of religious splendor. As it turned out, competition among the regional hierarchies of the Catholic Church worked in the masons' favor, as each faction wanted to build bigger and more impressive churches and cathedrals than the previous faction.

When one takes into consideration the building of such massive structures and the danger involved in working with stone, it's easy to see why the cathedrals built by masons were indeed regarded as tremendously inspirational works of art. England's Westminster Abbey, France's Notre Dame, and Spain's Santiago de Compostela are ageless reminders of the artisanship of the Gothic, Medieval, and modern-day stonemasons.

The Protestant Reformation

One might ask what a religious upheaval such as the Protestant Reformation has to do with Freemasonry. As it turns out, it had a direct impact on the masons of the day, who were primarily employed by the Catholic Church to build, among other things, many grand cathedrals, churches, and monasteries.

The sixteenth century saw a major shift in religion in Western Europe, which at the time was primarily guided by the Roman Catholic Church. It's no mystery that theological changes throughout history have resulted in persecution, war, and general mayhem. During the Crusades, for example, many individual lives were lost in the name of God.

The Protestant Reformation of the 1500s was a religious rebellion that sought to reform the Catholic Church. The result was a division of faith, the primary establishment being Lutheranism, and what would become the Lutheran Church. The movement began as a result of one man and his bold actions to incite reform.

By definition, Protestantism is faith founded on the principles of the reformation, acceptance of the Bible as the true source of revelation, and the universal priesthood of all men equally. In its simplistic form, it refers to the religious movement of separation from the Roman Catholic Church.

Martin Luther

The trigger for the Protestant Reformation was an Augustinian monk and German theologian named Martin Luther. A professor at the University of Wittenberg, Luther felt so strongly about the subject of religious indulgences that he took to outright rebellion. It is said that on October 31, 1517, Luther went to Wittenberg's Castle Church and nailed to the castle door his ninety-five theses for all to read and debate.

This spawned a quick outbreak of discontent, as the theses were translated into a number of languages, and because of the new technological advances of the printing press, they were widely distributed throughout Europe. Within two months Luther's faith-based words were spread throughout the continent, and a mire of religious discontent became a major point of contention for the papacy and the Catholic Church. During this time, British Freemasons remained loyal to the Catholic Church, but this religious movement would eventually come to a head in England with King Henry VIII.

King Henry VIII

King Henry VIII is perhaps best known for his fondness for wives—all six of them—and the beheading of wives Anne Boleyn, and Katherine Howard, number two and five respectively. The amorous king also left a lasting historical mark in regard to the Protestant Reformation. As such, it should come as no surprise that the king came to blows with the Papacy over the dissolution of his first marriage to Catherine of Aragon.

It all began when the Catholic Church refused the king's request to dissolve his first marriage, which would enable him to marry his then-mistress

Anne Boleyn. By 1533, Henry ignored Catholic doctrine and married Boleyn. Several months later, he had his marriage to Catherine annulled and his new marriage validated. As a result of Henry's chicanery, Pope Clement VII excommunicated the king from the Roman Catholic Church. In response, Henry put forth the Act of Supremacy in 1534, which in effect separated him from the Vatican and made him the head of the Church in England.

QUESTION?

Was Shakespeare a Mason?
The question of whether William Shakespeare was part of the Brotherhood has given rise to much speculation. Many theorists draw attention to Masonic references in Shakespeare's work, with lines such as: "The nobility think scorn to go in leather aprons."

As a result of the king's proclamation, monasteries, church properties, and land became the possession of the crown, which effectively halted the further construction of churches and as a result, the need for masons. It is said that this decline marked the beginnings of the shift from operative to speculative Masons, thus beginning a new phase in the as yet unofficially recognized Brotherhood.

Freemasonry Before 1700

Despite the fact that the first official Grand Lodge was created in 1717, which is generally accepted as the beginning of Freemasonry as an organized fraternity, there is quite a bit of evidence that shows the Brotherhood could perhaps have existed much earlier. Historians often point to the formation of the Masons Company of London in 1356, but there is no solid proof that exists. Other possible sources indicating an earlier origin are the Cooke Manuscript, the Schaw Statutes, and Elias Ashmole, an alleged early initiate into the Brotherhood in 1646.

The Cooke Manuscript

In 1861 Matthew Cook transcribed a document believed to have originated circa 1450. This document was allegedly written by a speculative Mason, and is said to contain the Constitution of German stonemasons. The manuscript also makes reference to seven sciences that were used by George Payne, who was serving as Grand Master when he compiled his version of the general regulations. Whether by coincidence or not, the number seven is one of the numbers Masons favor (see Chapter 13).

These are the seven sciences according to one transcription:

The first, which is called the foundation of all science, is grammar, which teacheth to write and speak correctly.

The second is rhetoric, which teaches us to speak elegantly.

The third is dialectic, which teaches us to discern the true from the false, and it is usually called art or sophistry (logic).

The fourth is arithmetic, which instructs us in the science of numbers, to reckon, and to make accounts.

The fifth is geometry, which teaches us all about mensuration, measures and weights, of all kinds of handicrafts.

The sixth is music, and that teaches the art of singing by notation for the voice, on the organ, trumpet, and harp, and of all things pertaining thereto.

The seventh is astronomy, which teaches us the course of the sun and of the moon, and of the other stars and planets of heaven.

The Schaw Statutes

In its simplest form, the Schaw Statutes were an attempt to organize the structure of Freemasonry. King James VI of Scotland, who would eventually become King James I of England, appointed William Schaw as Master of the Work and Warden General in 1583. Schaw then issued the first of his Schaw Statutes in 1598, which outlined to both lodge members and the public, the duties of all Masonic members.

FACT

As a matter of historical interest, King James was famous for an endeavor in addition to his appointment of William Schaw—he commissioned the King James version of the Bible, which was first published in 1611.

In 1599, Schaw created a second statute, the significance of which lies in reference to stonemasonry and the existence of esoteric, or secret, knowledge. The statute also makes reference to the Mother Lodge of Scotland, Lodge Mother Kilwinning, No. 0, which was supposedly active at that time. Schaw's writings also provided a set of instructions for all lodges that certain activities, such as record keeping and the dates of lodge meetings, must be written and recorded. Depending on the theory, it is said that Schaw was the founding father of modern Freemasonry.

Elias Ashmole

The name Elias Ashmole is constantly mentioned when discussing Freemasonry and its history. The reason for his significance is his admission into a lodge in 1646 as a speculative Mason, a practice that is theorized to have occurred long before that time. It was said that admissions of non-Masons to the fraternity exacerbated a panic that caused operative lodges to destroy records for fear of their information falling into the wrong hands.

Ashmole was a politician, collector, and antiquarian with a thirst for knowledge, especially when it came to alchemy and astrology. He was, in fact, an avid student in the study of alchemy, and in the 1650s he was able to compile and publish many manuscripts that were formerly only part of private collections. In later years, Ashmole even consulted on astrological matters with King Charles II and his court.

Rebuilding London

On September 2, 1666, Thomas Farrinor, the baker for King Charles II, neglected to extinguish his oven before retiring for the evening. Hours later, a fire broke out and it would prove to be the most deadly in British history. Four days later, the fire had destroyed over thirteen thousand homes, over eighty churches, and forty-four company halls. The fire consumed 373 acres and destroyed everything in its path. The catastrophic destruction the fire left in its wake was unthinkable.

English architect, mathematician, and scientist Christopher Wren had the daunting task of rebuilding the great city of London. Wren was a founding member of the Royal Society who designed and built over fifty churches and buildings throughout Oxford and Cambridge. One of his greatest accomplishments was the construction of St. Paul's Cathedral which he personally oversaw from 1675 to 1710. Wren was also a Freemason and Grand Master of an operative lodge. Records show he was initiated in 1691.

The London Fire was tragic, but unfortunate as it was, it gave masons years and years of steady employment. Wren's decision to rebuild the city with brick and stone required a strong contingent of masons, many of whom were brought in from all over the British Isles. With Wren's guidance, they met in lodges and began rebuilding the city. Included in the massive reconstruction was St. Paul's Cathedral, which took thirty-five years to build.

Operative and Speculative Freemasonry

The terms *operative* and *speculative* are very common when reading anything on the subject of Freemasonry and it can sometimes be confusing. In a nutshell, operative Masons are individuals who were masons by trade. It is commonly assumed that modern-day Freemasonry evolved from the operative Masons. Speculative Masons comprise the majority of the present-day Brotherhood. In short, they are individuals who are not part of the masonry trade.

When in doubt, it's the language of Latin that ultimately helps in the understanding of this Masonic distinction. *Operative* is derived from the Latin word for "work," or *operari*. *Speculative* is derived from the Latin word *specere*, which means "to see," or "to look about." Operatives were the workers of the trade while the speculatives were taught the knowledge, understanding, and theories of the trade often through allegory, ritual, and symbolism.

One of the things that distinguishes operative from speculative Masons is the use of symbols. Most Masonic symbols are tools related to the mason and his trade, including the square, compass, plumb, and level.

The terms *operative art* and *speculative science* are also common. Operative art refers to the Middle Ages and the practices of stonemasons. Speculative science refers to the modern-day practice of Freemasonry.

Operative Masons

Operative Masons were the hands-on stonemasons who used the actual tools that would later become symbols and icons of Freemasonry. Their operative art reflects a high skill level. They built structures for both private and commercial use, as well as churches, monasteries, temples, and cathedrals. As a group of men they were much like those in any other trade—they traveled to where work was most abundant. For as long as there have been buildings and monuments, so have there been masons to carve stone into structure.

The Etymology of Freemasonry

When it comes to the subject of Freemasonry and its origins, nothing is, ironically, written in stone, and the origin of the actual word *freemason* is no exception. Many different definitions are available when perusing the history books, some more commonly accepted than others as being the most likely meaning.

One of the more common explanations points to a material called *freestone*, a soft form of limestone that hardens to durability with age. Masons who worked with this material were naturally called *Freestone Masons*, which is assumed to have evolved into *Freemason*.

One possible translation of the word Freemason is of French origin: "Frere Mason" (Brother Mason), which could have evolved into the English "Freemason."

The word *free* is typically the cause for the dispute in the name. Some speculate that the name is derived from the actual freestanding stones masons worked with. Others surmise that a possible explanation is simply that masons who weren't under the control of local guilds were, in fact, free masons.

Speculative Masons

In the late 1600s, masonry had gone into decline. The religious turn to Protestantism in the mid 1500s by King Henry VIII, which resulted in fewer cathedrals being built, had set the wheels in motion. By 1665, the British population was succumbing to the horror of the Great Plague which it's estimated killed up to a hundred thousand people—a fifth of London's population. A year later was the London fire, which resulted in a resurgence in the masonry trade, but it was short-lived.

Masonry virtually came to a halt in the first years of the eighteenth century. Only a handful of operative lodges remained and their members were in disagreement over allowing non-tradesmen into their groups. That changed in 1716 with the death of architect and Grand Master Christopher Wren. By the following year, the four lodges of London made the decision to form a Grand Lodge.

The formation of that Grand Lodge would definitively mark the shift from operative Masonry to speculative Masonry, thereby creating a more philosophical fraternity, one whose members sought to further their own education and spirituality. As a result of this shift, a wide range of individuals from politicians and artists to explorers and aristocrats entered the Craft.

The Grand Lodge of England

It is generally agreed upon that the formation of the Grand Lodge of England marks the official beginning of organized Freemasonry. In February, 1717, four London lodges, which included over one hundred masons, met for the first time. The lodges were:

- **Lodge No. 1:** The Goose and Gridiron Ale-house in St. Paul's Churchyard.
- **Lodge No. 2:** The Crown Ale-house in Parker's Lane near Drury's Lane.
- **Lodge No. 3:** The Apple Tree Tavern in Charles Street, Covent Garden.
- **Lodge No. 4:** The Rummer and Grapes Tavern in Channel Row, Westminster.

At the meeting, which took place at the Apple Tree Tavern, they decided that together they would form the Grand Lodge of England. In forming this official lodge, they would become a central authority and recognize three symbolic degrees. Four months later, on June 24, 1717, St. John the Baptist's Day, an assembly and feast was held, this time at the Goose and Gridiron. At that meeting, they elected Anthony Sayer, a member of Lodge No. 3, as their first Grand Master.

QUESTION?

How long was it before other Grand Lodges were created?
Four lodges followed England's lead—two in Europe and two in America. The Grand Lodge of Ireland was formed in 1725, followed by the Provincial Grand Lodge of Pennsylvania in 1731, and the Provincial Grand Lodge of Massachusetts two years later. By 1736, the Grand Lodge of Scotland was begun.

In 1718, George Payne was elected Grand Master, and he immediately began compiling ancient manuscripts, rituals, charts, and all texts pertaining to Freemasonry. Together with the documents collected by St. Paul's Lodge, Payne had enough information to write a code of laws and doctrines. Jean Theophilus Desaguliers served as Grand Master in 1719, but by 1720, when Payne again was serving as Master, was created the *General Regulations* (commonly known as the *Book of Constitutions*) which were approved by the Grand Lodge the following year. They would eventually be published in 1723 by Dr. James Anderson, and came to be known as *Anderson's Constitutions*.

An interesting shift took place in 1721, when John, the Duke of Montagu, was chosen by the lodge as its next Grand Master. This set in motion a trend that would endure for the next 278 years. In that time, no "commoner" would serve as Grand Master of the Grand Lodge of England. All who held the prestigious position would be of nobility or members of the royal family. The affluent association of gentry and aristocracy gave rise to an increase in fraternal membership. With only four lodges constituting the Grand Lodge in 1717 the number of lodges over the next eighteen years grew to 126.

Anderson's Book of Constitutions

James Anderson, a native of Aberdeen, Scotland, became a minister of the Presbyterian Church of Scotland when he was only twenty-three years old. Starting in 1709, he began ministrating in nonconformist chapels around London. It is said he was a man with considerable literary skills, but he is best known for having written the *Book of Constitutions of the Antient and Honourable Fraternity of Free and Accepted Masons,* which he wrote for the Grand Lodge of England in 1723. He also worked on a second, more elaborate, edition which was published in 1738.

There is no authoritative Grand Lodge, and Europe isn't the only place where Grand Lodges exist. In fact, there is a Grand Lodge in each of America's states and in most countries around the world.

It was 1721 when the Grand Master the Duke of Montagu enlisted Anderson's help in creating the *Constitutions*, in an effort to compile the relatively scattered history, regulations, and old charges of the fraternity so that it could be used as a universal code by all lodges. Anderson's *Constitutions* are still considered to be the basis of Freemasonry in regard to governing the fraternity. A Mason himself, Anderson became one of the Grand Wardens of the Grand Lodge in 1723 and later served as Grand Chaplain.

This constitution of Freemasons took into account the ancient charges of Masonry and tailored them to modern-day purposes. Anderson's charges addressed the following topics:

- God and religion
- The Civil Magistrate, supreme and subordinate
- Lodges
- Masters, Wardens, Fellows, and Apprentices
- The Management of the Craft in working
- Behavior

A Deist Controversy

Anderson's *Constitutions*, while historic to Freemasonry, was not without controversy. Historians and scholars debate whether Anderson advocated deism—the belief in a Supreme Being or existence of God without revealed religion—a belief of reason and the "light of nature."

The charge in question concerns God and religion, and is as follows:

A Mason is oblig'd by his Tenure, to obey the moral law; and if he rightly understands the Art, he will never be a stupid Atheist nor an irreligious Libertine. But though in ancient Times Masons were charg'd in every Country to be of the Religion of that Country or Nation, whatever it was, yet 'tis now thought more expedient only to oblige them to that Religion in which all Men agree, leaving their particular Opinions to themselves; that is, to be good Men and true, or Men of Honour and Honesty, by whatever Denominations or Persuasions they may be distinguish'd; whereby Masonry becomes the Center of Union, and the Means of conciliating true Friendship among Persons that must have remain'd at a perpetual Distance.

Historically, Masons were accustomed to the rules and ways of Christianity and the Roman Catholic Church. The suggestion that all other religions would be embraced by the Craft must have been a shock to traditionalists. On closer examination, Anderson's revisions of the charges of Freemasonry appear to reflect a remarkable tolerance to the religious diversity of the times. By deliberate and vague reference to any specific religion, Anderson's *Constitutions* opened Freemasonry to virtually any individual who believed in God no matter what their chosen faith might be.

Much of what Anderson wrote, in terms of historical accuracy in regard to the Brotherhood, is still heavily debated. The second edition of his *Constitutions* expanded the history of Freemasonry into undocumented and questionable territory. Regardless, Anderson remains a highly revered member of the fraternal organization who at the very least set a benchmark for the basic tenets of Masonic beliefs.

chapter 4

A Great Divide

As an essentially autonomous organization with independence and freedom of thought, it would be quite surprising had the Craft not seen changes in its long and varied history. Many of the divisions in the Brotherhood were brought about by internal differences in ritual. Many more were triggered by responses to the inevitable evolution of societies and social structures. There has always been a common theme to the schisms that have occurred, but it has been the innate desire of Freemasons to heal those rifts and move forward as brothers.

Ancient Free and Accepted Masonry

The terms *ancient free* and *accepted Masonry* are often used in the names of Grand Lodges and the lodges of their constituency to signify their historical ties. This chapter is devoted to describing the rift in English Freemasonry that resulted in the creation of separate Grand Lodges. Because the formal names of these Grand Lodges are a mouthful, it's best to refer to them in shortened, recognizable terms, and include their common nicknames.

The Premier Grand Lodge of England (the Moderns)

The Grand Lodge formed in England in 1717 was the first Grand Lodge in history. Formally titled, "The Grand Lodge of Free and Accepted Masons" under the constitution of England, this lodge became designated as the "Moderns" or "Premier" lodge after the establishment of a rival Grand Lodge in 1751. For clarity in this section, the lodge will be referred to as the Premier Grand Lodge of England, or the Moderns.

Ancient or Antient Freemasons

The Grand Lodge established to rival the Premier Grand Lodge of England is formally titled, "The Grand Lodge of Free and Accepted Masons of England according to the Old Institutions." This Grand Lodge is referred to by its well-established nickname, "the Antients."

FACT

Antient lodges spread throughout Scotland and Ireland, and became a significant Masonic influence in the British military. Through the military, Antient Masonry would find its way to the American Colonies.

Rifts in the Brotherhood

During the 1700s the popularity of Freemasonry grew in England and rapidly expanded worldwide. The first lodge in the Netherlands was founded in 1721, followed by lodges in Spain (1728), Poland (1730), the American Colonies (1731), Switzerland (1736), France (1738), Prussia (1740), Austria (1742), Denmark (1743), Norway (1749), and Sweden (1753).

A major division in Freemasonry would occur in 1751, ironically in its country of origin. The Premier Grand Lodge of London and the lodges in its jurisdiction had throughout the years been making gradual changes and innovations in its modes of recognition, and had expanded the two degree system to three.

Some historians believe that these changes were triggered by a combination of published "exposés" and the steady influx of immigrants from Scotland and Ireland. Many of these immigrants found it difficult to gain employment, and some were clever enough to exploit printed versions of Masonic symbolism and attempt to pass themselves off as Masons. These attempts, whether successful or not, threatened the privilege of charity that Freemasons extended to one another. It is also likely that the number of bona fide Freemason immigrants applying for charitable aid were straining the charitable sensibilities of the English lodges.

Loyalty and Turmoil

Alterations in ritual and recognition symbols effectively barred immigrant Freemasons from participation in local lodges, and spawned a great deal of resentment that traveled back to their home countries. As a result, disenfranchised Masons broke away to set up their own lodges, and many English lodges simply chose not to recognize the Premier Grand Lodge at all.

The parallel cause for the shift away from the Premier Lodge of England is both philosophical and cultural. By its very nature, early Freemasonry in England was revolutionary and bold, and arguably helped to spawn the Age of Enlightenment that would eventually sweep through Europe, affecting the attitudes of commoners and the ruling nobility, and influencing the social and political structures of entire nations. Through Masonry, the social status quo was being broadly challenged, given that the tenets of Masonry suggested that equality among men was an achievable birthright, and that knowledge and self awareness were concepts open to everyone.

Cultural Shifts in Masonry

During the early 1700s in England, Masonry provided a venue for the emerging middle classes to engage in open discussion and debate. The quest for philosophic and scientific understanding was no longer confined to the elitist hierarchy. The attraction to this novel and powerful avenue of expression spread quickly through all of the cultural classes, and would soon foster conflicting results for Freemasonry itself.

Within the boundaries of the lodge, Masons were not the subjects of an established regime—they had, in effect, become citizens with a voice. This shift in social consciousness would leave an indelible mark on the future of England, Europe, and the American Colonies.

Freemasonry was effectively growing into a microcosm of a democratic society. While individualism was held in the highest regard, self government was an essential. Laws, constitutions, symbolism, and rituals were all open to discussion and could be altered at will by a majority vote.

As membership in lodges under the jurisdiction of the Premier Lodge of England expanded into the middle and upper classes, the hierarchy of the lodges grew increasingly elitist. The religious undertones of traditional Masonry were also becoming more obscure and shifted toward philosophical Deism. Intellectually, the Premier Lodge of England was losing much of its grip, and much of its influence on the common man.

The Ancients and the Moderns

The most significant group of Masons to compete with the Premier Lodge of London established a new Grand Lodge in 1751, and called themselves the "Grand Lodge of Free and Accepted Masons of England according to the Old Institutions." Because this group chose to adhere to the old and long established passwords, customs, and rituals of Freemasonry, the Grand Lodge of Free and Accepted Masons of England according to the Old

Institutions assumed the nickname, "the Antients." The established Premier Lodge of London, although the oldest organized group of Freemasons, became known as "the Moderns."

The Antients offered a traditional alternative to Modern Freemasonry. The Antients actively sought the support of nobility, and became adept at casting an anti-religious cloud over the Moderns. The attraction for the working classes was immediate.

This rift in British Freemasonry would continue unabated for sixty years. In the early 1800s, overtures were made between the two branches that culminated in the union of the two grand lodges in 1813. The compromise returned the modes of recognition to pre-division days, although it was ambiguously worded in a fashion that simultaneously provided elements of "wiggle room" for both parties.

The compromise avoided standardizing all the rituals, allowing individual lodges to continue incorporating their own established customs. The union of lodges became the United Grand Lodge of Ancient Freemasons of England. Today the Lodge is formally known as the United Grand Lodge of Free and Accepted Masons of England, and informally called the "United Grand Lodge of England."

The Colonial Effect

The division of the Antients and Moderns had limited effect on Freemasonry in the American Colonies. Although both branches had granted charters in the colonies, they tended to act independently of one another. A number of lodges were formed in the colonies that were completely independent of the English Grand Lodges. The earliest chartered Grand Lodge in the colonies was formed almost twenty years before the English rift took place, but it would soon create a rift of its own.

The first Grand Lodge in the colonies was formed in Boston in 1733 by an Englishman named Henry Price, who would become known in later years as the father of American Freemasonry. Although there is little information about Price's date of birth or early life, it's known that he was a successful merchant and tailor when he emigrated from London to Boston in 1723.

In London, Henry Price was appointed Provincial Grand Master of New England, effectively giving him the authority to establish a new Grand Lodge in the colonies, and to charter new lodges as he saw fit.

Price became associated with Masons who were operating without a charter from the Premier Grand Lodge of England, which had been established only a few years earlier. In 1732, Price set sail from Boston back to London, and one of his goals was to obtain a warrant from the Premier Grand Lodge, allowing him the authority to form a chartered lodge in Boston.

The First American Grand Lodge

After his return to Boston, Henry Price immediately organized and established the new Provincial Grand Lodge that was named Saint John's Grand Lodge. On the very same day the Grand Lodge granted a charter to a group of Boston Masons, making them the first officially constituted lodge in the colonies. This would become known as the First Lodge.

Over the next year, Henry Price's authority was broadened to cover all of North America, and Price went on to charter dozens of new lodges. One of those lodges would be in Philadelphia, with Benjamin Franklin as the appointed Grand Master in 1743. In addition to the First Lodge, four more lodges were also chartered in Boston.

Contempt Breeds Rivalry

The First Lodge in Boston was, quite by coincidence, following a similar path to the one taken by the Premier Grand Lodge of England (the Moderns). Membership of the First Lodge had become decidedly elitist, admitting only the prosperous upper class. This prosperous upper class had another commonality, consisting largely of loyalists to the British. The working class was turned away, and their response was nearly identical to that of the disenfranchised English Antients.

The Masons in Boston who were unable to gain admission to the chartered lodges in Boston soon formed a lodge of their own. Probably because the Antients in England had garnered support from the Grand Lodges of Ireland and Scotland, the new lodge applied to the Grand Lodge of Scotland for a charter. The Grand Lodge of Scotland (probably with great glee) agreed to the charter on St. Andrew's Day in 1756, with the suggestion that the lodge be named St. Andrew's Lodge.

The charter for the new lodge arrived in 1760, and St. Andrew's Lodge became official.

FACT

One of the first orders of business for the newly created St. Andrew's Lodge was to admit a twenty-five-year-old silversmith named Paul Revere into their ranks.

Rival Unity

St. Andrew's Lodge joined ranks with three British military lodges stationed near Boston in 1769, and successfully petitioned the Grand Lodge of Scotland for the appointment of their own Provincial Grand Master. Doctor Joseph Warren was installed as Provincial Grand Master of the new Massachusetts Grand Lodge on December 27, 1769, which is St. John the Evangelist's Day. There is unsubstantiated speculation that this day was chosen specifically to irritate the rival St. John's Grand Lodge.

Joseph Warren was a Harvard graduate, and one of the most prominent physicians in Boston. His enthusiasm and social stature brought publicity and success to the Massachusetts Grand Lodge during his five years as Grand Master.

Revolutionary Joseph Warren

During this same time period, Warren was one of the most outspoken critics of British authority in Massachusetts. He developed close relationships with John Hancock and Samuel Adams, and authored a number of published articles, including the Suffolk Resolves, that the British considered seditious.

It was Warren who volunteered to speak publicly at the Old South Church after hearing from British officers that anyone who dared do so would surely lose his life. And it was Joseph Warren who on April 18, 1775, dispatched William Dawes and Paul Revere on their famous midnight ride. In May, Warren was unanimously elected as President of the Massachusetts Provincial Congress.

On June 14, 1775, Warren was appointed as the second Brigadier General for the Massachusetts military forces. He presided over the Massachusetts Provincial Congress on June 16, and upon hearing of the British troops' arrival in Charlestown, rode directly to Bunker Hill to offer his services as the British attacked. After repelling two assaults, the American forces were overwhelmed and Warren was killed by a musketball.

QUESTION?

What happened to Joseph Warren's body?
Joseph Warren was unceremoniously buried in a mass grave by the British troops, but his body was recovered some months later. Badly decomposed, his body was identified by Paul Revere.

The Legacy Lives On

Joseph Warren was replaced by Joseph Webb, who would hold the position of Provincial Grand Master for another five years, seeing the end of hostilities between the newly formed United States and the British. In 1782, the members of St. Andrew's Lodge became divided in their position toward retaining allegiance with the Grand Lodge of Scotland.

In 1784, the members voted on the question, resulting in a ballot of twenty-nine votes for retaining Scottish allegiance and twenty-three members voting for independence. The twenty-three dissenting members were subsequently dropped from membership by the majority. The minority group immediately formed a new lodge under the jurisdiction of the St. John's Grand Lodge, resulting in enormous confusion and animosity between the former members of St. Andrew's, the Massachusetts Grand Lodge, and the St. John's Grand Lodge.

Finally, in 1792, the rival lodges reached a diplomatic agreement and formed a single Grand Lodge, which is now known as the Grand Lodge of Masons in Massachusetts. Paul Revere served as Grand Master from 1794 to 1797.

The union of the Grand Lodges in Massachusetts, and resulting union of their constituent lodges created a great deal of confusion in the numbering system. Traditionally, constituent lodges are assigned numbers in the order of their charter dates. With eighty-one constituent lodges in place at the time of the union, the complications proved to be insurmountable. The numbers were simply discarded, and the lodges remain uniquely unnumbered.

Vive la Masonry!

The first reliably documented lodge in France is recorded around 1738, dubbed the English Grand Lodge of France. Its exact origins are unknown, other than the probability that Freemasonry was imported into France in the 1730s by either the English, the Irish, or the Scots. France would become a beacon for the Age of Enlightenment, and Freemason popularity exploded in the 1740s. However, confusion and French-Masonic anarchy also ran rampant, with Masters governing lodges and granting charters in any fashion they chose.

French Masonry Factionalized

The Grand Lodge of France changed its name in 1772 to the Grand Orient of France, and adopted the statutes of the Royal Order of Freemasonry in France. Masons who disagreed with the changes simply broke away and continued as the Grand Lodge of France. The two groups quarreled relentlessly until the French Revolution effectively shut down Freemasonry in 1789. Ten years later, a union was formed between the two factions, and the Grand Lodge of France rejoined the Grand Orient of France.

Under Napoleon Bonaparte, Freemasonry expanded and continued to grow in popularity. However, significant variations in membership requirements, rituals, and philosophy would eventually separate French Freemasonry from that of England and the United States. In the 1870s, England effectively broke off ties with the Grand Orient of France for relaxing its references to the Grand Architect and effectively allowing atheists to become Masons. On most levels in France, lodges had been given complete autonomy regarding the inclusion of religious symbolism in their rituals.

FACT

In the eyes of the English, French Freemasonry had taken the Craft to an untenable extreme, and that view continues to the present day.

Modern French Masonry

Today, nearly half of the Freemasons in all of Europe are operating in France under a number of jurisdictions. The Grand Orient of France is the largest, with nearly 44,000 members. The second largest jurisdiction is the Grand Lodge of France, with approximately 30,000 members. The third largest jurisdiction is the National Grand Lodge of France, with an estimated 20,000 members. The National Grand Lodge of France is currently the only Grand Lodge recognized by Grand Lodges in the United States.

chapter 5

Members Only

Arguably the most misunderstood aspect of Freemasonry is the degrees its members attain and the rituals and ceremonies associated with those degrees. In truth, there's nothing mysterious about Masonic ritual, and when understood in context it's a fascinating study blanketed in allegory and symbolism. The three degrees of Ancient Craft Masonry are the foundation stones of the organization that launch an initiate on his journey through the Craft.

What Qualifies a Mason?

When tagged with the ominous term *secret society*, it's easy to see how some would naturally wonder how a Freemason initially became part of the Brotherhood. Were they nominated? Were they bribed into it? Did they have to forfeit their firstborn or sell their soul to the devil? Or do those individuals applying to the fraternity simply wish to enhance their own knowledge and spiritual enlightenment toward their personal well-being and that of their community?

There are several factors that come into play when an individual applies to the Brotherhood, but in truth, there's nothing secret or sinister about it. Hundreds of organizations require that individuals qualify for membership, and uphold certain rules and regulations once they are inducted. Freemasonry is one such organization.

Separating the Men from the Boys

It must be said that rules and regulations for an individual's admittance into the fraternity vary throughout Masonic jurisdictions. A common misconception is that individuals are recruited to the organization. In truth, the opposite is the case. Rules do vary, so it is possible that some jurisdictions require that a potential member is highly recommended, but in general, an individual will not be asked to join, but rather must decide to join a lodge of his own accord. The best way for an individual to find out about joining is simply to ask a Mason.

People are often confused by the term *lodge*. A building in which Masons meet is called a lodge. As a group, they are also called a lodge. The term *blue lodge* refers to many lodges in the United States wherein the lodge ceiling is painted blue.

There are several general qualifications that must be met in order to join the Freemasons, and they are considered to be moral, spiritual, and physical in nature. The moral guidelines refer to the ideals of society, and the physical qualifications are viable as each individual must be responsible for his actions and be able to make life decisions. The spiritual necessities serve to enhance the structure of the Brotherhood and the religions represented by its members.

The basic qualifications for becoming a Freemason are:

- A man interested in becoming a Mason must apply to the organization of his own free will.
- Individuals must profess a belief in a Supreme Being and immortality of the soul.
- The individual must be of sound mind and body, and in possession of good morals.
- Individuals must be male and of a certain age. This varies among jurisdictions, but in general the minimum age is anywhere from eighteen to twenty-five.
- Individuals must be "born free," which translates to not being a bondsman or slave. Naturally, this requirement is no longer necessary in the modern world.

One of the common misconceptions of the Craft is that it's a religion. Freemasonry is indeed not a religion and there is no particular Deity or Supreme Being its members worship. In regard to religious affiliation, members can subscribe to any religion of their choosing. The Brotherhood accepts all theologies and beliefs aside from atheists, and in some jurisdictions and countries even atheists are allowed admission.

Approval and Induction

When an individual applies to a Masonic lodge, he is first investigated and then his admission is voted upon by the lodge's membership by way of secret balloting. This historical voting custom, known as the "Ordeal of the Secret Ballot," is accomplished using black and white cubes (or in some cases, balls). Current members of that lodge cast their vote by selecting one of the cubes. Though voting rules can vary slightly depending on the jurisdiction, a potential Mason must be voted into the Brotherhood unanimously.

Some lodges or jurisdictions allow for a potential candidate to receive one negative vote, and still be inducted into the Masonic order.

The Masonic fraternity prides itself on the fact that it accepts members from all walks of life and individuals of all religious faiths. Once a member is accepted into the Craft, they begin their journey through the first of three degrees of Freemasonry, also referred to as Ancient Craft Masonry.

Degrees of Freemasonry

There are three main degrees, or levels, of Freemasonry to which a member can ascend. The first degree is Entered Apprentice, the second is Fellowcraft, and the third is Master Mason. Any member can complete these three degrees and simply remain at that level, or they can continue to earn additional degrees by entering one of the two branches of Freemasonry, the Scottish or York Rite. In general, an individual who is referred to as a Mason has typically achieved all three degrees. (The degrees of Freemasonry are akin to a staircase—with each step an individual ascends to a higher level of educational and spiritual enlightenment.)

Once accepted, the individual will have an initiation ceremony and begin his fraternal journey as an Entered Apprentice. Each degree is designed to enlighten an initiate using allegory, ritual, and symbols, most of which have evolved from the Operative Masons and the tools of their trade.

It is said that the three degrees are a rite of passage celebrating youth, manhood, and age. During the first degree a member is born into the Brotherhood and begins the learning process. During the second degree he becomes more enlightened as to the ways of the Craft, and by the third degree he increases his moral value and virtue.

Another common description of the three degrees is body, mind, and soul. The first degree revolves around the body as it relates to an action-filled world and a man's ability to hone his relationship with that world. The second degree deals with perfecting the mind through the use of liberal arts and science. The third degree involves perfection of the soul as a result of understanding the mysteries of the Craft.

It is said that a potential member of the fraternity is prepared in his heart, and then enters into the Brotherhood in order to discover "light," or knowledge.

Entered Apprentice

The *Entered Apprentice* is the first degree of Freemasonry and in many ways it symbolizes an individual's spiritual birth into the fraternity, and begins his quest for "light," or knowledge. It is a preliminary degree which serves to prepare the individual for the second and third degrees that will, in succession, elevate his level of fraternal education, understanding, and enlightenment.

In order to obtain each degree, a member must participate in a symbolic ritual before he can continue on to the next degree. This begins with the Entered Apprentice degree and the first of an initiate's *catechisms*, or questions and examinations. Typically, a new member will work with an existing member to aid in the memorization of the questions and answers that relate to that degree. When a catechism is completed an initiate can move on to his next degree.

Each degree has certain symbolism associated with its level. These symbols, or *working tools*, are meant to represent the morals and forces necessary in building and rebuilding the nature of humankind. Philosophically, the tools, by their very nature, are meant to show that well-meaning and gratifying work, with proper guidance, can be accomplished. The working tools of the Entered Apprentice degree are the common gavel (a tool of force) and the twenty-four inch gauge (a tool of calculation and measurement).

As an Apprentice, an individual is introduced to the lodge and the internal structure of the fraternity. The lessons he learns begin with his initiation rite where he must be prepared to embark on a personal journey of educational and spiritual fulfillment. Once an individual is duly ready to accept this journey, he can proceed to the second degree, or Fellowcraft.

In Masonic lodges the world over, Entered Apprentice is the first degree. In German it is called *lehrling*, in French, *apprentiz*, in Spanish it is *aprendiz*, and in Italian, *apprendente*. In all cases the word apprentice finds its etymology in the word "learner."

Fellowcraft

Individuals who earn the second degree of Freemasonry, called *Fellowcraft*, are symbolically entering into the adult phase of the Craft. At this stage, members seek to acquire the knowledge and spiritual tools necessary to build character and improve society. The symbolism associated with the second degree differs from the first in that more science is introduced to the individual. Additional allegories and symbols serve to further enhance the initiate's intellectual prowess and reasoning capabilities.

The Fellowcraft degree symbolizes life and the emergence into spiritual adulthood. In keeping with his progressive fraternal education the initiate is taught more history of the Craft, and the legacy of Operative Masonry from biblical to Medieval times. During this symbolic period of manhood Fellowcraft initiates use the lessons they learned as an Entered Apprentice to broaden and strengthen their horizons.

The primary symbol associated with a Fellowcraft Mason is a winding staircase, which is used to ascend to new spiritual heights. He is also introduced to pillars and the letter "G," which holds special significance for the Brotherhood.

Master Mason

Throughout the fraternity it is a commonly held belief that there is no higher degree conferred on an individual than *Master Mason*. Degrees earned beyond Master through one of the concordant bodies such as the York and Scottish Rites, are generally considered to be educational and symbolic.

The Master Mason is symbolically linked to the soul and his own inner nature and belief system. His spiritual and physical growth is enhanced when achieving this degree, as he climbs the winding stairs of adulthood in an effort to learn more of the Divine Truth. The degree is richly laden with allegory and symbolism that dates back to the building of the Temple of Solomon, and the rites associated with the degree are taken very seriously in regard to a brother's spiritual and educational teachings of the Craft.

Additional Degrees

Once an individual has become a Mason, meaning he has completed the first three degrees and is now a Master Mason, he is free to continue his education by joining the Scottish or York Rite. The Scottish Rite consists of thirty-two degrees and an honorary thirty-third degree which is by invitation only and is conferred by the Supreme Council.

The York Rite features three additional Masonic bodies—Royal Arch Masonry, Cryptic Masonry, and Knights Templar—that confer degrees within their ranks. Master Masons also have the option of joining one of Masonry's social groups such as the Shriners (discussed in detail in Chapter 19).

Masonic Rituals

Masonic rites are serious, dignified ceremonies rich in allegory and symbolism. Freemasonry isn't a religion, but its rituals are held in the same regard as one holds ceremonies and rites associated with various churches and religions. Each allegory, symbol, or legend used in Masonic rituals and ceremonies holds great meaning within the Brotherhood. Some symbols, like the apron or a gavel may seem out of context, but their meaning is highly symbolic to ancient Masonry as the tools of the trade.

When a member is initiated into the Brotherhood he enters a world filled with ritual, allegory, symbolism, and history. As he progresses through the three main degrees of Freemasonry, his knowledge and enlightenment increase the higher he climbs. Initiation rites require preparation, including the various catechisms individuals must take to heart and memorize.

ALERT!

Englishman Samuel Prichard was the first non-Mason to expose allegedly secret Masonic rituals to the public. In 1730 he printed *Masonry Dissected*. Until that time Masonic rituals had been memorized and passed on within the Brotherhood by means of oral communication. Ironically, many Masons purchased the book in order to study their own rituals!

A candidate's primary initiation into the Craft is highly significant, and the rite he endures signifies his earnest, heartfelt promise to be taught, learn from those he teaches, and ultimately lead a better life as a result of those teachings. Initiates are encouraged to pay close attention to ceremonial proceedings, as with each degree the allegory and symbolism impart additional history of Freemasonry.

Initiation of the First Degree: Entered Apprentice

The initiation rite of the Entered Apprentice, called the Rite of Destitution, is replete with symbolism and mystery, but only an inkling of what is to come during the course of an initiate's Masonic career. For starters, the initiate is "duly and truly" prepared, which means he will wear garments that the lodge provides. This signifies an initiate's sincerity in joining the Brotherhood, as the focus is on his presence as a man and lacks any designation of personal honor and wealth.

One of the principles of Freemasonry is charity. By symbolically stripping a man of his wealth or perceived wealth, an initiate learns what it is to be in dire need. It is said that this ritual opens the initiate's eyes to the obligations one has to help mankind in order to bring him out of his desperate plight and help him regain his dignity.

The Rite of Destitution itself is interesting, as it relates to ancient times and planetary characteristics. In long ago times, it is said, that men adhered to a belief that the soul was descended from planetary bodies with innate qualities specific to each sphere. Each of the planetary attributes were associated with a type of metal, and as such, initiates rid themselves of all metals prior to ceremonies so that potentially disturbing planetary influences would not pollute the proceedings. In modern times, the rite instead focuses on the shedding of one's image, in a sense, and leaving any prejudice or extreme view out of the lodge so as to retain fraternal harmony.

Hoods and Ropes?

Part of the initiation rites for the various degrees involve a *hoodwink*, which refers to a blindfold or hood, and a *cable tow*, which is a rope used for restraint or towing. Looking at the ritual from the outside, the use of these items may conjure up images of violence or hanging, but that is certainly not the case. The cable tow, which is also a measure of distance, symbolically binds each Mason to all of his brethren. The tie is as strong and lengthy as the Mason and the personal abilities he brings to the Brotherhood.

Being hoodwinked represents the veil of silence and secrecy surrounding the mysteries of the Brotherhood. It is also meant to symbolize the ignorance or "mystical darkness" of an uninitiated member. The hood symbolically remains in place until the initiate is prepared to encompass the "light," or knowledge which is about to be imparted to him. Being blindfolded or hoodwinked also enables the initiate to completely focus on the ceremonial words being spoken without visual distraction. Taken literally, the terms *hood* (as a verb, to "cover"), and *wink* (an archaic reference to the eye) together mean to cover one's eyes.

The cable tow has several symbolic meanings, one of which is an umbilical cord, a necessary factor in the beginnings of life which is severed upon birth, but born with the potential for love and growth. The cable tow is also regarded to be a symbol of acceptance—complete and voluntary—by the initiate, who in doing so also pledges to comply with whatever the fraternity has planned for him.

Entering Into the Light

When the initiate is "duly" clothed and hoodwinked, he is led into the lodge by the cable tow. Entering into the room in this manner allows the initiate to symbolically leave the darkness and destitution of the world behind him and find embrace in the warmth of light. Initiation rites are highly confidential and are taken very seriously among members. The structure of this rite is meant to reinforce to the initiate that actions have consequences and that virtue plays a large part in gaining entrance into the fraternity and the mysteries surrounding it.

QUESTION?

Is this ritual some kind of hazing?
It's easy to see why the thought of hoods and ropes in confined quarters is unnerving to those not involved in Masonry, but it's all highly symbolic to the organization and is in no way harmful to any initiate. Individuals enter into the Brotherhood of their own free will.

Lodge meetings always begin and end with a prayer issued by a Chaplain or lodge Master. Because Masonry forbids the discussion of religion or politics, the prayer is universal. It simply pays homage to Deity and typically ends with the phrase "So mote it be," or "So may it ever be."

Within the lodge there is generally a central object or point (an altar) which the initiate must walk around. This ancient practice of *circumambulation* is meant to show that the initiate is prepared to embark on his journey. Walking in a clockwise direction around the object mimics the path of the sun—moving east to west via the south—as it is seen from an earthly perspective.

Altars are symbolic of faith and worship. In approaching and circumambulating the altar in the presence of his fellow brothers, the initiate offers himself to mankind and to the *Supreme Architect of the Universe*. It is said that the Master's wisdom travels from his eastern position out toward the altar.

It is important the initiate realize that Freemasonry, and the truths it teaches him are not secret. What is secret is the manner in which the Craft teaches those truths.

Obligations to the Brotherhood

At the center of the Entered Apprentice degree is the *Obligation* rite the initiate performs, which for the duration of his life binds him to the Brotherhood and his duties to the Craft. In its essence, the man's obligation proves to his brethren that his intentions are sincere. The rite also serves to protect the Brotherhood from members revealing instructive symbolism or modes of recognition.

When a man completes his initiation and becomes an Entered Apprentice, his rights within the Brotherhood are limited. He obtains knowledge of secret modes of recognition and is entitled to a Masonic funeral, but he is not allowed to vote in lodge proceedings or become an officer. Only when he becomes proficient enough in the first degree can he move on to the second.

The Holy Bible, the Square, and the Compass

Integral to the Apprentice initiation rite are the *Three Great Lights of Masonry*. The *Volume of the Sacred Law*, the *square*, and the *compass* acknowledge man's relationship to Deity and are another holy trinity of Freemasonry, similar in interpretation to the three degrees. It is said that each Great Light is a guiding principle of nature, with the square symbolizing the body, the compass representing the mind, and the Sacred Law serving as the soul.

The first of these lights is the Volume of the Sacred Law, and depending on the lodge and the area or country it can be a number of sacred texts. In the United States, that volume is typically the Bible, but initiates are given the option to have the sacred book of their choosing on the altar during their initiation ceremony. The book is placed on the altar and is open, which is highly significant as it acts as a guide to faith and to acknowledge man's relationship to Deity.

The square and the compass are the most recognizable symbols in Freemasonry, and their evolution is apparent in many ancient works (see Chapter 14). The square signifies earth and the compass symbolizes an "arc of heaven." This heaven and earth relationship is often shown in conjunction with the Sacred Law as a representation of God's heavenly and earthly creations. These three Great Lights are highly regarded by Freemasons as symbols steeped in revelation, righteousness, and redemption.

The First Stone

In the masonry trade, the northeast corner holds a special place, as it marks the spot where the first stone, or cornerstone, of a building is placed. Symbolically, an Entered Apprentice takes his place during the ceremony in the northeast corner of the room, signifying that from that spot he will build his own temple according to the principles of the Brotherhood.

There are several interpretations of the significance of the northeast positioning of an Apprentice. In Freemasonry, north represents darkness while east represents light, which makes the northeast corner the midpoint between the darkness and the light. It is also said that this light/dark dichotomy is reflective of the equal balance of night and day during the Spring equinox.

Finishing Touches

During the initiation rite, the Worshipful Master, the leader of a lodge, gives lectures to the potential brother which further explain particular phases of the ritual in which he has taken part. This is meant to help the initiate understand the lessons taught in the Craft as well as to introduce the *four cardinal virtues* of temperance, fortitude, prudence, and justice. In addition he is told of Brotherly Love, Relief, and Truth and the trio of tenets associated with them.

Do Masons discuss religion and politics during their meetings?
The subjects of religion and politics are not allowed to be discussed in a lodge. Brothers are all entitled to their own opinions, but in the lodge the objective is for all members to be on common ground.

At the closing of the initiation ceremony, the new Brother is given a "charge" which explains his Masonic duties in relation to the degree he has achieved. He then begins a series of questions and answers called a *proficiency*, which he must memorize before he can ascend to the next degree.

The proficiency is meant to teach the language of the Brotherhood, the structure of his degree, and help him make the distinction between his points of obligation. It also serves to present the initiate with historic methods of contemplating his degree, and aims to establish contact with a current member of the Brotherhood.

Once an Entered Apprentice completes his initiation he receives a white lambskin apron as a mark of distinction. For the new Apprentice it is a badge and an innocence dictated by clean thought processes, obedience, and goodwill toward his new brethren. An Apprentice is then born and takes his first spiritual steps into the light. When he pursues the second degree, he moves higher up the staircase and enters into his fraternal adulthood.

Initiation of the Second Degree: Fellowcraft

The second degree, or Fellowcraft, marks an individual's spiritual ascendance into adulthood in the Craft. Like the Entered Apprentice the Fellowcraft degree is highly symbolic, but in ways that illuminate, grant passage, and offer instruction and elevation toward "the East." The second degree is about advancement, assuming new responsibilities, and using the Three Great Lights to further an individual's connection to the Brotherhood.

The primary symbol of the second degree, a winding staircase, leads to the "Middle Chamber of the Temple." The seven steps symbolize the seven liberal arts and sciences. Other symbols also mark an individual's ascension including ladders, staircases, mountains, and vertical ropes. Additional benefits (wages symbolically represented by corn, wine, and oil) are offered to Fellowcraft initiates, and their working tools—the square, the level, and plumb—become instruments used for testing purposes in order to ascertain the true from the false.

ALERT!

The number three is a revered number in Freemasonry as it relates to groupings, science, history, and especially geometry. This is first introduced in the second degree and, like most Masonic symbols, implies deeper meaning than the obvious.

As the Entered Apprentice symbolically focuses on the body, the Fellowcraft focuses on the mind and perfection of faculties through the mediums of art and science. The teachings of this degree are profound, as they allow initiates entrance into new areas of the Brotherhood and further education into the symbolism associated with a Fellowcraft Mason.

The Square, the Level, and the Plumb

The Apprentice learns that the square symbolizes earth. It is plain and its sides are of equal measure and it is used for testing angles. The Fellowcraft initiate increases his awareness of the square as a symbol representing honesty, morality, and truthfulness. Two sides of a square form a right angle, mimicking stones used to build strong upright structures. The square is accurate but the angle is such that it forces one to follow the correct path.

The level by its very nature is symbolic of spiritual balance and equality. It is meant to show that though all men may not be on equal ground, they all have the opportunity to achieve greatness. The plumb represents rectitude or "uprightness of conduct." Thought of in terms of a plumb line it is said to relate to justice in that all individuals shouldn't be judged by the standards of others, only by their own sense of right and wrong.

The Pillars of Solomon

Other important symbols introduced to Fellowcraft initiates are the *pillars on the porch*, which are historically linked to the Temple of Solomon. These two pillars, which represent power and control, were located at the porchway, or entrance to the Temple, and it is speculated that globes atop the columns alternately represent the celestial (heaven) and terrestrial (earth) respectively.

FACT

The two pillars at the entrance to Solomon's Temple actually have names. The pillar on the left is called Boaz, and the pillar on the right is named Jachin.

It is said that the pillars also relate to the Three Great Supports of Masonry. Wisdom (south) and strength (north) denote the pair of columns, and the potential Fellowcraftsman at his initiation is a third column which symbolizes balance or beauty.

One Step at a Time

The winding staircase is the primary symbol associated with the second degree. It is said that eighteenth century Masons adopted the symbol from the First Book of Kings which makes reference to the middle chamber.

While the Entered Apprentice is but a child in the Craft, the Fellowcraftsman, when standing before the winding staircase, begins the life of a man by passing through the pillars on the porch and starting his ascent of the stairs in ultimate pursuit of the Divine Truth to which all Masons aspire. It is said that with each step, he strives to improve himself, taking careful notes of the symbols surrounding him, and learn as much as his journey through life provides. The reward for successfully completing this intellectual and moral quest is heightened character and ascension into a higher life. It is a difficult passage made successful with instruction and ultimate wisdom.

The winding stairs are also used as a symbol in one of the degrees of the Scottish Rite, where it is called *cocleus*, or a spiral staircase.

The number of steps comprising the winding staircase has been debated over the years, but a common belief is that it contains seven stairs that correspond to the ancient Seven Liberal Arts and Sciences. Another possible source are faith, hope, and charity, a triad of theological virtues said to be a heavenly ladder. Combined with the four cardinal virtues from the first degree they comprise seven steps.

The four cardinal virtues of temperance, fortitude, prudence, and justice are considered to be earthly virtues and therefore horizontal. The virtues of faith, hope, and charity represent ascension into the light and are vertical, symbolizing the climb up the stairs.

Seven Educational Steps

The year 330 marks the formulation of the Seven Liberal Arts and Sciences, which Christian scholars adopted in France in the twelfth century. It is said that the study of the Seven Liberal Arts and Sciences was a "means to the knowledge of God."

The Seven Liberal Arts and Sciences are:

- **Grammar:** The art of correct writing and skillful speech.
- **Logic:** The art and science of "proper" thinking.
- **Rhetoric:** The art of using language to invoke specific impressions on others.
- **Arithmetic:** The science of theories involving numbers.
- **Geometry:** The science and art of abstraction.
- **Astronomy:** The science of the metaphysical and celestial.
- **Music:** The art and science of harmony evolved from mathematics.

These seven disciplines, said to represent an ideal education toward understanding the Supreme Being, are highly embedded in the Craft, and each are seen as equally important. Proficiency in these areas is required for Fellowcraft initiates, for when they ascend the seven steps to reach the other doors of the middle chamber, they are furthering their path to enlightenment.

As reward for his ascension of the seven steps, an initiate has earned a symbolic wage of corn, wine, and oil, which represent an enhanced richness of the mental and spiritual world. Corn symbolizes nourishment or resurrection, wine portrays health and refreshment or "divine intoxication," and oil represents joy and happiness or consecration. Together they constitute a full life.

God or Geometry?

Initiates into the second degree are introduced to one of the more prominent symbols of Freemasonry, the letter "G." There is no definitive explanation for its true meaning but it is thought to have first represented geometry and then evolved to include God. It has also been interpreted as Grand Architect of the Universe or Great Architect of the Universe. Regardless, the interchangeability of God and geometry has a certain symmetry to the Craft as both are prominently figured and as such, "G" remains a powerful symbol.

FACT

Both the letter "G" and the number three are significant symbols for Freemasons. In the Greek and Hebrew alphabets, where letters are assigned numeric values, the letter "G" is equal to the number three.

The Fellowcraftsman is first introduced to geometry in his studies of the Seven Liberal Arts and Sciences, but in that particular science, his studies must be furthered. Because geometry is heavily entrenched in the trade of masonry, it is recognized for its importance in the symbology of Freemasonry. Its mathematical and metaphysical origins dating back to ancient Egyptian and Greek eras provide an initiate with an enormous amount of information to ponder and from which to draw conclusions. The combined principles of numbering, ordering, proportion, and symmetry are all a part of geometry, and that makes the science a powerful entity that is further revealed to those pursuing the third degree.

Initiation of the Third Degree: Master Mason

An initiate entering into the third degree will have bestowed upon him the central mystery of Freemasonry which refers to the soul and its arrival at perfection. Commonly called the "Crown of the Blue Lodge Masonry," the degree of Master Mason is a culmination of all the teachings an individual has absorbed during the first two degrees and another step toward attaining fraternal enlightenment. Those completing the third degree are also entitled to a Masonic funeral as well as rights of relief (charity) and visitation (to other lodges).

For his tenacity in achieving the first two degrees, the Master Mason is rewarded full symbolic use of all the working tools of the trade. The trowel in particular holds special meaning for the Master, as it relates to the spread of "brotherly love." The third degree is characterized as the "sublime climax of symbolic Freemasonry." In keeping with this, an initiate into the third degree is raised to the Sublime Degree of Master Mason. Once raised, a brother can remain at this level or continue his studies of the Craft by joining one of its appendant bodies.

It is said that by this stage of Brotherly evolution, an individual has learned to balance his inner nature, developed stability, purified his physicality, and broadened his mental faculties. The beginning of the initiation rite of the Master Mason is similar to that of the previous degrees, yet worlds apart. He enters the lodge in darkness, but for this rite he is fully prepared to enter sacred territory. Fortunately, he is given the tools to do so.

Drama in Antiquity

Central to the initiation rite of the Master Mason is a symbolic dramatic enactment that brings the Temple of Solomon and the Legend of Hiram Abiff to the forefront. Often mentioned in the rituals of the Brotherhood are the three Grand Masters involved in the building of Solomon's Temple. The first is Solomon, the king of Israel, the second is his friend the king of Tyre, and the third is architect and Master Mason Hiram Abiff, whom the Tyrian king sent to Solomon to help construct the Temple. These three Grand Masters serve to represent the Divine Truth which all Brothers strive to achieve.

It is said that Hiram Abiff was seen as the father of those workers who built Solomon's Temple. One translation of the name Abiff is "his father," so the name is often referred to as "Hiram, my father."

During this enactment, the Master initiate plays the role of Hiram Abiff, a man of mystical and highly symbolic meaning within the Craft. Hiram's death, at the hands of three ruffians seeking to obtain the Divine Truth, is a symbolic representation of man's ignorance, passion, and attitude—virtues he seeks to quell. Hiram's death and the fact that he took Divine secrets with him left a void in the search for ultimate enlightenment. His resurrection and reburial, however, is an allegory that denotes ultimate victory and immortality. Masonic ties to the Divine Truth are strong and an initiate's participation in this drama serves to reinforce one of the primary beliefs of the Brotherhood.

Symbols of the Master Mason

Like the previous two initiation rites, the ceremony of the Master Mason is blanketed in symbolism. With a rich historic legacy from which to draw, the Master learns the deeper meanings of these symbols and how they apply to his spiritual journey of the Craft. The gavel, twenty-four-inch gauge, and setting maul are part of the Master's working tools, and a sprig of acacia is used as an ancient symbol of rebirth.

Emblems introduced during the rites of the Master are rife with meaning. A pot of incense signifies purity of heart, prayer, and meditation. The beehive is representative of industry and the need for constant work for the good of mankind, and the book of constitutions serves to remind initiates of law and morality. Also part of the rite is the *Sword Pointing to a Naked Heart*, which singles out the need for justice in heart and in practice. The all-seeing eye is also apparent as it reinforces the presence of God.

The Forty-Seventh Problem of Euclid is a symbol which finds its roots in Egyptian legend. It is a triad linking Osiris (vertical) to Isis (horizontal) and Horus (the diagonal).

Three additional symbols are featured in the Master Mason ritual. The anchor and the ark focus on well-being and stability in a life that is truthful and faithful. The hourglass symbolizes time and how quickly life passes, as does the scythe which furthers the element of time, and ultimately severs the cord of life thereby presenting man to eternity.

chapter 6

Structure of a Brotherhood

To Freemasons, the lodge is a magical place. It provides a safe haven amid trusting brethren bound together by common goals and interests in making the world a better place. The inner workings of a lodge and Grand Lodge are similar to that of most organizations. They have officers and assigned duties, and carry out meetings in typical fashion, but it is the symbolism and tradition of the lodge that is fascinating, from the attention paid to directionality to their use of the color blue.

Lodges Defined

The term *lodge* is one that often confuses those not familiar with Freemasonry. The meaning of the word *lodge* is two-fold, as it refers to both a group of Masons, and the building in which they meet. Masonic buildings are often called temples, which is more symbolic in meaning and pays homage to the construction of Solomon's Temple. In this case, the word *temple* does not bear religious significance, instead deferring to the actual masonry trade. In ancient masonry, specifically in regard to the construction of cathedrals, stonemasons during the construction process would build structures against the sides of a cathedral. When building operations would halt during the winter months, the masons would live in these "lodges."

One expert traditionally defines a lodge as follows: "A lodge of Masons is an assemblage of brothers and fellows met together for the purpose of expatiating on the mysteries of the Craft, with the Bible, square and compasses, the Book of Constitutions, and the warrant empowering them to act."

With the establishment of the Grand Lodge of England in 1717, the word *lodge* became multidimensional. Prior to that time, operative Masons often held meetings in private homes or at inns or taverns.

Masonic lodges are specific in their physical structure, which focuses on geometry and directionality. The buildings are generally oblong squares (rectangles) with the longer sides stretching from east to west, and the width of the structure running from north to south. At the time of Solomon's Temple the earth was thought to have the form of a rectangle. The directions related to the rectangle, if placed on a map, serve to symbolically locate the world surrounding its form. As such, it is said that the world is representative of a Masonic lodge. Its members work and thrive in that world.

The Blue Lodge

One of the most common terms in Freemasonry is "blue lodge," and it is primarily used in the United States and Canada. The color blue is highly symbolic to the Craft and is evident in their teachings, their attire, and in the lodge itself, as the ceilings of many meeting rooms are literally painted blue. It is symbolic of the three degrees of Freemasonry, and is emblematic of the virtues of universal friendship, benevolence, and charity. In Masonic terms the color blue is symbolic of the blue vault, or arch of heaven. The ceiling of a lodge is often called a "canopy of heaven."

FACT

During the time of Hitler's Germany, when the Brotherhood was being persecuted, Freemasons used the blue forget-me-not flower as a way of recognizing one another.

The color blue is also a representation of truth, fidelity, and universality. Blue lodges, with their dedication to the three degrees are true to the educational and spiritual journey they make through the Craft. Like any other lodge in the Masonic world, blue lodges are sanctioned, or warranted, by Grand Lodges. Degrees achieved in a blue lodge are commonly referred to as *blue lodge degrees*, but they are no different than any other Masonic lodge. The distinction to be made here is simply a matter of rhetoric as it is most commonly used as a North American term. Blue lodge degrees are *Ancient Craft Degrees*.

The Fraternal Jewels

The six *jewels* given to each lodge, three *moveable* and three *immovable*, are both literal and symbolic of morals and virtue. The *rough ashlar*, *perfect ashlar*, and the *trestle board* are the movable jewels that are not confined to a specific area of a lodge. The rough ashlar is a squared block of building stone which requires refinement in order to become perfect ashlar. The trestle board was used by operative Masons to secure designs and blueprints. Together they are emblematic of a moral plan and successful journey.

The square, level, and plumb are the immovable jewels of a lodge, placed in specific locations within a lodge where brethren can meditate upon them. In North American Masonry, the square is placed in the east, the level in the west, and the plumb in the south. In English Masonry, the jewels are reversed. In their lodges, the three movable jewels (square, level, plumb) are passed from officers to their successors, with the jewels typically worn around the neck by a ribbon or chain.

Lodge Hierarchy

The hierarchy of a typical lodge or blue lodge is similar to that of a Grand Lodge, only the names are different. One way of looking at it is the Master of a lodge is basically the leader or president. His wardens would be first and second vice president, and so on. The head of a lodge is called the *Worshipful Master* or in some jurisdictions a *Right Worshipful Master*, and he is an individual who has passed through the three degrees and become a Master Mason. The position is elected and is generally a one-year term.

The *Senior Warden* is second in command of a lodge. The jewel of his office symbolizes equality and impartiality. He assists the Master in governmental matters of the lodge, and he also regularly attends meetings and takes over as leader should the Worshipful Master be absent and a Past Master unavailable. If the Master dies during his term or is rendered incapable, the Senior Warden assumes his position until the next election.

The *Junior Warden's* jewel is emblematic of the upright conduct he is to display in working with his Master and Senior Warden. He is third in the chain of command and his duties primarily involve acting as liaison and coordinator of lodge activities.

The *Senior Deacon's* duty is to welcome and introduce brothers who visit the lodge. He also carries out various duties as required by the Worshipful Master. The jewel of the deacon is a dove, which is emblematic of peace.

The *Junior Deacon* is the messenger of the Senior Warden and among his other responsibilities he is stationed by the lodge door during meetings to make certain those entering or leaving have permission from the Master or Senior Warden.

Positions vary among lodges, but in general the three principal officers are wardens, deacons, and stewards, who are all elected. Then there are appointed secretaries, treasurers, a chaplain, and a tyler.

The *Senior Steward* assists the deacons and other officers of the lodge with various duties. He is generally in charge of maintaining refreshments and making sure each brother is comfortable. The *Junior Steward* serves as his assistant.

The *Tyler* of a lodge is very important. His symbolic jewel is his sword, which is used to guard the lodge from non-Masons. He attends all meetings and makes certain the lodge is in order, acts as host to visiting brethren, and makes certain all brothers are properly clothed when entering the lodge. Symbolically, he is a reminder that only worthy thoughts, words, and deeds should be spoken within the lodge.

Lodges So Grand

There are Grand Lodges in countries all over the world and in the United States there is one in every state. In order to become an official Masonic lodge, a warrant or charter must be issued by the Grand Lodge in that jurisdiction. Lodges under the umbrella of a regional Grand Lodge are recognized by their name and lodge number.

Edward VII, son of Queen Victoria, served as Grand Master of the Grand Lodge of England from 1874 to 1901. He was a huge proponent of Freemasonry and was renowned for his attendance at public Masonic ceremonies.

Grand Lodges have governing bodies within the lodge that include a Grand Master and his staff which varies from one lodge or one jurisdiction to another. Grand Lodges deal with the governmental aspects of the Craft. They have the power to enact regulations and laws in order that the ancient landmarks of Freemasonry remain true. They can also decide upon all matters relating to individual lodges or brothers and delegate authority should circumstances warrant a particular action. Grand Lodges also have the power to expel brethren or lodges themselves. Basically, they are the governing bodies of Freemasonry and establishments that all other lodges can seek out for all matters relating to the Craft.

Grand Lodge Hierarchy

The titles of the various officers within a Grand Lodge differ from those of the lodges within their jurisdiction. However, the positions of the officers are basically the same. The highest ranking individual of a Grand Lodge is called the *Grand Master*. It is an elected position and one of great prestige within the Craft. His powers vary depending on the jurisdiction, but in general he is the head of the Grand Lodge and its officers. The length of a Grand Master's term varies depending on location. In England, the Grand Master is typically a member of nobility or royalty and the position is for life. In some jurisdictions in North America, the position is held for a year.

In general each Grand Lodge has a *Deputy Grand Master* and various levels of wardens, stewards, deacons, secretaries, treasurers, and chaplains in the same structure as regular lodges. Grand Lodges typically meet once a year, and the positions held within a Grand Lodge are members of the lodges under their jurisdiction. In other words, individuals can hold positions in both their lodge and a Grand Lodge.

Symbolic Directions

The directionality of a lodge and the ornamentation and furniture within the lodge are of great symbolic importance to Freemasons. In general, directions are referred to as the *four cardinal points*. Each point has symbolic and mystic meaning, with east representing wisdom, west indicating strength, south reflective of beauty, and the north given to darkness.

Masonic buildings run east to west. The east has throughout history been considered sacred as it represents the light of the rising sun, or the daily birth of the sun. In the lodge, the Worshipful Master sits in the eastern part of the lodge usually on a raised platform, which is considered to be the most honorable area of a lodge. The Volume of the Sacred Law is placed on a pedestal or altar also in the eastern direction.

The west part of the lodge is where the Senior Warden stands, his position representing a show of strength. Symbolically it also marks the end of the day and the hope within each individual that hard work will provide well-earned reward.

If the orientation of the lodge building does not allow for the Master to sit in the true eastern side of the lodge, he is still considered to be symbolically in the east.

The north in Freemasonry is a place of darkness. In ancient masonry, the north marked the spot where the foundation stone of a new building was laid. Symbolically, those in the north are as yet uninitiated. The northeast direction, where the cornerstone is laid is crucial to a building and to a newly initiated Apprentice who is said to symbolically be in the most superficial area of the Craft. The south, the more esoteric of the four directions, symbolizes beauty.

Proceedings Behind Closed Doors

Secrecy and Freemasonry are often used in the same sentence, so when it comes to lodges and meetings among brethren the public at large remains morbidly curious, especially in regard to ritual ceremonies. But the bottom line is that Masons enjoy each other's company—after all they are a fraternity—and so they look forward to working on projects that benefit the community.

Within a lodge there are two different types of meetings, one simply for business and the other for degree ceremonies. Masonic business meetings run much the same as other membership-based organizations with minutes read, votes taken on various issues, and charitable functions or events planned. The degree ceremonies are much more formal. Most lodges are open to the public for various events and special meetings supporting the community.

Amity and Autonomy

Freemasonry as an organization is unusual in that each jurisdiction is sovereign and independent of each other. Typically, jurisdictions are divided geographically by territory, and as such there is no central guiding authority. However, jurisdictions do keep track of other jurisdictions that they officially recognize. The term "amity" in relation to Masonry means that two jurisdictions who recognize each other allow their members to freely visit and attend closed lodge meetings. This camaraderie usually indicates that both jurisdictions have similar landmarks and fraternal characteristics in common.

Grand Lodges and the lodges within their jurisdictions have the sole authority to grant the three basic Masonic degrees of Entered Apprentice, Fellowcraft, and Master Mason. *Concordant* bodies are organizations of Freemasonry that can confer additional degrees. Generally speaking, *appendant* bodies are organizations that only allow Masons or those related to Masons into their membership.

There are a number of appendant organizations associated with the Brotherhood including the Shriners and the Daughters of the Eastern Star (see Chapter 19). The two largest concordant bodies of Freemasonry are the Ancient and Accepted Scottish Rite and the York Rite, both of which offer a wide range of additional degrees that a Master Mason can achieve.

chapter 7

The Scottish and York Rites

The Ancient and Accepted Scottish Rite and the York Rite are the two largest concordant bodies of Freemasonry. Rich with history and symbolism, they both confer additional degrees that afford Masons the opportunity to continue their study of the Craft. Highly revered and allegorical rituals are part of both Rites, which continue the legends and lessons a Mason learned during the first three degrees of Craft Masonry.

The Scottish Rite

The Ancient and Accepted Scottish Rite, or Scottish Rite, is one of the most popular concordant bodies of Freemasonry. It is available to all Masons who have completed the three degrees of Ancient Craft Masonry and is entirely optional. Origins of the Scottish Rite are unclear, but it is generally believed to have originated from the French Scottish Rite of Perfection. The Scottish Rite offers thirty-two advanced degrees and a thirty-third degree which is both nominated and honorary.

The Scottish Rite is difficult to explain, given that it differs in certain countries and from Northern to Southern jurisdictions in the United States. Unlike typical Craft Lodges, which are governed by Grand Lodges, the Scottish Rite is governed by a Supreme Council for each jurisdiction. Listed below are the degrees for the Southern jurisdiction which includes four divisions—the Lodge of Perfection, Chapter of the Rose Croix, Council of Kadosh, and Consistory.

Lodge of Perfection

The Lodge of Perfection is the first division of the system of Scottish Rite degrees in the Southern jurisdiction. Here an individual can earn the fourth through fourteenth degrees which are commonly referred to as ineffable, or indescribable degrees. In this section, the rituals focus on the Temple of King Solomon and Master Mason Hiram Abiff.

Fourth Degree: *Secret Master*

The lessons of this degree emphasize secrecy, fidelity, and integrity in all confidential relationships. The accompanying ritual involves King Solomon's Temple and the king's selection of seven expert masons to protect the inner sanctum and its contents.

Fifth Degree: *Perfect Master*

The primary focus of Perfect Master is that trustworthiness and honesty are the basis for fraternal honor. The ritual of this degree focuses on the demise of Hiram Abiff and the respect that should be paid to a deceased brother.

Sixth Degree: *Intimate Secretary*

This degree focuses on faithfulness and devotion to friends, and the zeal in performing one's duties. Also that one must take care to respect the privacy of a fellow brother. The ritual depicts King Solomon sparing the life of an alleged spy.

Seventh Degree: *Provost and Judge*

These lessons center around impartiality, equity, and justice, so that laws and customs apply to everyone and justice is tempered with mercy. In this ritual, King Solomon appoints several judges to try the murderers of Hiram Abiff.

Eighth Degree: *Intendant of the Building*

The Intendant degree teaches the virtues of benevolence and charity, and that each act moves one a step closer to moral perfection. The ritual for this degree relates the cessation of building King Solomon's Temple after the murder of Hiram Abiff, and the king's subsequent appointment of five super-intendents to continue construction.

Ninth Degree: *Master Elect of the Nine*

The focus of this degree is caution and avoidance of enthusiasm in enacting justice even if the cause is just. This ritual tells of how King Solomon randomly chose nine masons for an investigation so that the perpetrators would be appropriately punished.

Tenth Degree: *Master Elect of the Fifteen*

This lesson involves the potential evils of ambition and envy, and that those who do wrong to further their own interests will be found out and brought to justice. This ritual continues the lessons already taught, by focusing on the incarceration and punishment of Hiram Abiff's murderers.

Eleventh Degree: *Master Elect of the Twelve*

This degree focuses on the virtues of honesty and sincerity and earnest citizenship, and that rewards will come to those who show respect for others. The ritual here recounts the reward bestowed upon twelve of the fifteen individuals who sought justice for Hiram Abiff's murderers.

Twelfth Degree: *Grand Master Architect*

This degree teaches that perfection in the use of the tools of the mason's trade are parallel to the perfection achievable in all aspects of life through contemplation and virtue. The ritual is reflective of the schooling of the builders of King Solomon's Temple.

Thirteenth Degree: *Royal Arch of Solomon (Master of the Ninth Arch)*

This degree teaches that difficulties should not impede a brother from seeking perfection, and that the best in life does not come easily or without effort.

Fourteenth Degree: *Grand Elect and Sublime Mason*

The final degree of the Lodge of Perfection teaches the Mason to create his own inner Lodge of Perfection, in which the essence is God and reverence for His name.

Chapter of the Rose Croix

The Chapter of the Rose Croix is the second division of degrees of the Scottish Rite. This includes the fifteenth through eighteenth degrees.

Fifteenth Degree: *Knight of the East or Sword*

This degree deals with loyalty to one's personal convictions and the dedication to do what is right. This biblical ritual tells of the captivity of Jews in Babylon, their return to Jerusalem, and their subsequent building of a new temple under King Cyrus.

Sixteenth Degree: *Prince of Jerusalem*

Truth and fidelity are the focus of this degree in relation to one's duty. The ritual relates the hardship of building the new temple, with trowel in one hand and sword in the other.

Seventeenth Degree: *Knight of the East and West*

This degree reaffirms that man's primary allegiance is to God and that the governments of man who dispel the belief of God will fail. Man's temple is in his heart and must be built and dedicated to God.

Eighteenth Degree: *Knight of the Rose Croix*

This degree establishes principles of faith, tolerance, and universality in which the spirit of God's love will guide the journey of all men.

Council of Kadosh

The Council of Kadosh comprises the third segment of the Scottish Rite degree system. This includes the nineteenth through the thirtieth degrees.

Nineteenth Degree: *Grand Pontiff*

This degree focuses on the conflict between good and evil. It strives for the spiritual unity of believers who possess a hope of immortality regardless of the religion or creed they follow.

Twentieth Degree: *Master of the Symbolic Lodge (Master ad Vitam)*

This degree seeks to confront disloyalty and the act of treason. The initiate in this instance is taught that governing hinges on selection and intelligence as learned through patience.

Twenty-First Degree: *Patriarch Noachite (Prussian Knight)*

This degree ensures that evil deeds cannot be shielded by membership in the Brotherhood, and reaffirms that one of the main supports of the fraternity is justice.

Twenty-Second Degree: *Knight of the Royal Axe (Prince of Libanus)*

The lesson emphasized in this degree is the honor of labor and the intent to improve working conditions for all who labor. The ritual relates a story of the building of Noah's Ark, and those who cut cedars from Lebanese forests.

Twenty-Third Degree: *Chief of the Tabernacle*

This degree teaches that selfish and unworthy ambition can corrupt a man, who must never ignore his duty to family, country, and God, lest he be left in moral and spiritual ruin.

Twenty-Fourth Degree: *Prince of the Tabernacle*

This degree asserts that men will be bound together in society and the Brotherhood by a mutual belief in God. It also teaches the importance of historic symbolism in terms of theology.

Twenty-Fifth Degree: *Knight of the Brazen Serpent*

Based on a ritual of the Israelites' fortieth year in the desert, this degree calls for individual faith as well as faith in God and fellow man.

Twenty-Sixth Degree: *Prince of Mercy*

This degree instills in an initiate the quality of mercy necessary to survive offending deeds and the capacity to treat offenders with compassion.

Twenty-Seventh Degree: *Commander of the Temple*

This lesson focuses on the virtues of humility, temperance, honor, and generosity, and teaches that initiates uphold these knightly virtues as did the warriors of ancient times.

Twenty-Eighth Degree: *Knight of the Sun*

Using the symbolic tools of architecture this lesson focuses on high moral standards and teaches that through the Brotherhood a man can help the world achieve unity and goodness.

Twenty-Ninth Degree: *Knight of St. Andrew*

The degree teaches that one must respect others' opinions while remaining true to our own convictions, and that Masonic lessons are based on toleration and equality.

Thirtieth Degree: *Knight Kadosh*

This degree focuses on the tests and rituals that symbolize the trials an initiate must endure in order to build excellent character.

Consistory Degrees

The Consistory is the final segment of the Scottish Rite system of degrees, which includes the thirty-first and thirty-second degrees. This Consistory group, which includes elected officers, meets to confer the final degree of the Scottish Rite, the thirty-third degree. This degree is honorary and by invitation only. Individuals must have completed the first thirty-two degrees and cannot be younger than age thirty-three.

FACT

In any Supreme Council Jurisdiction there can be only thirty-three Masons awarded the thirty-third degree.

The thirty-first degree is *Inspector Inquisitor Commander* and the focus of his lesson deals with impartial justice, and that every man should be afforded the benefit of innocence and purity of intent. Initiates to this degree are meant to first judge themselves before they can judge others and in doing so learn to forgive an individual in the hope they can be reformed.

The title of *Sublime Prince of the Royal Secret* is awarded upon completion to an initiate of the thirty-second degree. This level of the Scottish Rite system focuses on a spiritual victory over human frailty thereby elevating morality and reason. The symbol associated with this degree is a historic double-headed eagle which represents virtue, and guards an individual as they journey through life.

An individual who is awarded the thirty-third degree of *Inspector General* is one who has proven excellence both in the Brotherhood and in his community, and who exemplifies a faith in God. He must be elected unanimously, usually at an annual meeting of the Supreme Council.

The York Rite

An individual who has completed the first three symbolic degrees of the Craft and is now a Master Mason has the option of joining the York Rite. The name York is said to be taken from the English city of York and the legend surrounding King Athelstan and the first Grand Lodge meeting held in 926 A.D., which is contained in the Regius poem—more commonly known as the Halliwell Manuscript (see Chapter 2)—and the Cooke Manuscript (see Chapter 3). The York Rite is rich in history and many of its symbolic teachings emanate from the Crusades and the Knights Templar.

Like the Scottish Rite, the York Rite offers additional degrees through which an individual can ascend to continue his spiritual education in the Craft. There are three bodies, or branches, of the York Rite: the Royal Arch Chapter, the Council of Cryptic Masonry, and Commanderies of Knights Templar. Nine additional degrees are offered in these three branches. The Royal Arch Chapters are governed by Grand Chapters. The Cryptic Council is overseen by Grand Councils, and the Knights Templar are governed by Grand Commanderies.

The Royal Arch Chapter

Royal Arch Masonry consists of four degrees: Mark Master, Past Master, Most Excellent Master, and Royal Arch. These degrees are referred to as *capitular*, as it relates to a capstone, which is the final stone laid on a wall. The Royal Arch degrees are often said to be profound and the most replete in terms of symbolism. They are offered to Master Masons who wish to become further enlightened to the mysteries of Freemasonry.

The degrees vary in Canada, the United Kingdom, and the United States. For example, the Holy Royal Arch degree conferred in the United Kingdom was, until 2004, part of the third degree of Craft Masonry. In that system the Mark Master and Most Excellent Master degrees were entirely separate bodies within the York Rite.

ALERT!

One difference in the degrees offered in Canada and the United States is that in Canada, the Virtual Past Master degree was at some point in time eliminated.

The first three degrees of Royal Arch Masonry are considered preparation for the final sublime degree of Royal Arch Mason which is said to be the most important and impressive of the degrees. In 1813, the United Grand Lodge of England in its Act of Union proclaimed that "Pure Ancient Freemasonry consists of but three degrees and three degrees only, namely, that of Entered Apprentice, Fellowcraft, and Master Mason, including the Holy Royal Arch." This statement enabled the Royal Arch degree to remain part of the ancient three degrees of Craft Masonry in the United Kingdom.

Mark Master

The first Royal Arch degree of *Mark Master* is often considered to be the oldest and in many ways most respected degree. In this degree, the lessons a man learned in the first three degrees, particularly the Fellowcraft, are furthered in regard to the labor he must endure in order to continue building his own inner temple. He will learn the importance of labor and that he must never claim the work of others.

The degree of Mark Master teaches order, regularity, and discipline, and that all labors should be dutifully accomplished through precision and punctuality.

The symbolic lesson taught to the Mark Master initiate involves the labors of building the Temple of Solomon and detecting impostors seeking craftsman's wages. In this case, the initiate is a novice stonemason who is required to put his individual mark on each carving. When he approaches his overseers, they are unimpressed with his work. The reason for distinctive marks was to determine which mason was responsible for faulty workmanship. Defective masonry resulted in punishment to the worker, while perfect work was rewarded with craftsman's wages. The initiate in this case learns that hard labor is rewarded if he is truly industrious and faithful.

Past Master

After earning the degree of Mark Master an individual can move on to the second degree of *Past Master*, sometimes called *Virtual Past Master*, which focuses on obedience and learning how to govern oneself before attempting to govern others. An initiate is taught to explore every opportunity for personal development or deal with unfortunate consequences. Originally the fourth, or Royal Arch, degree could only be given to a Mason who had served as a Master of a lodge. Later, the degree was expanded to include those individuals who had not served as Master, hence the term Virtual Past Master.

Most Excellent Master

The degree of *Most Excellent Master* symbolically revolves around the completion and dedication of Solomon's Temple. It is said to be a beautiful, colorful, and dramatic degree that has its origins in American Freemasonry in 1783. Amid the pageantry of this degree, initiates learn that their own inner temple must properly house Divine goodness and truth, and that much exaltation and joy will result when this is accomplished. Only then will they become Most Excellent Masters.

Royal Arch

The *Royal Arch* degree is considered to be the capstone of the first three ancient Craft degrees, as it marks the climax of those degrees, and is the pinnacle of Masonic symbolism. Often referred to as the "root and marrow of Freemasonry," it is said that a man's character within the Brotherhood cannot be complete without the knowledge gained by the Royal Arch.

The ritual of the Royal Arch focuses on a later history of the Jews in which various objects were preserved, then later discovered and restored. A "word" which was lost to initiates in previous degrees is now revealed to those completing the Royal Arch degree.

The Council of Cryptic Masonry

Previously known as the Council of Royal and Select Master, it is now simply referred to as Cryptic Masonry. This body of the York Rite consists of three degrees: Royal Master, Select Master, and Super Excellent Master. In order to qualify for the Cryptic degrees, an individual has to have completed the three degrees of Craft Masonry and the degrees of the Royal Arch Chapter. The Cryptic degrees, however, are not a prerequisite for entering the Commanderies of the Knights Templar.

FACT

The Royal Master and Select Master degrees are often called Degrees of Preservation, with the three degrees together denoted as the "three little jewels." Historians disagree on the origins of the Cryptic degrees, though it is often said that it is the smallest but most curious of all the Rites.

The symbolic focus of the Cryptic degrees are legends surrounding a vault or crypt hidden beneath Solomon's Temple which was said to contain certain treasures meant for a particular purpose. The name *cryptic* first came about in the 1800s. It has been speculated that the Cryptic degrees evolved from the French Rite of Perfection, which later became the basis for the Scottish Rite.

Royal Master

The first degree of Cryptic Masonry is *Royal Master*, which allegorically extends the knowledge an initiate gained when earning his Fellowcraft degree and seeks to further his spiritual enlightenment in the Craft. The ritual of this degree finds the initiate in the council chamber—represented as King Solomon's private quarters—where, as legend tells it, he met with two builders who helped construct the Temple. Symbolically, the initiate is one of those men who met with the king in order that he impart to them the secrets of a Master Mason.

The lessons of the Royal Master degree relate to death and the events that occurred causing the secrets to be hidden in the vault where they will be discovered at a later time. Once this degree is earned, a Royal Master Mason can continue his journey in order that he may be found worthy to have secrets revealed to him.

Select Master

The ritual of the second degree, *Select Master*, continues the legend from the Royal Master, only this time the initiate is inside the secret vault where he discovers arches that contain various secrets. The initiate in this ritual is one of King Solomon's well-known masons who accidentally finds the secret vault, interrupting a trio of Grand Masters who are inside holding a meeting. They relate to the intruder the consequence of his discovery.

In Freemasonry there are two symbolic temples. The first relates to Ancient Craft Masonry and represents life in the present. As such, it must be destroyed. The second temple relates to the higher degrees, in particular the Royal Arch. It symbolizes eternal life, which must be built on the foundation of the destroyed temple.

Super Excellent Master

The degree of *Super Excellent Master* is technically not a Cryptic degree, but rather an honorary one that is meant to prepare an initiate for the Order of the Red Cross which is the first degree of the Knights Templar. The ritual in this case has no relation to the vault under Solomon's Temple. Instead it is set during the time of the first destruction of the Temple, including the siege of Jerusalem and the eventual release of Jewish captives. It is said that the ritual for Super Excellent Master is the most profoundly beautiful in its telling of the continued tale of Solomon's Temple.

Commanderies of Knights Templar

The third body of the York Rite, Commanderies of Knights Templar, is unique to the Masonic order. Unlike previous degrees of Freemasonry where only a belief in a Supreme Being is required, those joining the Knights enter into a strictly Christian order. Initiates must possess a belief in the doctrine of the Trinity, much like the Templars of Medieval times. One of the group's mottos is: "Every Christian Mason should be a Knight Templar."

FACT

William Davis was the first Templar initiated in the United States in 1769. Davis earned the degrees of Excellent, Super Excellent, Royal Arch, and then Knight Templar at the St. Andrew's Royal Arch Lodge. Paul Revere became a Templar in 1769, and Revolutionary hero Joseph Warren became one in 1770.

Degrees within what is termed *Chivalric Masonry* are replaced by *orders* out of respect to Knightdom. The ceremonies as such are replete with Christian symbolism. A connection between the original Knights Templar and Freemasonry continues to be debated, and it should be said that while Masonic Templarism makes no claim on the Knights of old, they do pay homage to their virtues and traditions (see Chapter 2).

There are three orders of Chivalric Masonry, including the Illustrious Order of the Red Cross, the Order of Malta, and the Order of the Temple. Some jurisdictions require that an individual entering the Chivalric order have already completed the degrees of Cryptic Masonry.

Illustrious Order of the Red Cross

The divine attribute of truth is the focus of the lessons initiates learn when entering the *Illustrious Order of the Red Cross*. Initiates learn that truth is the foundation of every virtue and only the truth will set one free. They learn this through a story which takes place prior to the Crusades during the reign of King Darius.

During the Crusades, the original Knights Templar wore white surcoats upon which were emblazoned a red cross on the chest or over the heart.

In the ritual, the initiate represents a Mason called Zerubbabel who attempts to convince the king that he is committed to the Jews. He is then asked to participate in a discussion which hopes to answer the question of whether wine, women, or the king have the most power in the kingdom. In the end, the initiate puts forth the virtue of truth as an option that pleases the king.

Order of Malta

Also known as the *Knights of Malta*, this order is the first Christian order of Chivalric Masonry and the oldest charitable organization. It is also a Catholic organization. By way of history, the Knights of Malta were originally called the Knights Hospitallers of St. John of Jerusalem. It is said they existed as an Order in the year 1099 A.D., and were the first organization whose aims were to care for injured soldiers.

The present-day order ceremony focuses on the arrival of St. Paul on the island of Melita (the current Malta), and subsequently, the Knights of St. John. The history described to the initiate is compared to the birth, life, death, resurrection, and ascension of Jesus. The Knights of Malta claim their symbolic lineage from knights who fought in Palestine during the Crusades.

The Order of the Temple

The ultimate achievement of York Rite Masonry is the *Order of the Temple*, which is admired for its solemn and inspirational experience. The ceremony is divided into three parts—novice, installation, and consecration. On occasion the orders are conferred at the same time, but typically they are completed individually. In the ceremony, the initiate represents a knight of the Crusades who has vowed to visit the Holy Sepulcher. In a trial of worthiness, he must make a seven-year pilgrimage, including preparation and penance. The ceremony teaches lessons of Christ's death and ascension.

chapter 8

Famous International Masons

Europe, along with many other parts of the world, has a long legacy in the Brotherhood. Unlike the United States, which is still in its infancy, the list of famous international Masons includes a historic roster of prime ministers, royalty, composers, writers, artists, and distinguished members of the military. From Mozart to Rudyard Kipling to Frederick the Great, Freemasonry's international contingent has secured a place in history and legend.

Heads of State

History shows that Canadian prime ministers have a particular affinity for the Craft, as did Winston Churchill and his father. With the shift to speculative Masonry, a range of gentry and members of royal families also joined the growing fraternity.

A number of prime ministers and heads of state have been members of the Craft. Arguably one of the most influential men in twentieth-century Britain and perhaps the entire world, was a Mason. Legendary politician, soldier, and author Winston Churchill served as Britain's prime minister in the 1940s and 1950s, at a time when the world was embroiled in World War II and its aftereffects. Churchill's inspirational speeches remain indelible marks in history, as was his cross-Atlantic relationship with fellow Mason and American president Franklin Delano Roosevelt.

The Brotherhood also includes a strong contingent of Canadian leaders. Sir John A. MacDonald has the distinction of being the first prime minister of the Dominion of Canada. MacDonald, who served from 1867 to 1873 and again from 1878 to 1891, played an integral part in the British North America Act which led to the Confederation of Quebec and Ontario and the birth of the Canadian Dominion. Mason MacDonald also has the distinction of having created the Canadian Pacific Railway.

Prime Minister John G. Diefenbaker, another Canadian Mason, served as prime minister from 1957 to 1963. Prior to becoming prime minister, Diefenbaker led the Progressive Conservative Party of Canada. In the 1960s, he also played an integral part in the installation of the Canadian Bill of Rights.

Other Canadian prime ministers who belonged to the Brotherhood include:

- **Sir John J. C. Abbott,** the prime minister of Canada from 1891 to 1892.
- **Viscount R. B. Bennett,** the prime minister of Canada from 1930 to 1935.
- **Sir Robert L. Borden,** the prime minister of Canada 1911 to 1920.
- **Sir Mackenzie Bowell,** the Canadian prime minister from 1894 to 1896. In later years, the British-born Bowell led the Conservative opposition.

A host of international Masons have served their countries in myriad capacities. South American revolutionary leader Simón Bolívar is a revered Latin American hero and Mason. Bolívar led the fight for independence in what is present-day Panama and Bolivia, the country which was named for Bolívar in 1825.

FACT

Freemason Manuel Quezon served as the first president of the Commonwealth of the Philippines. Known for his humanitarian acts, Quezon worked with the United States High Commissioner in the 1940s to help Jewish refugees who were escaping European fascist regimes enter the Philippines.

Distinguished cleric and British Mason Geoffrey Fisher served as the Bishop of London in 1939. By 1945, Fisher became the ninety-ninth archbishop of Canterbury, and was renowned for his ecumenical works and for his reorganization of the work of the Church of England after the second World War. From 1946 to 1954, Fisher also served as president of the World Council of Churches.

Other notable Masonic leaders include:

- **Emilio Aguinaldo,** the former Philippine president, who in 1898 declared his country's independence.
- **Charles H. Allen,** the first American appointed Governor of Puerto Rico.
- **Edvard Benes,** the second president of Czechoslovakia and leader of the independence movement.
- **Edmund Burke,** Irish statesman and author who served as a Whig in the British House of Commons.
- **George Canning,** British foreign secretary who in 1827 briefly served as prime minister.
- **Benito Juárez,** a Zapotec Amerindian who was the only Native American to serve as president of Mexico. He served two terms in the late 1800s.

- **Bernardo O'Higgins,** the revolutionary who in 1817 became Chile's first supreme director.

As evidenced by the list above, some of the most influential leaders have been members of the Brotherhood.

Royal Masons

When the Brotherhood made the move from operative to speculative Masonry it is said that the fraternity proved attractive to gentry and those of royal blood. One of the more influential proponents of the Craft was Edward VII, son of Queen Victoria, who from 1901 to 1910 was king of Britain and Ireland, as well as the king of Commonwealth Realms and emperor of India.

For the duration of his adult life, King Edward, the former Prince of Wales, was an active Mason and contributor to the Brotherhood. In 1874 he was named Grand Master and was renowned for attending ceremonies for public buildings and laying the foundation stones. His participation gave the Freemasons of the day an abundance of publicity.

Edward's younger brother Prince Arthur William Patrick, third son of Queen Victoria, was also a member of the Brotherhood. When Edward became king in 1901, Prince Arthur succeeded him as Grand Master of the United Grand Lodge of England. He served as Master until his death in 1942.

QUESTION?

Was Jack the Ripper a Freemason?
One Masonic conspiracy theory is the so-called royal conspiracy, which implicates Prince Albert Victor Edward (son of Mason King Edward VII), the Duke of Clarence, and Queen Victoria's physician William Gull (who was also a Freemason) in the Jack the Ripper murders.

Edward VIII, the son of King George V, was also a Mason, although he is perhaps better known for his short reign as British monarch. Edward became king in 1936 upon his father's death. At the time he was involved in an affair with American Wallis Simpson. By the end of that same year after his attempts to officially marry Simpson were rejected, King Edward abdicated, and a year later he and Simpson were married in France.

George VI was crowned king of England after his brother Edward abdicated, and like his brother, George was also a Freemason. King George reigned from 1936 until his death in 1952, and was perhaps best known for his leadership during the fight against Germany in World War II. He was also the last reigning British monarch to rule Ireland and India.

Arguably one of the greatest German rulers, Freemason Frederick II, or "Frederick the Great," served as king of Prussia from 1712 to 1786. A great patron of the arts and literature, Frederick was a composer, and renowned military commander during the War of Austrian Succession.

The Arts

The Brotherhood has been blessed with a historic membership in regard to the international artistic community. Dozens of composers, writers, and artists have made their mark on the Craft, and their names alone—Mozart, Conan Doyle, Kipling, and Voltaire—are legendary.

Musical Masons

Arguably one of the most famous Freemasons is Austrian composer Wolfgang Amadeus Mozart, who is considered to be one of the most talented and prolific composers in history. During his short life, Mozart composed hundreds of works including *Don Giovanni* and *The Magic Flute*, which he produced in 1791 and is said to contain many references to Freemasonry.

FACT

As was the case for Winston Churchill, Freemasonry was part of Mozart's family. His father Leopold Mozart, himself a composer and violinist, was also a Mason.

Fellow Austrian and composer Franz Joseph Haydn was a Mason and friend to Mozart. A career court musician, Haydn distinguished himself as a leading composer of the Classical Period. Revered throughout Europe in the 1700s, his original symphonies became legendary, eventually earning him the title of "Father of the String Quartet."

Finnish composer Jean Sibelius holds particular endearment to the Brotherhood. In 1927, he composed *Musique Réligieuse Opus 113* to which he later added *Praising Hymn and the Ode to Fraternity*. Both pieces are Masonic ritual music that encompass the three main degrees of Freemasonry.

Other musical Masons include:

- **Johann Christian Bach,** German classical composer and eleventh son of famed composer Johann Sebastian Bach.
- **Dmitry Stepanovich Bortnyansky,** renowned and highly prolific Russian composer.
- **Sir William S. Gilbert,** British playwright and lyricist. His comic operas, which he composed with partner Sir Arthur Sullivan, include *The Mikado, The Pirates of Penzance,* and *H.M.S. Pinafore.*
- **Franz Liszt,** nineteenth century Hungarian virtuoso pianist and composer, considered to be one of the world's greatest virtuosos.
- **Giacomo Meyerbeer,** German opera composer who studied with Antonio Salieri.
- **Sigmund Romberg,** Hungarian-born Jewish composer famous for his operettas.
- **John Stafford Smith,** British composer and organist who composed the music that eventually became the United States national anthem, "The Star Spangled Banner."

Prolific Brothers

The international community of Masons is represented by scores of talented and well-known writers and poets such as Sir Arthur Conan Doyle, Rudyard Kipling, and Robert Burns. Often referred to as the National Poet of Scotland, Burns was an avid participant in the Brotherhood. Considered to be a patriot and romantic poet his works are now legendary.

Masonry also attracted a pair of writers whose names may not be familiar, but whose works are highly revered the world over. In 1923, Austrian writer Felix Salten was inspired by a trip to the Alps. Three years later, he wrote *Bambi*, which he later sold (including rights) to Disney who released the movie in 1942. The Disney film *The Shaggy Dog* was inspired by another Salten tale, *The Hound of Florence*.

Italian writer, journalist, and Mason Carlo Collodi wrote an equally famous tale involving a boy marionette. *Pinocchio* was originally published in a children's newspaper in Italy in the late 1800s. Unfortunately, Collodi passed on before *Pinocchio* rose to fame and fortune in the Disney tradition.

QUESTION?

What does Freemasonry have to do with Lilliputians?
Gulliver's Travels, published in 1726, is a classic tale of travel and satire on the nature of humanity. Its author, Anglo-Irishman Jonathan Swift, was a Freemason.

British Mason and Nobel Prize–winning writer and poet Rudyard Kipling is perhaps best known for his children's stories in *The Jungle Book* and his poem "Gunga Din." Awarded the Nobel in 1907 he is still the youngest recipient to ever receive the award, at age forty-two. Kipling was recognized by the early Masons as one of forty living members of the Fellows of the Philalethes Society.

Another legendary Mason of the eighteenth century was François-Marie Arouet, better known as Voltaire. A French writer, philosopher, and Deist, Voltaire was renowned for his fight for civil liberties and his sardonic wit, philosophies, and criticism regarding the Church and French society of the day. Still considered one of the most influential French figures, his words and opinions to this day incite debate.

Freemasonry is often linked with intrigue and mystery, especially in literature. Legendary detective Sherlock Holmes no doubt gained insight from his creator, British writer Sir Arthur Conan Doyle, who was indeed part of the Craft.

Additional writers who were Masons include:

- **James Boswell,** the Scottish lawyer and diarist best known as the biographer of English poet Samuel Johnson.
- **Heinrich Heine,** highly revered German poet.
- **Gotthold Ephraim Lessing,** German writer, philosopher, and art critic during the Age of Enlightenment.
- **José Julian Martí,** Cuban poet and writer considered to be one of the greatest Cuban heroes.
- **Aleksandr Pushkin,** groundbreaking Russian poet and author of *Boris Godunov.*
- **Friedrich Schiller,** a German poet, philosopher, dramatist, and historian.
- **Sir Walter Scott,** renowned Scottish poet and historical novelist, who wrote *Ivanhoe.*
- **Alexandr Petrovich Sumarkov,** Russian poet and dramatist.

Artists

Given the historic roots of ancient Masonry, it is easy to see why sculptors, artists, and architects were drawn to the Brotherhood. Operative Masonry was highly creative and extremely hard work, all of which is commonplace for those in the artistic community.

Arguably the most important monument in the United States is the Statue of Liberty. She stands 305 feet tall overlooking New York Harbor, and was built from copper plates that were hammered onto wooden forms before being mounted on a skeleton of steel. Designed by French sculptor and Mason Frederic A. Bartholdi, the statue, modeled after Isabella Eugenie

Boyer (widow of sewing machine magnate Isaac Singer) was dedicated on October 28, 1886.

It is immediately apparent which monument Mason Gustave Eiffel created. The French engineer, architect, and builder erected the Eiffel Tower for the Universal Exposition in Paris which showcased its unveiling in 1889. Eiffel also designed the armature for America's Statue of Liberty.

British architect Sir John Soane is held in high regard by the Brotherhood. In 1813, Soane held the position of Grand Superintendent of Works for the United Grand Lodge of England. Together with Joseph Michael Gandy, Soane designed the London Freemason Hall.

Other artistic Masons of note include:

- **Jean Chalgrin,** French designer of the Arc de Triomphe in Paris, one of the world's most famous historical monuments.
- **William Hogarth,** renowned British painter, engraver, satirist, and cartoonist during the 1700s, who is considered to be a pioneer in Western sequential art.
- **Edmund Kean,** British actor revered as one of the greatest actors of his day.
- **Bertel Thorvaldsen,** Danish Neoclassical sculptor known for his statue of Copernicus.

Science and Exploration

Whether a goal involves inventing a cure for a deadly disease, or going where no man has gone before, Masonic representation is evident and impressive. A wide range of scientists and explorers were part of the Craft, and their individual accomplishments in life have left indelible marks on the history books.

Explorers

When it comes to extreme explorations, the Masonic fraternity is well represented. In fact, several Freemasons were in an epic race to discover the last place on earth—Antarctica. Masons Roald Amundsen and Robert

Falcon Scott both secured a place in history as they attempted to navigate the polar regions. For one Mason the end would be victorious, but for the other the journey would end tragically.

Amundsen was a Norwegian who in 1903 led the first expedition through the Northwest Passage between the Pacific and Atlantic oceans. After his successful journey he set his sights on the North Pole, but received word that it had just been discovered. So instead, he headed South. Scott, a British naval officer, learned of Amundsen's intentions while he himself was en route to the South Pole and the race had begun.

FACT

Freemason Giacomo Girolamo Casanova was an explorer and adventurer of a different kind. A flamboyant figure in eighteenth century Italy, his name is now synonymous with love and promiscuity.

In January 1912, Scott and five men finally reached the Pole, only to learn that Amundsen had been there a month earlier. While Amundsen celebrated his victory, Scott and his comrades endured slow and painful deaths during their attempt to return.

Irish polar explorer and Freemason Sir Ernest Shackleton had accompanied Scott on several unsuccessful polar expeditions starting in 1901, and led his own Antarctic treks for many years. His journeys resulted in many discoveries for which he became a knighted hero in Britain.

Freemason Sir Richard Burton was also a British explorer, but his adventures took him on a much different path. A translator, writer, and Orientalist, Burton made solo trips to Mecca in Arab disguise and spent time translating the *Kama Sutra* and the *Arabian Nights*. He then ventured on to discover sources of the Nile River and some of the great lakes in Africa. It is also said that he was considered the third best swordsman in Europe.

Scientific Masons

Masons who were part of the international medical and scientific communities made more than a few groundbreaking discoveries, from vaccinations to hypnosis to measuring the speed of light. One such trailblazer was English country doctor Edward Jenner who discovered the vaccine for smallpox. Jenner never patented his lifesaving discovery, as it was meant as a "gift for the world." By 1840, the government banned the use of other treatments for the deadly disease and used only Jenner's vaccine.

Another disease was averted by Belgian microbiologist and immunologist Jules Bordet who in 1906 isolated the cause of whooping cough. In 1919, this Mason was awarded the Nobel Prize for his immunization discoveries.

If the name Franz Anton Mesmer sounds familiar it is because this Mason discovered animal magnetism, which was ultimately termed "mesmerism." Thirty years after his death, Mesmer's research allowed James Braid to take it one step further and invent hypnosis.

The medical condition known as anaphylaxis earned physiologist Charles Robert Richet a Nobel Prize in 1913. Sufferers of asthma, allergies, and hay fever have this pioneering French Mason to thank for the ability to breathe freely. It wasn't long after Richet made his discovery that Scotsman Sir Alexander Fleming accomplished his own medical landmark. A Mason and bacteriologist, Fleming accidentally sneezed into a petri dish filled with bacteria, and in doing so eventually discovered penicillin. Flemming was knighted in 1944, and the next year he and his partners won the Nobel Prize.

Famous Masons of the sciences include:

- **Sir Joseph Banks,** British botanist and naturalist who accompanied Captain Cook on his first voyage of discovery. Over seventy-five species bear his name.
- **Jöns Jakob Berzelius,** the Swedish chemist considered to be a founder of modern chemistry.
- **Jean Theophilus Desaguliers,** the discoverer of the "properties of electricity." He also served as Grand Master and Deputy Grand Master of the Grand Lodge of England.

- **Samuel Hahnemann,** the German physician and founder of homeopathy.
- **Gaspard Monge,** French mathematician and inventor of descriptive geometry.
- **Sir Bernard Spilsbury,** renowned British pathologist who worked on thousands of criminal cases, among them the infamous Dr. Crippen murders.

Military Masons

Freemasonry has attracted many individuals who have served in the military, including men of all ranks from the naval and armed forces on both sides of the Atlantic. One of the more distinguished naval Masons is German Grand Admiral Alfred von Tirpitz, who during World War I served as Minister of State and Commander of the Kaiserliche (Royal) Marines. It is said that the "risk theory" that von Tirpitz developed in regard to submarine warfare marked the beginnings of a naval arms race between Britain and Germany. In 1939, the German battleship *Tirpitz* was dedicated in his honor.

FACT

Joseph Brant, chief of the Mohawks from 1742 to 1807, was a Freemason who also served as a British military officer during the American Revolution.

Several European Masons took part in the American Revolution, and the paths of three of them intersected with each other. Gilbert du Motier, better known as the Marquis de Lafayette, was a French aristocrat and lifelong friend of fellow Freemason George Washington. After leaving France as a rebellious young soldier, Lafayette eventually became a commander of American military forces and in 1781 was in charge of defending Virginia. He then returned to France and played a part in the French Revolution. A national hero in both countries, Lafayette is one of six individuals to be granted honorary American citizenship.

Less known is Mason Major John André, who played an infamous role in aiding fellow Brother Benedict Arnold during the American Revolution. A British officer, André's ploy to help Arnold surrender the fort at West Point to the British failed, and in 1780 he was hanged as a spy. Unlike Arnold, however, André was eventually revered for his participation (by the British).

Also a friend to George Washington was Mason Friedrich Wilhelm Steuben (Baron von Steuben), a Prussian army officer. Von Steuben also served with Washington during the American Revolution and is said to have taught troops the importance of military decorum. He was also a member of Major André's court-martial, and later took his place as the commander of Virginia, until the Marquis de Lafayette took his place. Von Steuben became an American citizen in 1783, and later had the USS *Von Steuben* named for him.

At the same time in Russia, Mason Mikhail Kutuzov, was making a name for himself as a field marshal. As commander-in-chief when Napoleon invaded Russia, Kutuzov was able to hold back the French. For his efforts, the renowned marshal is immortalized in Leo Tolstoy's epic *War and Peace*.

Movers and Shakers

Many men gifted with ambition in the blood have adopted the Craft. Free thinking and discovery often go hand in hand as many inventors and innovators can attest. The prevalence of these Masonic men of historic stature is perhaps a testament to the spiritual and educational enlightenment they received as members of the Brotherhood.

Innovators

International Masons have never fallen short in terms of innovation, and the Brotherhood attracted a host of patriots, revolutionaries, heroes, and humanitarians such as Swiss entrepreneur and Freemason Jean Henri Dunant. Also a social activist, Dunant has, among other achievements, a pair of impressive credits to his name. As a result of bearing witness to the horrors of war in Alegeria in 1859, he developed a plan of recovery, which evolved into the formation of the Red Cross in 1863. Dunant's visionary quality also gave birth to the Geneva Convention.

Swiss Freemason and circus clown Grock was highly revered throughout Europe for his amusing antics with the twenty-four musical instruments he played. In the early 1900s, he even performed for European royalty, and later formed a successful music publishing business.

Revered aviator, Mason, and politician Ramón Franco is considered to be a pioneer of Spanish aviation. Franco, the brother of the notorious Spanish dictator General Francisco Franco, earned international acclaim in 1926 when he piloted a trans-Atlantic flight in a hydroplane. It is said that when his general brother tried to become a Mason, Franco was among those who refused his membership into the fraternity.

Other tenacious international Masons include:

- **Father Francisco Calvo,** the Catholic priest who in 1865 introduced Freemasonry to Costa Rica.
- **Lord Elgin,** former Grand Master Mason of Scotland and worldwide head of the Royal Order of Scotland.
- **Paul Foelsche,** the first police inspector of Australia's Northwest Territories.
- **Giuseppe Garibaldi,** Italian patriot and nationalist.
- **Manuel Fernández Juncos,** revered Puerto Rican journalist, poet, writer, and humanitarian, and founder of the Puerto Rican Red Cross.
- **Lajos Kossuth,** a patriot, journalist, lawyer, and statesman, considered by many to be the "Father of Hungarian Democracy."
- **Giuseppe Mazzini,** Italian writer, politician, and revolutionary.
- **José Rizal,** revered patriot and linguist. Dubbed the "The Great Malayan," he is a national hero of the Philippines.
- **José de San Martín,** general and national hero of Argentina named with Simón Bolívar as one of the liberators of South America.
- **Matthew Webb,** who in 1875, in less than twenty-two hours, became the first man to swim the English Channel.
- **William Wyler,** German film director who won Best Director Oscars for his Best Picture films *Ben Hur* and *The Best Years of Our Lives.*

Inventors

The international Masonic community features a host of inventive and entrepreneurial men now famous for their innovative creations and actions. From the saxophone to doughnuts to methods of execution, these Masons have secured their historic fame and fortunes.

Tea drinkers will immediately recognize a Mason by the name of Sir Thomas Lipton. A Scottish merchant and yacht racer, Lipton established a chain of grocery stores in Britain in the 1870s. To keep his shops stocked he made many purchases, including plantations, which ultimately led to the birth of Lipton tea. An avid yachtsman, Lipton went yachting in the royal company of kings Edward VII and George V (both Masons), and for thirty-one years persistently challenged participants in the world-famous America's Cup.

Other inventive Freemasons include:

- **Eberhard Faber,** German founder of the Eberhard Faber Pencil Company.
- **Tim Horton,** legendary Canadian hockey player and founder of a chain of doughnut shops called Tim Horton's.
- **John Molson,** Canadian founder of Molson Breweries.
- **Jacques Etienne Montgolfier,** Frenchman who with his two brothers invented the Montgolfier hot-air balloon.
- **James Naismith,** Canadian-born educator who invented the game of basketball, and first introduced the helmet to the American game of football.
- **Antoine Joseph Sax,** the Belgian instrument designer and inventor of the saxophone.

Mason Joseph Ignace Guillotin has also become a household name, if only for his name's notorious history. Guillotin was a French physician, revolutionary, and persistent advocate who in 1789 sought a solution to the problem of more humane methods of execution. Unfortunately for Guillotin, the mechanized decapitator was named for him and made its first chop in 1792. The good doctor's descendants changed their name as a result of the infamous association.

Yet another French Mason made a name for himself with his mechanical engineering. In 1919, engineer Andre Citroen founded the Citroen automobile company, which by the early thirties was the fourth largest car manufacturer in the world.

chapter 9

Expanding Across the Globe

The United States of America is still an infant in terms of world history, but it is no less rich for the centuries of baby steps it has taken. The practice of American Freemasonry differs from its European counterparts, but its fraternal ties remain strong whether the climate is revolutionary, industrial, or modernized. Eighteenth century American brothers took great care in assembling their New World brethren, while at the same time reaffirming the legends, rituals, and historic and spiritual teachings of the Craft.

American Freemasonry

The study of Freemasonry in the United States is in many ways a tour of early American history with a focus on legendary individuals such as Benjamin Franklin, John Hancock, and George Washington, and events surrounding the American Revolution, including the Boston Tea Party, and the signings of the Declaration of Independence and United States Constitution. A European fraternity taking root in the New World is no surprise, but the journey it has taken from infancy to adulthood has proven to be fascinating through all its successes and turbulent times.

In contrast to its European brethren, American Freemasonry has a historical advantage in that its origins are slightly easier to establish, but as with all things related to a secret society there are dozens of theories and conspiracies waiting in the wings. In regard to its earliest origins one expert directs attention to a flat stone slab which has cut into its face the year 1606, and a square and compass. Found in the Annapolis Basin of Nova Scotia, on the shore of Goat Island, it is thought to be a gravestone of a French stonemason who had settled in the area in 1605.

One of the first recorded Freemasons in America was a Scotsman by the name of John Skene who was No. 27 on a 1670 roster of Aberdeen No. 1 in Scotland. Skene, who settled on a plantation in Mt. Holly, New Jersey, in 1682, was a Quaker who served as Deputy Governor of the Colony of West Jersey from 1685 to 1690.

New World Lodges

Londoner Daniel Coxe, a student of medicine and law, arrived in Burlington, New Jersey, around 1701 where he became active in local politics and served in various governmental capacities. On June 5, 1730, Coxe was awarded a historic position in American Masonry when the Duke of Norfolk, Grand Master of the Grand Lodge of England, appointed Coxe Provincial Grand Master of the Provinces of New York, New Jersey, and Pennsylvania.

FACT

In 1799, upon the death of George Washington, the Grand Lodge of Massachusetts made an unusual request of his widow. In deference to their wishes she gave them a lock of her husband's hair. Sealed in a gold urn made by silversmith Paul Revere, its safekeeping is charged to all Grand Masters upon their appointment.

There is little known about Henry Price before he emigrated to Boston from London, but records show that he was a successful merchant tailor and a Freemason. Clearly a man on a fraternal mission, he set off for England from Boston in 1732 in order to secure a warrant from the Grand Lodge of England, which was required in order to make a lodge official. His mission was a success. English Grand Master Lord Viscount Montague, named Price Provincial Grand Master of New England, which gave him the authority to establish charters in New England. A year after he became Grand Master, his position was expanded to include all of North America.

On July 30, 1733, a group of Boston Masons met with Price at the Bunch of Grapes Tavern, at which point Price selected officers for America's first Grand Lodge. Now the oldest official lodge in the Western world, it was named St. John's Lodge. When his authority expanded, Price granted a petition from Benjamin Franklin and the contingent of Philadelphia Freemasons to form their lodge, of which Franklin served as their first Master. Over the years, Price continued chartering many lodges all over the colonies, and several in Canada, Dutch Guiana, and the West Indies.

As with most membership-based organizations, however, it was only a matter of time before rivalry reared its eternal head. At that point in time, members of the fraternal order were generally men of means—business owners, merchants, manufacturers, and individuals based in art and science. The working class was often omitted from joining the Brotherhood. As such, working individuals formed their Grand Lodge under the auspices of following traditional Masonic practices. This, as it's been told, led to a great divide among brethren that saw lodges bitterly divided between antient and modern groups (see Chapter 4).

The Lightning Rod of Masonry

Arguably one of the most famous and industrious Americans is Benjamin Franklin. An inventor, printer, scientist, philosopher, author, and exceptional diplomat and statesman, Franklin is revered not only by posterity, but also by his fellow brethren both past and present. A man with only two years of formal education, Franklin's achievements in the colonies and as a diplomat abroad were nothing short of astounding. From 1729 to 1765 he edited and published the *Pennsylvania Gazette*. He also: learned several languages, formed the first police force in the colonies, introduced hospital services, founded the first public library, and is credited with a wide range of inventions including the lightning rod and bifocals.

In 1753, Franklin was appointed postmaster general and four years later moved to England to serve as the chief representative of the American colonies. By the time he returned to America over a decade later, and despite his efforts in Britain, the Revolution had begun. As a member of the Second Continental Congress he served on a committee of five individuals who were chosen to draft the Declaration of Independence. Franklin was also a key player in obtaining funds from France's Louis XVI, and eventually helped negotiate a commerce and alliance treaty with France that helped turn the tide of the American Revolution.

After Benjamin Franklin invented the furnace stove, he created the first fire company and fire insurance company. As postmaster, in an effort to better calculate routes of service, Franklin invented an odometer which he attached to his carriage.

In 1730, Franklin made mention of several Freemason lodges in the *Gazette*. Shortly thereafter, he became a member of the St. John's Lodge. Six months later on St. John the Baptist's Day of 1732 he became Junior Warden of the Grand Lodge in Pennsylvania, only to be chosen Grand Master two years later. A free thinker, Franklin then began his correspondence in an effort to secure a Masonic charter.

The majority of Franklin's lodge gatherings were held in Philadelphia at Tun's Tavern and also in a Videll Alley building. It was in the latter in 1786 that the Grand Lodge of Free and Accepted Masons of Pennsylvania declared its independence from the Grand Lodge of England. Franklin continued his long and extraordinary career as a diplomat and trailblazer of the American Brotherhood. Near the end of his life, he was still fighting for a cause, this time the abolition of slavery.

Not long after having signed the United States Constitution, Franklin died, but his multifaceted legacies continue to thrive. Even in the 2005 film *National Treasure*, which features Freemasonry, the protagonist played by Nicolas Cage is named Benjamin Franklin Gates.

The Boston Tea Party

One might wonder what the infamous Boston Tea Party has to do with Freemasonry. As it turns out, there's quite a Masonic mystery attached to the notorious tea dumping that set the stage for the American Revolution.

As history tells it, the phrase "no taxation without representation" became a mantra for colonists who were angered over the 1765 Stamp Act and the Townshend Acts of 1767. One of the loudest protesters was Freemason John Hancock, who later organized a boycott of tea from the British East India Company.

Despite the British government passing the Tea Act, which eliminated the colonial tea tax, ships continued to be turned away from American ports. Then on the night of December 16, 1773, a group of Bostonians calling themselves the Sons of Liberty boarded the ships *Dartmouth*, *Eleanor*, and *Beaver*. Disguised as Mohawk Indians, they boarded the three ships and dumped 342 crates of tea into Boston Harbor, after which they swept the decks clean and made certain the Sons of Liberty were named the perpetrators.

No one knows with any certainty who actually conceived of the infamous raid, so one legend is as good as another. One alternate claim to the Boston Tea Party boasts a significant Masonic spin. In this case, connection to the brethren starts with the Green Dragon Tavern, a building that was purchased by the St. Andrew's Lodge in 1764. Sometimes dubbed the "Headquarters of the American Revolution," the downstairs tavern and upstairs meeting rooms were said to have served the Grand Lodge of Massachusetts as well as the Sons of Liberty.

The Green Dragon Tavern is still standing at 11 Marshall Street in Boston, Massachusetts. Although no longer a Masonic lodge, it does still serve beer and food such as Mohawk trail chicken fingers and Red Coat spicy buffalo wings.

Allegedly, the Tea Party was planned at the Green Dragon and executed with the help of the Masons. Involved in the planning were Grand Master Dr. Joseph Warren, and fellow Brothers John Hancock and Paul Revere. It was, in fact, Warren who sent his good friend Revere on his infamous ride to warn colonial troops of British incursion on April 18, 1775. And the men Revere delivered his messages to? Revolutionary Samuel Adams and Freemason John Hancock.

The American Revolution

Like most aspects of Freemasonry, participation of the brethren in the Boston Tea Party remains a source of debate. There are all kinds of intriguing conspiracy theories based on various allegations that all the founding fathers and all of George Washington's generals were part of the Craft. Some assert that the majority of signers of both the Declaration of Independence and United States Constitution were Masons. Even the Boston Tea Party remains a mystery, as it is theorized that Freemasons either planned or participated in the legendary turning point.

What is known is that many Freemasons took part in the Revolutionary War. Masonic brethren served as military leaders, soldiers, politicians, patriots, revolutionaries, and statesmen, but in general, their numbers were small as compared to the non-Masons who participated in the war. Much of the speculation and subsequent conspiracies surrounding Masonic involvement is perhaps due to the fact that a handful of highly influential individuals were indeed Masons.

Were Thomas Jefferson, Patrick Henry, and Samuel Adams Freemasons?
Often listed as members of the Craft, there is no evidence that any of the three were ever initiated into the fraternity. Adams was a close associate of Paul Revere and John Hancock who were well-known Masons. Jefferson also had documented Masonic connections, but Henry did not.

Due to their stature or famous incidents involving them, men such as George Washington, Benjamin Franklin, John Hancock, Paul Revere, John Paul Jones, Ethan Allen, Baron von Steuben, and the Marquis de Lafayette brought Freemasonry to the forefront simply by association. The same goes for infamous Masons like Benedict Arnold and Major John André.

Founding Fathers

For Americans, the term "Founding Fathers" holds special meaning, as it refers to a remarkable group of men who served their country as statesmen, leaders, and patriots. Their stories are fascinating and their perseverance in achieving liberty no matter the cost earned them a legendary place in American history. These men signed the Declaration of Independence, the United States Constitution, and many took part in the American Revolution. A number of these forefathers were also Freemasons.

It is a common misconception that all of the founding fathers were Masons. This is hardly the case. It is true that many prominent Masons took part in the war and at least twenty signed the Declaration and Constitution, but there were many more non-Masons who participated in these events. Arguably the most famous American Mason, Benjamin Franklin, did indeed lend his penmanship to both documents. Mason John Hancock was a signer, and so was George Washington. Out of a total of ninety-five signatures on the two documents, twenty-one were those of Freemasons.

Those given to conspiracy often claim that the U.S. Constitution is based on *Anderson's Book of Constitutions*. They also attribute Masonic connections to individuals, like Thomas Jefferson and Patrick Henry, who have never been part of the Craft. Another popular myth is that every one of the generals serving under George Washington during the war were Freemasons. In truth there were only thirty-three Masons who served under Washington's command, which was quite extensive in number.

Another common conspiracy is that when Washington was inaugurated as president, all of the governors of the original thirteen colonies were Freemasons. Masonic research shows that of the thirty individuals who served as governors, ten were members of the Craft.

Famous American Signatures

The subject of how many Masons signed the Declaration of Independence and United States Constitution remains a constant source of debate. Lodge records have been able to confirm that a number of Masons did indeed sign both landmark documents, and other scattered records show that a number of the individuals involved entered the Brotherhood sometime after the signings occurred.

FACT

In the film *National Treasure* starring Nicolas Cage, the Declaration of Independence contains a clue that leads to a treasure trove the Knights Templar procured and the Freemasons kept hidden.

Perhaps the single most important document in American history is the Declaration of Independence. On July 4, 1776, the document was ratified by the Continental Congress, and in its eloquence stated, with apt justification, that the thirteen colonies were declaring themselves independent of the Kingdom of Britain. A committee of five men were responsible for the writing of the Declaration, one of whom was Mason Benjamin Franklin.

A total of fifty-six delegates ultimately signed the famous declaration, and of those, nine were Freemasons:

- **William Ellery,** member of the First Lodge of Boston (1748).
- **Benjamin Franklin,** Grand Master of Pennsylvania (1734).

- **John Hancock,** became a Mason in the Merchant's Lodge No. 277 in Quebec, and then moved to St. Andrew's Lodge in Boston (1762).
- **Joseph Hewes,** member of the Unanimity Lodge No. 7 in North Carolina.
- **William Hopper,** member of the Hanover Lodge in Masonborough, North Carolina.
- **Robert Treat Payne,** member of the Massachusetts Grand Lodge (1759).
- **Richard Stockton,** Charter Master of St. John's Lodge in Princeton, New Jersey (1765).
- **George Walton,** member of Solomon's Lodge No. 1, in Savannah, Georgia.
- **William Whipple,** member of St. John's Lodge in Portsmouth, New Hampshire (1752).

By 1787, the time had arrived to create a governmental structure for the newly independent nation and a number of Freemasons played an integral part in the process. The Constitutional Convention was held in May in Philadelphia and after a unanimous vote by the fifty-five delegates, George Washington became presiding officer. Also in attendance as a delegate was octogenarian Benjamin Franklin.

QUESTION?

Why is John Hancock's signature so famous?
Freemason Hancock, a statesman who served as president of the Continental Congress, was the first signator of the Declaration of Independence. His signature was very large as compared to the others. Legend has it that Hancock did that intentionally so that King George III could clearly read his signature.

It was a debate that led to the eventual outcome of the United States Constitution, and of the five primary men leading the debate—Washington, Franklin, John Adams, Thomas Jefferson, and Edmund Randolph—only Adams and Jefferson were non-Masons. The document was to replace the Articles of Confederation and create a federal union of sovereign states and a federal government. After being ratified in each of the thirteen states became official on March 4, 1789.

Out of the original thirty-nine individuals who signed the Constitution (fifty-five was the eventual total of those who signed), thirteen were Freemasons. Known Masons who signed include:

- **Gunning Bedford Jr.,** the first Grand Master of Delaware.
- **John Blair,** the first Grand Master of Virginia.
- **David Brearley,** the first Grand Master of New Jersey.
- **Jacob Broom,** an officer in his lodge in Delaware.
- **Daniel Carroll,** the Maryland Mason who with George Washington participated in the Masonic cornerstone laying of the United States Capitol building.
- **Jonathan Dayton,** a member of Temple Lodge No. 1 in Elizabethtown, New Jersey.
- **John Dickinson,** a lodge member in Dover, Delaware.
- **Benjamin Franklin,** Grand Master of Pennsylvania.
- **Nicholas Gilman,** a member of a St. John's Lodge No. 1, Portsmouth, New Hampshire
- **Rufus King,** a member of the St. John's Lodge in Newburyport, Massachusetts.
- **James McHenry,** a member of Spiritual Lodge No. 23 in Maryland.
- **William Paterson,** a member of Trenton Lodge No. 5 in New Jersey.
- **George Washington,** was raised in the lodge at Fredericksburg (now Fredericksburg Lodge No. 4), Charter Master of Alexandria Lodge No. 22, in Virginia.

George Washington

The name George Washington is known and revered by all American citizens as a brilliant military leader, statesman, founding father, and the first president of the United States. Washington is also famous for being a Freemason, a fact that inspires pride in all of his American brethren. It wasn't so much that he was heavily involved in the Craft, but that he was steadfast in his moral virtue. Oddly, Washington's participation in the Brotherhood is a source of debate, with some theorizing that he never was a Mason.

Records from the lodge at Fredericksburg, Virginia (which is still in possession of the records), show that Washington was initiated as an Entered Apprentice on November 4, 1752, and further became a Fellowcraftsman on March 3, 1753. By the following August, he was raised to the Sublime Degree of Master Mason. It has also been speculated that Washington further went on to earn the Royal Arch degree.

In response to an address from the Grand Lodge of Massachusetts, it is said that Washington stated, "My attachment to the Society of which we are members will dispose me always to contribute my best endeavors to promote the honor and prosperity of the Craft."

By 1775, Washington was unanimously chosen commander-in-chief of the Colonial Army. At the Federal Convention in Philadelphia in May of 1787, Washington presided as the United States Constitution was framed. On April 30, 1789, Washington was sworn in as first president of the United States by fellow Mason Robert Livingston, the chancellor of New York, and Grand Master of Free and Accepted Masons.

The year before his presidential victory, Washington was appointed Master of Alexandria Lodge No. 22 in Virginia. Later that year he was elected Master but no records exist of his presiding over any lodge. When Washington passed away on December 14, 1799, he did receive, at his widow's request, a Masonic funeral.

A Black Sheep Brother

Like most organizations, the Brotherhood is not without its infamous members. One individual in particular is so reviled that the mere utterance of his name on American soil is synonymous with traitorhood. Benedict Arnold, a brother shown to have been initiated into the Brotherhood in New Haven, Connecticut, in 1765, served as a general in the Continental Army during the American Revolution.

A former druggist and bookseller turned West Indies trader, Arnold was ambitious and increasingly aware of the British presence in the New World. For the first part of his military career Arnold served with distinction until his command was given to another by the Continental Congress after the Battle of Ticonderoga in 1775. Arnold's bitterness over that decision, made worse by future altercations, would years later result in his defecting to the British military and in 1780 devising a plot to deliver the American fort at West Point, New York, to British control. Arnold's plan proved unsuccessful, but for the effort he was monetarily rewarded and made brigadier general in the British Army. Fellow Masonic Brother and conspirator Major John André was not so lucky.

A British Army soldier at the age of twenty-one, André found his way to Canada where he was captured and held prisoner until 1776 in Pennsylvania. Two years later he was commissioned as a major and became a popular individual in New York and Philadelphia society. At one point he even lived in the house of fellow Mason Benjamin Franklin. By 1780, however, Major André's destiny would turn when he entered into Benedict Arnold's West Point plot.

FACT

General Arnold and Major André had more in common than just Freemasonry. In 1779, Arnold met and married eighteen-year-old Peggy Shippen who during the British occupation of Philadelphia was being courted by Major André!

After meeting with Arnold, André was dispatched carrying documents meant for the British, which told how the fort could be taken. Unfortunately for the major, his endeavor proved futile as he was captured, tried as a spy, and hanged. Said to have been a gallant officer, André's remains were moved in 1821 to the famed English site "Hero's Corner" at Westminster Abbey.

The William Morgan Mystery

In regard to the history of American Freemasonry, there is perhaps no more intriguing a tale than the mysterious demise of William Morgan. The mix of circumstances, evidence, hearsay, public speculation, and alleged abduction and murder weave a fantastic tale perfect for a made-for-television movie. The fact that the case was so much in the public eye is arguably the most crucial element of the mystery, as the eventual outrage and exposure of the Brotherhood and its secrecy led to widespread anti-Mason sentiments and the formation of the Anti-Masonic Party.

A native of Culpepper County in Virginia, William Morgan left his home to spend time working various jobs in Canada and areas of New York. It was 1824 when Morgan settled in the small town of Batavia, New York, and began work as an itinerant stonemason. Referring to himself as "Captain" Morgan, he cited his distinctive military service in the War of 1812.

Whether Morgan actually did serve in the armed forces is still questioned by historians, and many accounts of the Morgan mystery vary widely.

Some historical accounts show that in 1825 in the Western Star Chapter No. 33 in LeRoy, New York, Morgan was awarded a Royal Arch degree. Experts disagree as to whether he was ever really a Mason (most assert he wasn't) or had simply lied his way into the fraternity for his own evil gain. Other accounts tell that Morgan showed up at the lodge claiming he was already a brother, which definitely incited suspicion among that lodge's brethren.

No matter whether he was a true Mason or not, several accounts state that Morgan spent time visiting other lodges and eventually was part of a group which was petitioning for a Royal Arch chapter. However, when the chapter was started, Morgan was denied membership, which unbeknownst to everyone marked the beginning of a powerful public scandal that would shock fraternal brethren around the world.

Secrecy Threatened

Morgan's omission from the new Batavian charter group resulted in arguments and Morgan leaving the fraternity. At that point, he made his intentions clear—he was writing a book that would reveal all the secrets of Freemasonry including their rituals and procedures, and had, in fact, been paid a great sum in advance of the book by David Miller, publisher of local newspaper, the *Batavia Advocate*. Morgan's contract for the book involved Miller, a Mason who for twenty years did not progress beyond Entered Apprentice and was assumed to bear a grudge against the Brotherhood, Morgan's landlord John Davids, and a man called Russell Dyer.

Rumors of a payment as high as a half-million dollars led Morgan to exacerbate the issue with continual boasting, which only gave rise to anger among the brethren. In order to avert the potential crisis, local Masons ran advertisements in other publications which informed the public to be watchful of Morgan and his undesirable attributes.

As one historian tells the tale, it wasn't long after that a local innkeeper was asked by a Mason to provide a meal for fifty of his brethren who apparently had no problem revealing that their intention that evening was to attack the *Batavia Advocate*'s offices. After hearing of their plan, Miller got the word out that he and others were armed and prepared for any attack. The Freemasons never did execute their plan as reported, but the incident did set off a chain of events that led up to the sordid events that followed.

It is said that several Masons then approached Morgan at his residence and arrested him for debts he owed them. He was taken to a local jail in the charge of a jailer who also happened to be a Mason. Miller, upon hearing of Morgan's incarceration, set about finding the jailer so as to pay off Morgan's alleged debt; however, it was a Friday evening and the jailer had conveniently departed, leaving Morgan behind bars until Monday.

FACT

William Morgan's wife Lucinda became heavily involved in the anti-Masonic movement. In 1830 she married anti-Mason George W. Harris and then became intimately involved with Joseph Smith, founder of the Mormon Church. Records show that while Lucinda was still married to Harris, she was also "sealed," or married, to Smith.

With the jailer absent, the Freemasons returned to confront Morgan about his scandalous exposé, telling him that if he gave them the book he would go free. After refusing to do so, they went to his home and engaged in a futile attempt to recover Morgan's work. From there, matters only got worse. By Monday morning Miller paid Morgan's "debt" and he was released. The Freemasons then turned around and had him immediately arrested for stealing a shirt and tie, and owing another small debt in the town of Canandaigua, about fifty miles east of Batavia, to which he was driven in a carriage and again incarcerated. At the same time, an unsuccessful attempt was made to jail Miller.

A Masonic Kidnapping

As it is told, the entire affair took a major turn on September 13, 1826, when a man claiming to be Morgan's friend showed up at the jail to pay the alleged debt and secure Morgan's release. Lotan Lawson, Morgan's "friend," encountered the jailer's wife who cleared the charge and released a highly suspicious Morgan from his captivity. Once outside the building Lawson supposedly insisted that Morgan join him in his carriage, at which point two fellow Freemasons called Chesebro and Sawyer forced the reluctant man into the coach. It is said that those who witnessed the encounter heard Morgan shout "Murder!" as the carriage disappeared from sight.

When the Morgan affair took place, kidnapping was a mere misdemeanor in the State of New York. Governor Clinton, as a result of the disparaging circumstances, later signed a bill elevating the punishment to up to fourteen years.

Where the carriage traveled for the next two days is a source of speculation, but investigators of the day attest that Morgan and his kidnappers made their way over one hundred miles from Canandaigua to Fort Niagara (between the United States and Canada). At some point the kidnappers were joined by Freemason and High Sheriff of Niagara County, Eli Bruce, and made a stop in the town of Youngstown where witnesses heard Morgan inside the carriage.

The fort at Niagara, which formerly contained the federal government's department of defense, was empty when the carriage arrived on September fourteenth. Investigators later asserted that the fort's caretaker (who was a Mason) granted them access. For the next few days, Morgan was held inside the fort. It is said that at one point, he was taken by boat across the river to the Canadian border by four Freemasons. According to a ferryman, a meeting between several American and Canadian Masons ensued at which time the American men were willing to transfer Morgan to their cohorts to eliminate him by undetermined means. No plan was apparently reconciled and Morgan was returned to the fort and never again publicly seen.

As with modern-day murder, it is difficult to prove guilt with the absence of a body, and William Morgan's body was never found. His abduction, however, was witnessed by many individuals and that crime could be proven.

Body of Evidence

The outcome of William Morgan's disappearance was greatly marred by speculation, hearsay, and hysteria. Back in Batavia rumors, innuendo, and accusations were spreading. Friends of Morgan were alerting the press to his absence, as others were asserting that in order to prevent his book from being published the Freemasons had murdered him. Smelling the makings of what did become an immediate bestseller, publisher David Miller took the opportunity to promote Morgan's book.

Those who believed Morgan to have been murdered theorized that when the Canadian Masons refused to take Morgan the kidnappers weighted his legs and tossed him into the Niagara River. Another theory suggested he was taken over the Canadian border, and given a horse and five hundred dollars to disappear. The Freemasons countered that Morgan and Miller had concocted the entire event in order to generate a fervor over Morgan's exposé. In an effort to quell growing public outrage over the event, past Grand Master and now New York Governor DeWitt Clinton offered a three hundred dollar reward for Morgan's return or information concerning his disappearance.

Did Morgan's book have any impact on the public?
David Miller printed William Morgan's book and sold it for one dollar. By the time he produced the second edition, competition forced his price down to fifty cents. By 1932 there were well over a hundred anti-Masonic newspapers in print in the United States.

The public outcry increased when a body washed ashore on the banks of the Niagara River several weeks later. At first it was believed to be Morgan and was identified as him at an inquest, only to have that decision refuted at a second inquest when rumors of inconsistent markings on his body were touted, and a Canadian woman questioned whether the victim was her missing husband. At a third inquest the woman definitively identified the body as that of her husband and the matter was laid to rest.

When all was said and done, and without a body to prove murder, kidnappers Lawson, Bruce, Chesebro, Sawyer, and another Mason called Sheldon were convicted of Morgan's abduction. Protests then ensued over the leniency of their sentences and imprisonment which ranged from one month to just over two years.

Birth of the Anti-Masonic Party

The Morgan Affair began an anti-Masonic fervor that would not be easily subdued. Freemasons in general to this day maintain that Morgan was not murdered but instead struck a financial deal with the American Masons and, with the help of Canadian Freemasons, disappeared into obscurity. A wide measure of theories have been surmised since the incident, but no one can say with any certainty what really happened to William Morgan.

What can be said is that anti-Masonic sentiment continued to grow at an alarming rate, with the Brotherhood falling under close public scrutiny. Several anti-Mason meetings were held in 1828, and set forth a cycle that focused on everything from the secrecy of the fraternity to the alleged blood oaths in which they participate.

FACT

As is the case with martyrdom, Captain William Morgan became the poster boy of anti-Masonry. Up until 1882 many monuments were built and dedicated to the man who was supposedly murdered by the Freemasons before he could reveal their secrets.

Persecution of the Brotherhood

The sociopolitical climate at the time of the Morgan Affair was primed for upheaval and that measure of discontent manifested itself in a third political party called the Anti-Masonic Party. Andrew Jackson was enormously popular and the most prominent Democrat in the country. Though he failed to win the presidency in 1824, his stature was unscathed and he was set to once again run for office in 1828. A lawyer, statesman, and military leader, Jackson was also a Freemason—a Grand Master of the lodges of Tennessee. Naturally, this added fuel to the fire.

The Anti-Masonic Party grew quickly. Several of its candidates even held governorships in Vermont and Pennsylvania. But political and social campaigns against Masons were bitter affairs, and as persecution in society took hold, Masons and their families were denied many freedoms, including no longer being allowed entrance to their schools or churches. The idea that Freemasons considered themselves above the law coupled with their secret blood rituals was unacceptable to the public, and created an atmosphere of paranoia. As a result, the fraternity suffered greatly.

QUESTION?

Was Millard Fillmore an anti-Mason?
In his youth, Fillmore was indeed an anti-Mason. However, on July 4, 1851, during his term as thirteenth president of the United States, Fillmore invited the District of Columbia Grand Lodge to lay the cornerstone for the extension of the Capitol building.

One historian states that 227 lodges were under the Grand Lodge of New York in 1827. Eight years later, that number decreased significantly to only forty-one. In Vermont, every lodge either gave up its charter or simply became dormant. Even the Grand Lodge stopped holding meetings for several years. This decline was also apparent in Rhode Island, Massachusetts, and Pennsylvania.

Political Disparity

Despite any efforts made by the Anti-Masonic Party, Andrew Jackson won his 1828 presidential campaign against Whig John Quincy Adams. Four years later, the anti-Masons elevated one of their own at a national convention and presented former Mason William Wirt of Maryland as a presidential candidate. A three-way election between Jackson, Wirt, and Whig candidate Henry Clay gave President Jackson a decisive victory, and saw Wirt only carry the state of Vermont.

Though the Anti-Masonic Party began fading away in 1835, the damage had been done and would take over twenty years to undo. Lodge memberships decreased by the thousands in most states and in some cases lodges were abandoned entirely. The abduction and disappearance of William Morgan set into motion a devastating chain of events for American Freemasons, but it wasn't the first time the Brotherhood had been persecuted and like their European brethren, they would again see the Craft ascend from the ashes.

chapter 10

Famous American Masons

A list of famous Masons in the United States reads like a who's who of American history and ingenuity. Names associated with the Brotherhood run the gamut from presidents and diplomats to scientists and entertainers. Freemasonry most definitely took root and thrived in the open free-thinking environment of the New World, and its membership reflects that historical progression. From Benjamin Franklin to Bob Hope, American Masonry has enjoyed and continues to enjoy a diverse and highly innovative membership.

10

Franklin to Fitch

Over the centuries, the Brotherhood has taken pleasure in communing with hundreds of influential members of society from leaders of industry to presidents to a host of entertainers and historical groundbreakers. As noted in earlier chapters, arguably one of the most well-known American Masons of his day was Benjamin Franklin, who along with the Founding Fathers of the United States elevated Freemasonry to prominence in the New World.

Benjamin Franklin helped bring American Masonry to the forefront of American life. With an impressive career as a diplomat, scientist, printer, writer, and philosopher, he is often considered to be one of America's finest statesmen. In 1723, he published Freemasonry's Anderson's *Constitutions*, one of the first books to be published in the New World. In addition, Franklin was one of the thirteen Masons who signed the Constitution, and he served as Grand Master of Pennsylvania.

President of the Continental Congress and nine-term governor of Massachusetts, John Hancock is perhaps equally famous for being the first individual to sign the Declaration of Independence along with eight of his Masonic brothers.

The thrill of discovery and invention is a natural compliment to the Brotherhood, where Masons seek to enhance their communities and stretch their own educational wings. Many famous Masons carry recognizable names such as Ford, Macy, and Gillette, while others, like John Fitch, may not be as well known. Fitch was the inventor of the steamboat, a discovery that is often attributed to Robert Fulton, who was also a Mason.

Leaders of Industry

The lure of a "secret" fraternal organization such as the Freemasons would, without a doubt, be tantalizing for those taking part in an industrial revolution. It's no wonder that so many influential movers and shakers joined the Brotherhood.

One such Mason was David Sarnoff, a Russian-born American from modest means who started his career working with the Marconi Wireless Telegraph Company in 1906. Sarnoff then worked his way into radio broadcasting at the Radio Corporation of America (RCA) where he eventually organized their National Television Broadcasting Company. In 1929, he met Vladimir Zworykin, inventor of the all-electric camera tube and by 1953, RCA's color television became the mainstay in many American homes.

Household Names

A Mason named Lloyd Balfour may not be instantly recognizable, but for generations students have been purchasing their class rings from Balfour Jewelry. And that washing machine that works so hard for every American household? It was invented by Mason Frederick Maytag, whose company originally produced farm equipment, until he discovered a way to run the washer with an external power source.

FACT

The film industry also included several prominent Masons. Louis B. Mayer, the man behind the eventual merge of what became Metro-Goldwyn-Mayer (MGM), was a Mason, and Jack Warner of Warner Brothers Studios was also in the Brotherhood. Also part of the fraternity was Darryl Zanuck, who in 1933 cofounded 20th Century Productions.

Several prominent car manufacturers are also on the Masonic roster, including Walter Chrysler, founder of the Chrysler Corporation; Ransom E. Olds; and perhaps the most revered automobile manufacturer in history, Henry Ford, who invented the first gasoline-powered automobile. By 1903 he founded the Ford Motor Company and began mass producing his vehicles.

Another famous Masonic duo everyone is sure to recognize. Mason Harlan "Colonel" Sanders, made his mark when he founded his "finger lickin' good" Kentucky Fried Chicken, and Dave Thomas made Wendy's restaurants a household name with the catch phrase, "Where's the beef?"

Other influential industrialist Masons include:

- **Lawrence Bell** of the Bell Aircraft Corporation.
- **Herbert H. Dow,** founder of the Dow Chemical Company.
- **Charles C. Hilton,** hotel magnate.
- **Rowland Hussey Macy,** founder of R. H. Macy & Company, in New York.
- **James Cash Penney,** renowned retail entrepreneur who in 1902 founded J. C. Penney.

Masonic Inventors

A host of inventors also chose to join the Brotherhood. The name King C. Gillette is instantly recognizable as the Mason who developed a type of "safety razor." As a result, he founded the Gillette Safety Razor Company. Perhaps less known, but still highly significant, is John Loudon McAdam, a Mason who invented pavement made with layers of crushed stone (called macadamization).

A pair of firearms aficionados were also Masons. Samuel Colt patented his revolutionary revolving pistol in America in 1836, and his Colt revolvers are still manufactured to this day. Mason Richard Jordan Gatling founded the Gatling Gun Company in 1862, which merged with Colt in 1897. The Gatling gun was America's first successful machine gun.

Inventive members of the Brotherhood include:

- **John Fitch,** a clockmaker, brassworker, and silversmith who in 1786 built the first recorded steam-powered ship in America.
- **Richard March Hoe,** inventor of the rotary printing press in 1843, which revolutionized the newspaper printing industry.
- **Harry S. New,** journalist, politician, and Postmaster General who helped expand airmail service.
- **Simon Lake,** a mechanical engineer and innovator of submarine construction who held over two hundred patents for advanced naval designs.

- **George Pullman,** the industrialist who in 1864 invented and built the first railroad sleeper car.
- **Orville and Wilbur Wright,** renowned brothers and the inventors of the first airplane.

Political and Military Masons

Freemasonry has established an impressive legacy in the United States and has attracted a long list of powerful men. As a result, many politicians, statesmen, and individuals serving in America's military forces have belonged to the Brotherhood.

Presidential Prestige

Fourteen United States presidents have been Masons from George Washington to Gerald Ford. Given the high profile of their position, this gave Freemasonry an air of prestige akin to that of the Masonic royal members in Europe. Fourth president of the United States Andrew Jackson was a Mason, as was Harry Truman, and both Franklin and Theodore Roosevelt.

The following American presidents also belonged to the Masonic order:

- **James Monroe,** a Democratic-Republican, fifth president (1817–1825).
- **James Knox Polk,** a Democrat and eleventh president (1845–1849).
- **James Buchanan,** a Democrat and fifteenth president (1857–1861).
- **Andrew Johnson,** a Democrat and seventeenth president (1865–1861).
- **James Garfield,** a Republican and twentieth president (1881).
- **William McKinley,** a Republican and twenty-fifth president (1897–1901).
- **William Howard Taft,** a Republican and twenty-seventh president (1909–1913).
- **Warren G. Harding,** a Republican and twenty-ninth president (1921–1923).

Masonic Statesmen

The Brotherhood also welcomed many statesmen of note including Sam Houston, the first president of the Republic of Texas, and Thurgood Marshall, the first African-American Supreme Court Justice. Best known for his leadership of the Federal Bureau of Investigation from 1924 to 1972 was Mason J. Edgar Hoover.

Also distinguishing themselves in the Craft were a host of Hawaiian royalty. Several of the Kamehameha line of kings took part in the Brotherhood, including Kamehameha the Third, Fourth, and Fifth. King David Kalahaua, the last reigning monarch of the Hawaiian Kingdom, was also a Mason.

Statesmen who entered the Brotherhood include:

- **Samuel Ervin Jr.,** the North Carolina Senator best known for serving on committees for Joe McCarthy and for Richard Nixon during the Watergate scandal.
- **Barry Goldwater,** former Arizona Senator and 1964 Republican Party presidential candidate.
- **Jesse Helms,** five-term conservative Senator from North Carolina.
- **Reverend Jesse Jackson,** Baptist minister, American civil rights activist, and Democratic presidential candidate in 1984 and 1988.
- **Fiorello LaGuardia,** former mayor of New York who served from 1934 to 1945.
- **Sam Nunn,** former Senator from Georgia who served for twenty-four years.
- **Governor George Wallace,** infamous four-term governor of Alabama and presidential candidate who narrowly escaped assassination in 1972.

- **Earl Warren,** former California district attorney, governor, and Supreme Court justice from 1953 to 1969.

Military Leaders

Dedicated men in various branches of the American military services took part in Masonry. Naval officer, explorer, and aviator Rear Admiral Richard E. Byrd is best known for his 1926 flight over the North Pole with fellow adventurer Floyd Bennet, who was also part of the Brotherhood.

Also known for his distinguished career was Scottish-born John Paul Jones, who served as first admiral of the United States Navy. And not to be outdone, was Mason General Douglas MacArthur, commander of the Allied forces in the South Pacific during World War II.

FACT

Audie Murphy was an actor, singer, and songwriter, but he is best known for having been the most decorated American combat soldier of World War II. Murphy received thirty-three awards, among them the prestigious Medal of Honor. In 1955 he became a Mason, and eventually a Shriner.

Other Masonic military leaders include:

- **General Henry "Hap" Arnold,** American pilot who served as first general of the U.S. Air Force.
- **Omar Bradley,** the American general who played a crucial role in the Allied victory in World War II.
- **Brigadier General James Doolittle,** renowned World War II Air Force pilot.
- **John Joseph "Black Jack" Pershing,** revered army general who led American forces to victory in Germany during World War I. In 1920, he was awarded the unique rank of General of the Armies.
- **Eddie Rickenbacker,** legendary American Air Force ace during World War I.

Science and Aviation

The Brotherhood's zest for personal growth and exploration could likely account for their members involvement in planetary and other-worldly discovery. Several well-known astronauts were Masons, including Neil Armstrong, the Apollo 11 adventurer who on July 20, 1969, became the first man to walk on the moon. Fellow brother and lunar module pilot Edwin "Buzz" Aldrin became the second to take the giant leap.

Wally Schirra and Virgil "Gus" Grissom were two of the original Mercury Seven astronauts who had the right stuff. Grissom had his legendary lift-off in Mercury 4 and splashdown in Liberty Bell 7, but was unfortunately killed in 1967 in a launch pad fire when commanding Apollo 1. Mason Schirra has the sole distinction of being the only man to fly in the first three space programs—Mercury, Gemini, and Apollo.

ALERT!

Joel R. Poinsett is a Mason with a unique distinction to his credit. In 1922 Poinsett served as a special envoy to Mexico, but it is his association with a certain Christmas flower that makes him a household name. If it doesn't ring a bell yet, it will—Poinsett introduced the poinsettia into the United States!

The list of scientific and aviation Masons include:

- **Charles Lindbergh,** renowned aviator who piloted the first solo non-stop trans-Atlantic flight in 1927.
- **Dr. Charles Mayo,** who along with his father and brother founded the first official medical group practices in America, the Mayo Clinic. A Master Mason, he was active in the Rochester, Minnesota lodge.
- **Albert Abraham Michelson,** Prussian-born American physicist and Nobel Prize winner who in the late 1800s first measured the speed of light.
- **Andrew Still,** the physician considered to be the father of osteopathic medicine.

Also a brother is John Glenn, a former Ohio Senator and Marine fighter pilot who in 1962 became the first American to orbit earth. In 1998, Glenn made a second remarkable journey into space, securing his legacy as the oldest astronaut in history.

Arts and Athletics

The variety of entertainers, musicians, and athletes belonging to Freemasonry is impressive. The fraternity members range from Oscar-winning actors and composers to baseball legends, and all have left their mark on American culture.

Entertainers

One Mason in particular served both the Brotherhood and the world with class and stellar humor. A fifty-year Mason, Mel Blanc graced the world with cartoon character voices that only a legend could create. The voice of Bugs Bunny, Porky Pig, and Daffy Duck, among hundreds of others, was a true talent among men. In his distinguished company are other amazing brothers, including magician Harry Houdini who wowed the world with his astounding feats of escapism, and legendary silent screen swashbuckler Douglas Fairbanks.

FACT

Actor Ernest Borgnine, best known for his role in *McHale's Navy*, is a well-known Mason. He continues to serve as honorary chairman of a program which supports a Scottish Rite Childhood Center.

Many actors over the years have been Masons, including Gene Autry, Arthur Godfrey, Clark Gable, Tom Mix, Telly Savalas, and Will Rogers. A number of comedians also took their place in the Brotherhood, among them, Bob Hope, Red Skelton, and Oliver Hardy. Even the entire Ringling Brothers circus family—seven brothers and their father—were Masons.

Other entertaining Masons include:

- **Edgar Buchanan,** former dentist and actor best known for playing Uncle Joe in the classic television series *Petticoat Junction.*
- **Cecil B. DeMille,** legendary film director of such classics as *The Ten Commandments* and *The Greatest Show on Earth.*
- **Burl Ives,** revered singer and actor whose legendary voice can still be heard each Christmas season when he narrates *Rudolph the Red Nosed Reindeer.*
- **Al Jolson,** singer and actor who made history in 1927 acting in *The Jazz Singer,* the first talking picture.
- **Michael Richards,** actor best known for his role as Kramer on *Seinfeld.*
- **Roy Rogers,** actor and legendary cowboy.
- **Danny Thomas,** the actor and philanthropist who in 1962 founded St. Jude's Children's Hospital.
- **John Wayne,** actor and Hollywood legend.
- **Florenz Ziegfeld,** founder of the Ziegfeld Follies.

Musicians

Freemason Duke Ellington was considered to be one of the greatest composers of the twentieth century. His contributions to the music world as a jazz composer, bandleader, pianist, and orchestrator are legendary. Joining him in the Brotherhood is Irving Berlin, himself an exemplary songwriter and musical comedy genius best known for "White Christmas," "God Bless America," and "Alexander's Ragtime Band."

- **Eddie Arnold,** country music star internationally famous for his rendition of "Make the World Go Away."
- **William "Count" Basie,** legendary jazz pianist, organist, and orchestra leader.
- **Roy Clark,** singer and country-western star famous for hosting the television show *Hee Haw.*
- **Nat King Cole,** singer and jazz musician.

- **John Philip Sousa,** composer and former leader of the United States Marine Band.
- **Mel Tillis,** country-western singer, songwriter, and actor.

Athletes

Several remarkable athletes have served the Brotherhood with distinction, two of them legendary boxers. Professional Irish-American boxer Jack Dempsey had an exciting career during the early 1900s, as he eventually became a five-time heavyweight champion. His most famous bouts were with Gene Tunney. During World War II, Dempsey became a commissioned officer in the United States Coast Guard. Modern-day boxer and Freemason Sugar Ray Robinson was a six-time world champion in two weight classes. He is considered by many to be the best fighter of all time pound-for-pound.

One Mason in particular has been quite successful in the sport of golf. In the 1950s and 1960s, golf was not a major television event, but Arnold Palmer changed that. His charisma and tournament success led golf pros from America to the British Open and elevated the sport to new heights in popularity.

Ty Cobb and Cy Young, both Masons, secured their legacy in the game of baseball. Cobb was the first player ever elected to the National Baseball Hall of Fame. Young, arguably one of the greatest pitchers the game has ever produced, pitched for over two decades and earned additional distinction by pitching the first perfect game in modern-day history. "The Flying Dutchman," also known as John "Honus" Wagner, was a Mason and considered to be the greatest shortstop in the game's history.

Free Thinkers

Writers, artists, philanthropists, and a wide range of innovative and free-thinking individuals have taken part in the fraternal order. Writer and humorist Samuel Clemens, popularly known as Mark Twain, was a Mason, as was writer Alex Haley, author of the groundbreaking novel *Roots*.

At one time considered to be the richest man in the United States, Freemason and German immigrant John Jacob Astor served as Master of New

York's Holland Lodge No. 8. He later acted as Grand Treasurer of the Grand Lodge of New York. If the Astor name sounds familiar, it is because Astor's grandson, John Jacob IV, was lost in the sinking of RMS *Titanic*.

FACT

Another Mason of particular interest is author and illustrator Daniel Carter Beard, who founded the Society of the Sons of Daniel Boone in 1905. Five years later his group became the first organization of Boy Scouts in America.

One Mason who achieved great heights was Gutzon Borglum, a Freemason and sculptor who carved one of the most significant American monuments. Driven to create a fantastic and enormous portrayal of American nationalism, Borglum began carving Mt. Rushmore in 1927 with the help of over four hundred sculptors. It was finished by his son Lincoln in 1941. An astounding feat of masonry, Mt. Rushmore features the faces of Presidents Washington, Jefferson, Lincoln, and Theodore Roosevelt—two of whom were Freemasons.

Other innovative Masons of note include:

- **Ezra Ames,** prolific eighteenth century portrait painter who created over 450 works.
- **Brad Anderson,** famed cartoonist and creator of the comic strip *Marmaduke.*
- **Robert E. Baylor,** cofounder of Baylor University in Texas.
- **Reverend Norman Vincent Peale,** Protestant clergyman known for his groundbreaking book, *The Power of Positive Thinking.*
- **Booker T. Washington,** former slave and renowned educator who founded the Tuskegee Institute in 1881.

Historical Masons

Perhaps the best part of historical documentation are those pinnacle moments when astounding goals, feats, and personal journeys have been realized. In the past, there was so much about the planet and its inhabitants that was unknown, and the thrill of discovery was epic. As the modern age progresses, landmarks of history are often more about acts of self-discovery.

No matter the era, a host of Freemasons have, without a doubt, traveled a historic path, whether they were exploring the great unknown areas of the planet or the untapped resources of human interaction.

Adventurers

Freemasons have negotiated their way through all types of terrain, from the Great Plains to the frigid Arctic, and their adventures left an indelible mark on history. Even today, it's hard to conceive just how difficult their tasks were and the strength and perseverance required in achieving what many thought was impossible.

Joseph Smith, founder of Mormonism and the Mormon Church, and Brigham Young, for whom the famous Utah university was named, were both Freemasons.

Captain Meriwether Lewis and Second Lieutenant William Clark were both legendary frontiersmen, explorers, and Freemasons. Together in 1804, they embarked on their journey west and didn't stop until they reached the Pacific Ocean. Clark, the mapmaker of the duo, later served as governor of the Missouri Territory. Lewis, in addition to being named a national hero, became governor of the Louisiana Territory. He was also the first Master of a Masonic lodge in St. Louis.

Dr. Parker Paul McKenzie was a Freemason and a Kiowa Indian. When he passed away in 1999 he was the oldest living Kiowa, but that was not his only distinction. During his lifetime, he developed a written language for the Kiowa by creating an alphabet and then recording the words, grammar, and syntax.

Christopher "Kit" Carson and Davy Crockett were, in addition to being frontiersmen, part of the Brotherhood, as was William "Buffalo Bill" Cody. Renowned for being a scout and guide, Cody is perhaps best known for founding the Wild West Show, and for Cody, Wyoming, the city named in his honor.

Yet another famous duo conquered the great unknown, only theirs was a journey of a much different variety. In 1909, Mason and explorer Rear Admiral Robert E. Peary made the amazing journey to the North Pole, becoming arguably the first man ever to do so. It was an astounding accomplishment, one that most individuals felt was an impossible goal. One of Peary's companions on the trek was fellow Mason Matthew Henson, and together they made history.

Another polar explorer was Anthony Fiala, a former cartoonist and Spanish-American War correspondent who, as photographer on a 1901 expedition to the North Pole, took the first moving pictures of the Arctic region. In 1903, Fiala led his own expedition and succeeded in mapping various Arctic islands.

Breakthrough Masons

From epic moments in history to personal claims to fame, Masons have been driven to serve the self-betterment of the planet and its inhabitants. In some cases, Freemasonry served as a conduit for a better life, in others it showed that when individuals are presented with a challenge and are forced to overcome adversity, they rise to the occasion.

The name Robert Pershing Wadlow may not be instantly recognizable, but his participation in Masonry is well-known. Wadlow's claim to fame is the fact that at almost nine feet in height, he was the tallest human being on record. Wadlow was accepted into the Masonic youth group, the Order of DeMolay and eventually became an officer. It is said that the fraternity offered him acceptance, a welcome respite from the rest of the world, which at times was less than kind in regard to Wadlow's astounding height. He passed away in 1940 at age twenty-two.

FACT

Charles Stratton, better known as General Tom Thumb, was a Mason of the smallest order. An entertainer and circus performer for P. T. Barnum, Stratton stood only three-feet-four inches tall.

Immortalized as an American patriot is silversmith, engraver, and Mason Paul Revere, who during the American Revolution made his historic midnight ride to Lexington and Concord. It was April 18, 1775, and the warning he and two others delivered enabled American soldiers to hold back British troops. Revere's alleged shout of "The British are coming!" and his courageous ride was indelibly recorded in a poem by Henry Wadsworth Longfellow.

The name James Hoban may not be recognizable, but his work was vital in the building of America's capital city. Hoban, a Mason and architect, designed and oversaw the construction and later renovation of the White House in Washington, D.C. The Irish-born American was also one of the supervising architects of the Capitol building.

Other historic Masons of distinction include:

- **Francis Bellamy,** the Baptist minister who in 1892 penned the original Pledge of Allegiance.
- **Stephen F. Austin,** considered to be the Father of Texas. The city of Austin is named in his honor.
- **Rufus Easton,** the first postmaster west of the Mississippi River.
- **Francis Scott Key,** writer of the lyrics for "The Star Spangled Banner."
- **Frank S. Land,** founder of the Order of DeMolay, a fraternal youth group of Freemasonry for young men from the ages of twelve through twenty-one.

As head of the Central Pacific Railroad, the company responsible for building the first transcontinental line over the Sierra Nevada mountain range, Mason Leland Stanford made history on May 10, 1869, when he hammered in the famous golden spike signifying the final connection of the railways from east and west. He later went on to serve as governor of California and founded Stanford University.

chapter 11

Freemasonry and Religion

While members of the Brotherhood are, in fact, religious, the fraternity is nonsectarian. That is not to say that Freemasons haven't had historic battles with various churches and religions, because their chronicles clearly reflect opposition from several organized religions over the millennia, the Roman Catholic Church in particular. But as with all things that are perceived "secret" there is much to be learned when the subject is studied in the proper context.

Is Masonry a Religion?

One of the biggest misconceptions about Freemasonry is that it is a religion. It must be said that Freemasons do not claim to be a religion or some type of religious substitute. That doesn't mean its members aren't religious, because all of the brethren are required to profess a belief in a Supreme Being. This simply means they aren't an institutionalized system of worship. They're a fraternity that encourages its brethren to be active in whichever religion and church they belong.

For those unfamiliar with Freemasonry the religious aspects of the Craft can certainly be confusing. Writings about the Brotherhood often mention a bible, Masons meet in temples, many of their symbols have historically religious connotations, and some of their titles contain words like *worshipful* and *priest.* It's easy to see why misunderstandings occur. But in this case, a Worshipful Master has nothing to do with actual worship as a religious reference. It is, in fact, a title of honor, much like one would address the mayor of a city.

There are several basic elements to consider when analyzing Freemasonry in regard to religion. For starters, the organization has no dogma or central theology, and members are free to practice any religion to which they subscribe. Unlike most organized religions, the Masons have no sacramental offerings or ritual worship, and the Brotherhood does not offer salvation in the traditional religious sense of the word. All Masonic titles are purely symbolic and honorable.

ALERT!

Freemasons don't have a Masonic bible. They have a Volume of the Sacred Law, which is present and open at every Masonic gathering. During initiation ceremonies, a candidate can have on the altar or table whichever sacred text he wishes.

When speculative Freemasonry originated in the eighteenth century most of its members were Christian. As such, the Holy Bible, particularly the King James version, was the Volume of Sacred Law used in most lodges.

Freemasons, however, are tolerant of all religions. In lodges with memberships comprising a variety of faiths, several different sacred texts, such as the Koran or Torah, may be used.

A curious criticism, among others, in regard to the Masonic use of the Bible as Volume of the Sacred Law, is their reference to it as "furniture." This classification, which sounds odd to non-Masons (especially when taken out of context) is not meant to be disrespectful. The use of the word *furniture* is inclusive to Masons as it stands for "essential equipment" during lodge meetings. The sacred text is given a place of honor in a lodge, and lies open on an altar, table, or pedestal.

Grand Architect of the Universe

One of the basic qualifications an individual must possess when applying to become a Freemason is the belief in a Supreme Being and the immortality of the soul. The Brotherhood doesn't interfere with any member's religion, their only concern being that all members hold their own faith in a Supreme Being in high regard.

The letter "G" which is commonly used in Masonic symbolism with a square and compass alternately stands for geometry, God, or the Masonic preference, Grand Architect of the Universe. The latter addresses Deity in a nonsectarian manner, which gives brothers the ability to focus on their own Supreme Being. Differences in religion between the brethren don't really play a part in the fraternity, because religion and politics are not allowed to be discussed in a lodge.

Religion definitely plays a part in Freemasonry, but the organization strongly believes in religious freedom, which is why membership is open to individuals of any religion. It also believes that a person's relationship to Deity is both sacred and private.

The Mason's search for Divine Truth and Light is often misunderstood as being a search for salvation. That is not the case. Masonic references to "light" refer to knowledge in the ancient meaning of the word. Masons are in a search for knowledge, which includes educational and spiritual enlightenment and not salvation. In a similar vein, Masonry professes a hope in the concept of resurrection, unlike a religion which promises resurrection. Freemasons believe that a path to man's salvation is found not in their lodge, but in their chosen house of worship.

Freemasonry has also been questioned in regard to universalism, as it applies to Masonic writings. Given that universalism focuses on doctrines of universal salvation, which are part of the Church system, it again isn't something that Masons are involved with. Freemasonry doesn't have an "official" stance on the subject of salvation. All faiths and beliefs are welcome in the fraternity, but it is not one that teaches or preaches any type of religion.

FACT

The first Indian Mason was Omdat-ul Omrah the Nawab of Carnatic. He was initiated in the Marine Lodge in Calcutta in 1812. The first Hindu Mason was Ranganath Sastry, initiated in the Lodge Perfect Unanimity No. 233 in 1857, and the earliest Sikh Freemason was Duleep Singh who in 1861 became part of the Lodge Star in the East.

Atheism

Given that one of the qualifications in becoming a Mason is a belief in a Supreme Being, the question of atheism inevitably arises. As a rule, Freemasonry does not accept atheists. Much like any other membership-based organization, it has certain qualifications for their applicants. The only instances where atheists are accepted are in irregular jurisdictions, or those that are not officially warranted or recognized by a Grand Lodge.

Critics of Masonry are quick to point out a section of Anderson's *Constitutions* which states, "A Mason is obliged by his Tenure, to obey the moral Law; and if he rightly understands the Art, he will never be a stupid Atheist nor an irreligious Libertine." Of course, this was written in 1723, and the word *stupid* has since been dropped. However, the statement does make clear that Masons must have religious beliefs. They don't solicit members or force a particular belief on any member, but their varied lectures and rituals often refer to personal and spiritual self-knowledge and enlightenment, which assumes a man does believe in a higher being.

Deism

Deism and Freemasonry have an interesting history. Author J. G. Findel, who wrote *History of Freemasonry* in 1865, offered intriguing speculation about the relationship between Deists and Masons. Deists of the seventeenth and eighteenth centuries included many freethinkers like Voltaire, Descartes, Thomas Jefferson, Benjamin Franklin, and Lord Herbert of Cherbury, who is considered to be the father of English Deism.

QUESTION?

What is a Deist?
A Deist is someone who believes that reason should be the basis of one's belief in God, as opposed to revelation or tradition. Deists reject organized religion, and focus on reasoning being the key element to all knowledge. Deism is sometimes called natural religion or the religion of nature.

In his book, Findel asserted that these great thinkers had significant influence on Freemasonry and that they contributed to its transformation from an "Operative to a universal Speculative Society." Findel's speculation was certainly cause for Masonic debate. It is said that in Anderson's *Constitutions*, the term "irreligious Libertine" refers to the Deists of the time, which suggests they had little to do with the fraternal organization.

Also, during that era Freemasons were sectarian: Their religious allegiance, under the patronage of the Church, was dominated by Christianity. Of course now that has all changed with the modern era, and Freemasonry would not reject a member who is a Deist. No individual would be denied entrance assuming they have a belief in Deity and resurrection to eternal life.

The Catholic Church and Freemasonry

The independent nature of Freemasonry has historically run counter to the beliefs and tenets of the Catholic Church. Religious tolerance of Freemasonry, considered a virtue of universal nondenominational and nonsectarian acceptance by Masons, is considered to be religious indifference, in that the sovereignty of Christianity and the Catholic Church is unrecognized. Through a series of papal bulls and edicts, membership in Freemasonry has been grounds for excommunication from the Church since 1738.

While much of the Church's anti-Masonic rhetoric is ecumenical, there is no doubt that a significant element of the early Catholic condemnation of Freemasonry was politically motivated. The Catholic Church was gradually losing its overwhelming political and geographic clout in England and the whole of Europe, and the evolution of monarchies and governments was in constant motion. That evolution was inexorably slipping out of the hands of the Church.

Freemasonry, as a nonreligious, nonpolitical organization of progressive freethinkers championing the pursuit of knowledge and freedom of expression, has found itself the target of suspicion and repression for its very nature.

Masonic influence in the eighteenth century in England and Europe was inherently linked with the Protestant movement (see Chapter 3). By its inherent nonreligious and nonsectarian nature, Freemasonry became, in the eyes of the Church, just as much a threat to Catholic sovereignty. Ironically, the Protestant-based countries of Holland and Sweden enacted measures against Freemasonry in the 1730s, based not on religious grounds, but as reactions to perceived revolutionary threats.

Papal Intervention

The first papal bull against Freemasonry was issued by Pope Clement XII in April of 1738. The papal bull offers interesting insight into the Church's concerns over moral, social, and political issues in its condemnation. Pope Clement's papal bull begins by describing Masons as members of a society of any religion or sect who are joined together according to their laws by a strict and unbreakable bond, sworn to by oath and on the Holy Bible, and by threat of grievous punishment to an inviolable silence.

Clement continued that the Masonic society, which is held with the greatest suspicion, is depraved and perverted, and by their very secrecy must be engaged in doing evil. The papal bull went on to note that Masonry had been forbidden by civil authorities in several countries as being against public security, and "for some time past appear to be prudently eliminated."

QUESTION?

What is a papal bull?
A papal bull is a formal document issued by a pontiff and denoted by a bulla, or seal of authenticity, used exclusively by the pope.

The papal bull proceeded to incriminate anyone who supported Masonry, associated with Masons, or helped them in any way. The punishment for any of these acts was severe and immediate—excommunication, which is "incurred by the very deed without any declaration being required, and from which no one can obtain the benefit of absolution, other than at the hour of death, except through Ourselves or the Roman pontiff of the time." The papal bull concluded with an admonition for all Church authorities to actively pursue and punish anyone associated with Freemasonry.

Since 1738, nine Popes have issued seventeen pronouncements in support of Clement XII. These edicts variously encouraged Catholic and civil authorities to be more persistent in their mission to condemn Freemasonry. He deplored the civil authorities who were not paying attention to earlier edicts, and that the calamities of the era were due primarily to "secret societies." The last edict specific to Masonry in 1884 insists that the purpose of

Freemasonry is the overthrow of the entire religious, political, and social order based on Christian institutions, and the establishment of a new state.

Although the Church's official position has remained unchanged, there was a significant period of confusion in the early 1900s that lasted for decades.

Modern-Day Misunderstandings

In 1917, the Catholic Church issued Canon Law 2335 which stated, "Persons joining associations of the Masonic sect or any others of the same kind which plot against the Church and legitimate civil authorities contract ipso facto [immediate] excommunication." Taken literally, this law allowed any Catholic to become a member of any Masonic lodge that was not actively engaged in the overthrow of the Church or government. Since Freemasonry has never plotted or advocated the overthrow of any church or state, the door to Freemasonry appeared to be wide open to Catholics, and there is no question that a great many passed through it.

The Door Remains Ajar

In response to numerous questions from Catholic bishops about the meaning and enforceability of Canon Law 2335, a letter from Cardinal Francis Seper in 1974 stated that there would be no new law on the matter, that canonical law must be strictly enforced, and that the law regarding Masonic membership is reiterated. This decidedly unclear clarification continued to foster an interpretation of Church leniency toward membership in Freemasonry.

A new Canon code was introduced in 1983 that prohibited membership in any association that plots against the Church—without naming Freemasonry at all. The perception of this omission was perceived as a change in Church doctrine, but only for a short time.

The Door Slams Shut

Immediately following the release of the new Canon Code in 1983, Cardinal Joseph Ratzinger issued a new declaration, which stated that the Church's negative judgment of Masonry would remain unchanged, and that

Catholics who join the Masons are in a state of grave sin and may not receive Holy Communion. While the threat of excommunication from the Church was softened to denial of Holy Communion, the position of the Catholic Church was clear.

Cardinal Joseph Ratzinger, who clarified the Church's position on Freemasonry, became Pope Benedict XVI on April 24, 2005, after the death and decades-long reign of Pope John Paul II.

The proliferation of Freemasonry in historically Catholic countries, such as Mexico and most of Latin America, indicates that, despite the official position of the Catholic Church in Rome, Catholicism and Freemasonry coexist peacefully. The relatively long period of silence on the subject from the Church between 1917 and 1984, and the relatively benign punishment of withholding Holy Communion compared to immediate and unredeemable excommunication are further evidence that Freemasonry is currently considered to be an insignificant blip on the Catholic Church's radar.

Anti-Clericalism

It's important to bring up the subject of anti-clericalism in regard to Freemasonry, as the organization has many times throughout history been accused of its practice. Anti-clericalism, by definition, is a movement that stands against the power of religious institutions and the influence they have over politics and the public, as well as religious incursion of society in general. Those involved in anti-clerical practices strive to make religion a private matter with individual belief systems unfettered by external influences.

In the past, Freemasons have at times regarded Christianity to be the ally of those groups who defended the majority of the population in an effort to discourage the advance of human liberty. As such the Brotherhood has been equated to nineteenth century bourgeois liberalism, a perceived political and cultural threat. During that time lodges were also often accused of anti-clericalism.

It's no secret that various churches and governments have criticized and accused the Brotherhood of subversive activities. This was clearly the case during World War II, and with the P2 Lodge scandal in Italy (see Chapter 12). It was also evident in America with the murky case of William Morgan, which ultimately led to the birth of the Anti-Masonic Party. The two main criticisms of Freemasonry by established religions are the ecumenical aspect of its membership and the esoteric rituals it contains.

QUESTION?

Do Freemasons practice Gnosticism?
Built on doctrines of Jewish, pre-Christian, and early Christian sects that focused on the knowledge of God and the beginning and end of humankind, Gnosticism was considered heretical by the Roman Catholic Church. Few Gnostic communities survive today, so it's doubtful any Freemasons are Gnostics.

Some modern-day restrictions do still apply to individuals wishing to become a Freemason. Several Protestant denominations discourage their members from joining the Brotherhood, while the Eastern Orthodox church forbids it entirely. The Free Methodist Church was founded in the 1860s by individuals who felt that Masons and other "secret society" members were influencing the Methodists. A large contingent of Southern Baptists have additionally declared that its doctrines are incompatible with Masonic beliefs.

Sectarianism

Arguably one of the most prominent landmarks of Freemasonry addresses the issue of religious and political sectarianism, or narrow-minded attitudes in regard to those subjects. Freemasonry is most definitely nonsectarian and as such forbids the discussion of religion or politics in all lodges. In reality, this seeks to hone an individual's focus on his own educational and spiritual journey through the Craft, eliminating the distraction of potential conflicts that typically arise between those of varying beliefs.

When a man decides to join the Brotherhood and becomes an initiate, none of the brethren is allowed to question him as to his religious or political affiliations, and at no time do members take any actions publicly that associates Freemasonry with a particular alignment. Every Mason brings his own beliefs to the Craft, and while it is not a spoken virtue of the organization, he uses those beliefs to better understand the lectures and teachings of the various degrees.

Links to Ancient Mysteries

Freemasonry has long been associated with ancient mysteries and ancient cults. Though there is no proven link to any of the ancient mysteries, it is a popular and intriguing subject for historians, experts, and of course a contingent of conspiracy mongers. Theories and associations that have been speculated run the gamut including, among others, Hermeticism, Gnosticism, Paganism, and Cabbalism.

FACT

Hermeticists subscribe to the philosophy of a body of fourteen tracts of writings attributed to the ancient Greek philosopher Hermes Trismegistus. The influences of Hermeticism are thought to be Egyptian, Greek, Jewish, and Gnostic. Often considered to be the oldest esoteric philosophy in history, it is said to have influenced Plato, Pythagoras, and even Moses.

There is no doubt that the study of these religions is fascinating, and many thoughtful cases have been presented in regard to their possible connection to Freemasonry. One of the more intriguing of these mysteries in regard to the Brotherhood is Mithraism.

The Secret Cult of Mithras

From the first through the fourth century B.C. there was one dominant religion on the European continent, a "mystery" cult called *Mithraism*. For over two centuries this religion proved to be a powerful rival to Christianity. Mithras was known throughout Europe and Asia by many names, but he is commonly known as the Persian God of light and truth, who is often associated with the sun.

According to legend, Mithras came down to earth to gather his followers into an army. In a cave, he engaged in a battle against a fierce bull which took the physical form of the Spirit of All Evil. After defeating the bull, Mithras returned to the heavens to judge the dead and lead the righteous. In Mithraic art, he is typically shown sitting atop a bull, a knife in hand, often depicted with other animals.

Mithraism was an exclusive religion replete with symbolism, ritual, and rich ties to the astronomical world. Ironically, the Christians of the day equated Mithraism with their own doctrines and, having judged them to be similar, deduced that the Mithraics were a religion created by Satan for the purpose of leading souls astray.

So hated were the Mithraics by the Christians, that when the Christians finally overpowered the cult they annihilated everything associated with the religion, in fact rebuilding on their destroyed shrines. Only a few underground shrines survived and still exist in Europe.

Two of a Kind

What many Masonic and mainstream scholars have for many years pondered are the aspects of Mithraism that reflect the practices and symbolic rituals of Freemasonry. There is no solid proof of a connection, but given that Mithraism is a religion and a cult, and Masonry is a nonsectarian fraternity, it is curious that the two have so much in common.

The Mithraic cult was comprised solely of men, and its followers separated into seven "grades." Each of these grades had a symbolic ceremony in which initiates spoke vows, were baptized, and continued on to the next grade, each level imparting more knowledge to a individual and bringing him a step closer to Mithras. It has been speculated that these practices are very much in line with the rituals and ceremonies of Craft Masonry.

As with Freemasonry, Mithraics offered higher degrees that members could earn in order to achieve special knowledge and privileges. They also referred to one another as "brothers," and were focused on performing charitable and relief work.

Mithraics gathered in a cavern-shaped meeting place called a *mithreum*, in deference to Mithras fighting his legendary cave battle with the formidable bull. Mithreums, like Masonic lodges, had a president and a full range of presiding officers. Its membership was greatly varied in terms of class, but both slaves and men of liberty were afforded the same considerations and entrusted duties of equal accord.

Symbolic Symmetry

Symbolism was of great importance to the Mithraics, as they never recorded in writing any of their secrets or rituals. Freemasonry shares many of these common symbols—the sun, moon, stars, globes, and a ladder with seven rungs that symbolize the ascension of a candidate to higher degrees, much like the seven-runged ladder used in Craft rituals.

The astronomical symbols are of particular interest. In Mithraism, the seven grades are symbolic of the seven planets (Mercury, Venus, Mars, Jupiter, Saturn, and the sun and moon). The bull Mithras slays is representative of Taurus, with the other animals often shown with him translating to other signs of the zodiac, and subsequently, the constellations. Ancients looked to the stars and sun in order to track the equinoxes and summer and winter solstices. In addition to his other heavenly duties, Mithras oversaw the changing of the seasons and heaven's movement. His slaying the bull denotes the coming equinox.

Another commonality between Mithraism and Freemasonry is the symbolic death used in their respective rituals. The Mithraics used the legend of Mithras slaying the bull and representations of death and resurrection in their ceremonies, much the same way Freemasons use the Legend of Hiram Abiff, particularly in the initiation of the third degree, Master Mason.

FACT

In Masonry, one of the common ritual symbols is the point within a circle and the two vertical lines which appear on either side of the circle. One interpretation of the symbols joined together is the summer and winter solstice. It is said that the two vertical lines represent Cancer and Capricorn.

In context, it's easy to see why much time has been dedicated to the study of these two disciplines in combination, and while they do have many symbols in common, they have a great many differences in ideology. No definitive links have been proven and being that the majority of Mithraic history was destroyed, it's unlikely that a firm connection can be made. The possibility that Freemasonry descended from Mithraism, while highly fascinating, cannot at this point in time be firmly established.

chapter 12

Anti-Masonry

For as long as organized Freemasonry has existed, so has anti-Masonry. Like any membership-based organization, the Masons are subject to intense scrutiny, perhaps even more so as a result of the Brotherhood being termed a "secret society." As with many other groups and individuals, the Masons have endured their share of hatred, persecution, and scandal throughout history, arguably the worst of which occurred during times of war, both European and American.

Anti-Masonic Sentiments

Freemasonry is one of a handful of organizations that has stood the test of time. Whether one believes they evolved from the time of King Solomon's Temple or from operative stonemasons of the Medieval age is secondary to the fact that as a fraternity they remain bonded by the common goals of education and spiritual advancement both for themselves and their communities.

The burden of carrying around the term "secret society" has, however, resulted in all types of accusations, conspiracies, and persecution the world over. History has shown that over the centuries, more than a few powerful organizations, leaders, governments, and anti-Masonic groups have targeted Freemasonry for a host of alleged offenses including Paganism, Satanism, Luciferian worship, religious extremism, occultism, political corruption, murder, and control of powerful groups such as the Illuminati and Trilateral Commission who are bent on world domination.

QUESTION?

Who exactly are anti-Masons?
It is said that anti-Masonry can be broadly categorized into two factions, those who accuse the Brotherhood of anti-Christian or Satanic practices, and those who focus on the sociopolitical activities the fraternity allegedly exploits.

Being that the Masons are a fraternity based on the tenets of brotherly love, relief, and truth, those are fairly heavy accusations. But is any of it true? If one subscribes to anti-Masonic beliefs or various conspiracy theories, then yes, one would likely believe that Freemasons are the devil's concubines. As a historian, scholar, or expert on the subject, one is likely to focus on facts as they would any other historical subject and draw conclusions based on solid evidence. As a member of the general population whose knowledge of Freemasonry is limited, the choice of what to believe becomes highly individual and subject to the amount of research one does.

Conspiratorial Undertones

Organized anti-Masonic groups are a product of the eighteenth century that has evolved and now has reached considerable audience courtesy of the Internet. History, however, is replete with anti-Masonic activity ranging from pre-war paranoia to Nazi Germany to the present-day conspiracies surrounding such theories that, for example, Freemasons secretly created a pentagram when they designed the streets of Washington, D.C. (see Chapter 17).

A historical tour of the more prominent anti-Masonic actions, persecutions, and scandals will show that like any other membership-based organization, and most certainly with one that is dubbed secret, Freemasons have endured their fair share of strife, paranoia, hoaxes, and bad seeds within the organization who have added considerable fuel to anti-Masonic theories and accusations.

Early Inquisitions

Two of the earliest recorded cases of Masonic persecution recount incidents in Portugal and Italy. The first account surrounds the Roman Catholic Church and Tommaso Crudeli, who was a member of a lodge that was condemned on June 25, 1737, by the Chief Inquisitor of Rome. Two years later, on August 10, 1739, Crudeli was arrested and queried regarding his association with Freemasons. He was then subsequently tortured in the hopes that he would reveal secrets about the Brotherhood. Incarcerated for the next two years, Crudeli was finally released, but his time in prison combined with his torture sent him into ill health and in 1745 he died.

The second incident involves Swiss-born Freemason and jeweler John Coustos. Having lived in England since childhood, Coustos became a Mason in 1730. His initiation is of particular interest to the Brotherhood and their record books as it marks the first time a newly initiated Mason received a pair of white gloves.

FACT

John Coustos alternately made his mark on Masonic history, as he was the only English Mason targeted by the Catholic Inquisition.

Thirteen years after his introduction into the Craft, in 1743 Coustos founded and became Master of a lodge in Lisbon, Portugal, and it was there that his troubles began. Falling victim to the Catholic Inquisition, Coustos and two of his French brethren, Thomas Brasle and Jacques Mouton, were arrested and subsequently tortured over the course of two months. (Three other Masons had already been hanged in 1743.) Coustos survived and was sent to the galleys, but both his cohorts died. By 1744, with his release secured at the behest of King George II and carried out by a British minister, Coustos sailed for Britain, and later wrote a book recounting his harrowing experience.

Pre-War Condemnation

Many years prior to the start of World War II there were already anti-Masonic incidents occurring in Europe that would set the stage for the long period of Freemasonry persecution that would follow. One such intrusion would take place in Hungary starting in 1919 when the military forces of the Horthy regime began raiding Masonic lodges in order to pillage and destroy art, libraries, and records which were later displayed at anti-Masonic spectacles.

By the 1920s, the rumblings of anti-Masonry were already pervading Germany, as one of the country's World War I heroes, General Eric von Ludendorff, with the aid of his wife, began spreading both anti-Semitic and anti-Masonic propaganda. Their inflammatory publications, such as *Annihilation of Freemasonry through Revelation of Its Secrets*, divulged that the Jews and Freemasons were responsible for the German defeat during the first World War.

In 1928, the Spanish Grand Orient, one of two Grand Lodges in Spain, was closed after dictator Miguel Primo Rivera abolished Spanish Freemasonry. Individuals who were said to have been plotting against the government were arrested. Many of them were Masons, and when it came time for everyone to be released, five individuals and the Grand Master remained incarcerated.

Also during the twenties, Adolf Hitler was busy in prison writing his autobiography, *Mein Kampf*, in which he asserted that the Jews used the Freemasons to achieve their goals, especially with the influence that the Brotherhood had on high society. In his book, Hitler states that the Freemasons were responsible for the "general pacifistic paralysis of the national instinct of self-preservation."

Il Duce Versus Freemasonry

Italian Freemasons during the 1920s faced a new enemy in the form of dictator Benito Mussolini, whose Fascist Council on February 23, 1923, issued a decree which forced Freemasons who were Fascists to choose between the two affiliations. In response to the threat, the Grand Orient who had jurisdiction over Italian lodges, made clear that Masons were allowed to forfeit their membership in the Craft in order to remain loyal to their country. As a result, many did indeed give up the Craft.

An exception to the exodus was one of Italy's most prominent Fascists, General Luigi Capello, a World War I commander in the Italian army. When Mussolini issued his decree, Capello, who had at one time served as Deputy Grand Master of one of Italy's greatest lodges, the Grand Orient renounced Fascism instead of Masonry. Within the next year, the general—who was allegedly framed—was prosecuted in a lengthy and highly publicized trial in which he was convicted of conspiracy for having given money to individuals planning to assassinate Mussolini. His punishment was a thirty-year sentence of which the first six years was to be in solitary confinement.

By 1924, the persecution of Masons became more apparent as Mussolini issued a declaration stating that the names of individuals who were not Fascists and who belonged to the Brotherhood must be revealed. Committees were then formed to gather all information that could be found pertaining to Freemasons.

Mussolini's views became even more stern by 1925, when during an interview he asserted that Italian Masonry, under the rule of the Grand Orient of France, was simply a political institution. He did concede that English, American, and German Masonic organizations were charitable and based in philanthropy, but that apparently didn't apply to the Italians. As such, the

Italian Masons were accused by the dictator of being English and French agents who opposed the Italian military. Mass persecution ensued, and ultimately the assassinations of many prestigious Masons resulted.

FACT

The Italian Grand Orient managed to stay open until 1925, but by the following year, the lodge had been seized by the government. Comizio Torrigiani, Grand Master of the Grand Orient, stood up for democracy in an open letter to Mussolini after which Torrigiani was exiled to the Lipari islands where he died in 1932.

The Italian Brotherhood was entirely dissolved by Benito Mussolini in 1925, and for the next two years the infamous dictator's henchmen set forth to desecrate the domiciles of Masons in cities all over the country. During this onslaught, over a hundred Masons were murdered.

Freemasonry in Nazi Germany

Organizations or individuals who possess a certain degree of perceived power are always targeted by those striving for their own measure of power. This is nothing new when it comes to history as groups since the dawn of man have been made to endure all manners of persecution as a result of overpowerment. Like the millions of other individuals who were horribly persecuted in Germany during World War II, Freemasonry fell victim to the onslaught under the Nazi regime and its dictator Adolf Hitler.

Anti-Masonic sentiments were already present throughout the 1920s, so it's no surprise that Nazi party officials were in 1931 given a "Guide and Instructional Letter" which read: "The natural hostility of the peasant against the Jews, and his hostility against the Freemason as a servant of the Jew, must be worked up to a frenzy."

Brotherhood under Fire

It was January of 1933 when Adolf Hitler became the dictator of Germany. On April seventh of that same year Grand Master von Heeringen of the "Land" Grand Lodge of Germany was called to an interview with one of Hitler's top deputies, Hermann Göring, who at one time himself considered becoming a Freemason. At that interview, von Heeringen was informed that in Nazi Germany there was no place for Freemasonry.

Records show that Germany had nine Grand Lodges, which constituted a membership of approximately eighty thousand Freemasons. The three largest lodges were the Grand Lodge of the Three Globes, the National Grand Lodge of all German Freemasons, and the Grand Lodge Royal York of Friendship.

It is said that the Nazi government informed several Masonic leaders that their lodge activities would not be prohibited but that certain new rules must be instituted. In order for Freemasonry to continue, the words "freemason" and "lodge" would have to be banned, international relations and all secrecy must cease, the brethren must be entirely of German descent, and any reference to the Old Testament must be removed from ritual practices.

In compliance with Nazi demands, National Grand Master Dr. Otto Bordes (who later spent nine months in a concentration camp with his wife) and his officers changed their organization's name from Association of German Freemasons to the National Christian Order of Frederick the Great. The Grand Lodge of Prussia also complied and became the German Christian Order of Friendship.

From there, the situation continued to worsen. Before a large audience, the German Minister of Agriculture, Dr. Walter Darre, proclaimed Freemasons to be the "arch enemies of German peasantry" whose plan it was to sabotage the policies of the Nazi regime. This governmental anti-Masonic attitude resulted in Masons being barred from teaching and from performing other public services.

The Christian Grand Lodges, the Grand Lodge of the Three Globes, All German Freemasons, and the Royal York of Friendship—three of which were the oldest lodges in the country—were dissolved in 1934 under the order of the Premier of Prussia, Hermann Göring. The reason for the dissolution was, of course, that Nazi nationalism rendered the Masons unnecessary and due to their contact with international brethren they could potentially be hostile.

Fallout of Anti-Semitism

In Germany there had been for many years a highly voiced sentiment connecting Freemasons to the Jews. It is said that the rabid anti-Masonic and anti-Semitic movement was largely based on the feeling that the Masons and Jews were to blame for Germany suffering defeat in the first World War. Given that many Masonic rituals symbolically contained Jewish references, it's easy to see why so many Masonic lodges were under governmental attack.

By 1934, the Freemasons would find yet another opponent in Adolf Eichmann, a young Austrian sergeant in the *Sicherheitsdienst*, a secret security branch of the SS. Eichmann's work involved listing the names of high profile German Masons and delving into the international aspect of the Brotherhood. In doing so Eichmann became intimately familiar with what was termed the "Jewish question," and as a result, his ambitious nature soon made him an expert on the Jews.

FACT

During Hitler's reign, many Freemasons from various countries perished in concentration camps. One of them was founder and Grand Master of the Symbolic Lodge of Germany, Leo Muffelmann, whose lodge relocated to Palestine until the war ended.

Corrupt and Absolute Power

The final blow to Freemasonry came on August 8, 1935, when it was announced in Hitler's *Voelkischer Beobachter* newspaper that all Masonic lodges would be dissolved. In the paper, the Freemasons were blamed for the June 28, 1914, assassination of Austrian Archduke Franz Ferdinand which began World War I. They were also accused of wanting to initiate another war that would result in the creation of a "world republic."

Response to the announcement was swift, and included a decree—accusing Masonic lodges of subversive actions—issued by President von Hindenburg, and an order by the Minister of Interior that all lodges and their property be confiscated. The propaganda then continued as the German Nazi inspector of schools held town meetings to inform the public that in 1918, treasonous Masons who had worked in a German Army map department had passed military secrets to the British.

Heinrich Himmler was the head of the SS and the most feared man in Nazi Germany during World War II. His principal deputy Reinhard Heydrich made the claim that all organizations that were in opposition to the Nazi Party had been destroyed, but issued a stern warning that the "Judeo-Masonic world conspiracy" was still intent on destroying the German people.

Further propaganda was evident in 1936 when *Der Angriff,* the Berlin newspaper, published a report that American Freemasons were piloting over a dozen planes headed for Spain to fight General Francisco Franco's fascist military.

Gone but Not Forgotten

Even before the start of the second World War, many Freemasons were held in concentration camps. By 1937, many more would enter the camps as the Gestapo continued pillaging Masonic libraries and museums and gathering the names of anyone associated with the Craft. In keeping with the surge of anti-Masonic sentiment, Propaganda Minister Dr. Joseph Goebbels, a staunch anti-Semitist and perpetrator of the "Big Lie" moniker, opened Munich's Anti-Masonic Exposition in 1937 which, given all the looting that had occurred, featured totally furnished Masonic temples.

Apparently, the Nazi regime wasn't completely successful in their Masonic decimation because five destructive years later, in 1942 and with the war raging, Hitler issued a declaration that blamed the Freemasons and their allies, the "ideological enemies of National Socialism," for the war against the Germans. Again, the military ran roughshod through Masonic buildings in search of any accouterment they could find to fill anti-Masonic museum exhibitions. The following year, the propaganda machine continued to churn as Heinrich Himmler asserted in a speech that most of the espionage that had been committed against the Germans was primarily accomplished by the Jews and Freemasons.

Continental Persecution

Before, during, and after the war Freemasons in countries all over Europe were being killed, incarcerated, or scattered to the wind as a result of anti-Masonic governments and dictators. In the Netherlands, for example, there were over six thousand Masons in the country, but only a third of them survived the Nazi incursion. In Austria in 1938, the Grand Lodge of Vienna was taken over by the Gestapo who plundered the lodge and arrested Grand Master Dr. Richard Schlesinger (who died after his brutal incarceration).

In France a 1935 group sympathetic to Fascism called the Interparliamentary Group of Action Against Free Masonry issued a bold declaration that "Free Masonry must be struck down," and that national forces would fight to the death without "truce or respite." When the Germans defeated France in 1940, the Grand Orient and the Grand Lodge of France were dissolved and their property sold for later use in anti-Masonic museums.

Anti-Mason Bernard Fay, author of *Revolution and Freemasonry* was the Brotherhood's worst nightmare, as he was given the power to direct anti-Masonic activities. It is said Fay arrested thousands of Brothers, deported another thousand, and caused the deaths of a thousand more Masons.

Spanish Freemasons had their own problems, especially after the start of the Spanish Civil War in 1936 when troops under the order of Dictator General Francisco Franco began a Masonic onslaught by destroying temples and brutally executing members of the Brotherhood. In one town members of a lodge were made to dig their own graves before being executed.

Hundreds of Masons were killed or incarcerated throughout Spain and the Spanish territories of Morocco and the Canary Islands. By 1939, Spanish Freemasonry was outlawed and all offenders who did not repent involvement in the Craft were imprisoned. Franco's 1940 decree for the "suppression of Communism and Freemasonry" solidified the prosecution of every captured Mason in Spain. Military courts created specifically for purposes of Masonic suppression sent over two thousand Masons to prison for up to thirty years.

Scandal in Italy

The history of Freemasonry in Italy is not only a study of the Brotherhood, but a tempestuous chronicle of the country's political and societal evolution. The story of the P2 Lodge and the events spawned from its scandal are an anti-Mason's dream. The bottom line is that the truth of the matter is still not known, and while some facts may be accurate, the speculation remains, at best, just that.

In Freemasonry there exists what are called *irregular lodges,* meaning those not officially recognized by the Brotherhood. Italy and France have always been highly political countries, especially during times of revolution and, as such, many of their Masonic lodges were literally operated in secret. Italy had many irregular lodges, the country only having been truly united since 1870. Many Grand Lodges were created in the eighteenth century, but were suppressed until 1860 when Freemasonry was again revived and two Grand Lodges were formed.

From 1926 to 1945, however, Italian Masonry was banned, after which various competing groups emerged under the Grand Orient of Italy or the National Grand Lodge. American Grand Lodges officially recognized the Grand Orient of Italy and by 1972 it was further recognized by the Scottish, English, and Irish Grand Lodges among others. The National Grand Lodge remained irregular, with many of its members leaving to join the Grand Orient.

The P2 Lodge

One of the most common associations one makes to Italian Freemasonry is the modern-day scandal involving the Propaganda Due, or P2 Lodge in Rome. By way of history, the lodge evolved from the Propaganda

Massonica lodge which was issued a warrant from the Grand Orient in 1877. The lodge was more of a private club that was not on the official registers of the Grand Orient. The Grand Master of the Massonica had full control of whomever he initiated and as a result, the membership was comprised of many political and governmental individuals.

QUESTION?

Why is it called P2?
After World War II, the Grand Orient of Italy reopened and in an effort to name the new lodges under their jurisdiction, numbers were drawn and assigned to lodges. The Propaganda Lodge selected the number two and came to be known as P2.

Italy's P2 lodge was led by Master Lucio Gelli, a former soldier and Fascist who served in Mussolini's Italian Social Republic. It is said that in 1944, when fighting against Communist Partisans, Gelli led raids that resulted in the captured Partisan soldiers being executed. The ironic twist to Gelli's military success was that he felt as many other Fascists did at the time, that the Allies could win the second World War.

This school of thought led Gelli to incite a sympathetic backup plan that would ingratiate himself to the Allies. When the war ended, however, he portrayed himself as a member of a resistance movement but was unable to convince the anti-Fascists or the Communists, so he subsequently fled to Argentina in 1945. Upon his return to Italy years later, under the protection of an amnesty to Fascists, Gelli engaged in less-than-palatable Cold War business practices with Romania, including the black market.

Through his business, Gelli made powerful friends of all political alignments. When he took over the reins of the P2 Lodge, his membership grew to over a thousand and included cabinet ministers, high ranking military officials, civil service leaders, and journalists.

The trouble began when Gelli's dealings with Romania were revealed and an uproar ensued. In 1974, at a meeting of the Grand Orient Communication, the Grand Master of the Grand Orient of Italy proposed the measure to eradicate the P2 Lodge. With an overwhelming majority vote, P2 was erased.

The Puppet Show

Four months after P2 was expelled from the Brotherhood, Gelli made a bold accusation against the Grand Master, citing him for "gross financial irregularities." In an odd turn of events, a new P2 was warranted after which Gelli retracted his accusations. But this reinstatement was short-lived, as in 1976 a request was made to the Grand Orient by Gelli that P2 escape erasure by being merely suspended. This translated to Gelli retaining the power to control his membership without any involvement by the Grand Orient. Through all of this, the Grand Orient became public relations fodder, as their expulsion of P2 was seen as a fake maneuver—that P2 was working with the Grand Orient all along.

FACT

The Grand Master of the Grand Orient of Italy came under fire in 1978 when he was linked to suspicious financial activity. A financial campaign to elect an Immediate Past Grand Master was arranged by Gelli, but his candidate was not elected.

Italian Freemasonry had their fill of Gelli by 1980, when during a press interview he called Freemasonry a "puppet show" in which he was the puppeteer. The following year he was expelled from the Brotherhood by a Masonic tribunal which further stated that P2 had officially been erased in 1974, overriding the "illegal" actions of the previous Grand Master.

Italian police in 1981 had an open season on Lucio Gelli and his fraudulent activities. Raids on his home turned up all kinds of documents linking him to many influential people. A register of the P2 Lodge membership was recovered and revealed close to a thousand prominent names including statesmen, ministers, deputies, military officers, and politicians. This began a domino effect in Italian government as many government officials—including Prime Minister Arnaldo Forlani—were forced to resign. The government fell into chaos, and Gelli, the instigator, fled the country.

Freemasonry and the Vatican Bank

Lucio Gelli's documents provided a business connection between him and more than a few individuals of questionable repute. One of his colleagues was Roberto Calvi, president and chairman of the Banco Ambrosiano of Milan, an exclusive banking institution whose clients included Gelli and the Vatican. Another member of Gelli's P2 Lodge was Michele Sindona, a banker and alleged advisor to Pope Paul VI, who had ties to the Italian Mafia, Monorata Societa. Sindona was found dead in his prison cell in the 1980s, allegedly due to poisoning.

Calvi has been the subject of many anti-Masonic and conspiracy theories as his actions and mysterious death remain in dispute. In 1982, Calvi, who was known in the press as "God's Banker," was under fire when the Bank of Italy questioned him in regard to a large sum of money that was missing. When the Banco Ambrosiano collapsed, it was speculated that the funds in question ranged from seven hundred million to over a billion dollars. Calvi escaped to England and to what some experts surmise, a safe haven amid fellow Freemasons.

On June 19, 1982, Calvi was found hanging under London's Blackfriars Bridge (which some allege has Masonic connections). The cause of death was listed as suicide, but the circumstances surrounding his death took on new meaning when it was found that his pockets were filled with stones and drugs sufficient to cause his demise. A second inquest only served to fuel conspiratorial flames as it listed Calvi's death due to "causes unknown."

Masonic Murder

The death of Roberto Calvi became a sordid affair that spread suspicion throughout the Italian government and Freemasonry the world over. The fact that the Italian Parliament published its report on the P2 scandal two years after Calvi's death appeared to lend credence to theories that Freemasons were somehow involved. This, despite the fact that Parliament claimed that the Freemasons were not responsible for the P2 scandal and were in fact Gelli's primary target.

At that point, speculation that Calvi had been murdered accelerated and Lucio Gelli's associations and all the P2 information was again closely scrutinized to form all types of theories.

ALERT!

In 1992, Calvi's body was exhumed and the resulting conclusion was that he had been murdered. London Police reopened the investigation in 2003.

The tale of Lucio Gelli, the Grand Orient of Italy, and Roberto Calvi is replete with scandal, drama, intrigue, fraudulence, and murder all interwoven in the fabric of Italian Freemasonry. From the humble beginnings of the Propaganda Massonica lodge to the corruption of the P2 to the death of a Vatican banker, there is no lack of conspiracy and certainly nary a resolution as the case and the trials of those involved remain open to the present day.

A Reverent Forger

There is nothing anti-Masons enjoy more than a good scandal, and the case of Dr. William Dodd provided just that during the late eighteenth century in England. Both surprising and tragic, his tale was an eye-opening experience for all levels of society, which at the same time served up a bit of bad publicity for his Masonic brethren.

William Dodd was a man in possession of many impressive accomplishments, including a degree in mathematics, among other disciplines. He was also ordained in the Church of England, served as canon of the Priory church of St. John, and is said to have written over fifty books, poems, and theological works. In addition, Dodd was a renowned lecturer, tutored children of aristocracy, and was a major proponent of charitable organizations.

FACT

One of the charities Dr. Dodd founded was the Magdalen Home in Streatham for "fallen women" (the polite term for prostitutes). He was also instrumental in the Human Society for the Recovery of Persons Apparently Drowned, and in what would be an ironic twist, the Society for the Relief of Poor Debtors.

So what could a man of such upstanding character do to offend so many? In a word—forgery. William Dodd's life outside of his career was cause for speculation. Though married and of limited means, he had a propensity for throwing lavish parties. He had a town house and a country home, and wrote a novel that turned a few clerical heads, as it focused on sex.

A Clerical Error

Dodd's first mistake was a matter of bribery, a minor scheme which he initiated in 1774 in an effort to secure a fashionable—and free—residence in Hanover Square in London. The home, which had previously been used by a vicar who had recently been promoted and transferred, was given to Lord Chancellor Lord Apsley as a gift to do with as he saw fit. In a moment of stupidity, Dodd wrote to Lady Apsley asking her to persuade her husband to grant the home to an individual who would, after the agreement, be revealed. For her part she would receive three thousand pounds.

Dodd apparently failed in his efforts to write the letter anonymously, as Lord Apsley incited an investigation that ended up at Dodd's doorstep. When questioned, the investigators were convinced that Dodd was the culprit. As a result of the king hearing of Dodd's scheme from Lord Apsley, Dodd would be disgraced, as he was fired from his position as royal chaplain.

In the aftermath, Dodd sought and received help from a former pupil who was now the Earl of Chesterfield, and in no time he received new residence in the vicarage of Wing in Bedfordshire. Dodd was initiated into St. Alban's Lodge No. 29 on April 3, 1775, and was also a member of the Nine Muses Lodge. He had covered up his bribery debacle so well that he was accepted into the Brotherhood with no question. Soon after, a new position was created for Dodd and he became the first official Grand Chaplain of England.

Life and Death Debt

One would think that a man capable of such recovery from public scandal, who was a renowned preacher, humanitarian, and Freemason, would have lived happily ever after. Such was not the case. Having been appointed Grand Chaplain for a second term and comfortably situated in a new Freemasons Hall in London with an office created just for him, Dodd went on a

Parisian holiday. Not long after, the rumor mill made it known that he was living another life in France and spending a lot of money.

It is said that Dr. Dodd often frequented French racetracks and that he was connected to a high profile London prostitute.

In 1777, Dodd needed a loan and in attempting to secure over four thousand pounds, he offered the lender a bond which his friend Lord Chesterfield had issued. Dodd received his money, but the lender was suspicious and approached Lord Chesterfield. At that point, Dodd's forgery was uncovered, and despite all attempts to immediately repay the debt, he was charged and prosecuted. Dodd held out for clemency, feeling certain his former pupil Lord Chesterfield would not wish his prosecution, but that would not transpire.

Hanging High

In an elaborate trial speech, Dodd attempted to plead his case, but to no avail. Within ten minutes, a jury found him guilty, and being that the penalty for forgery at that time was death, he was sentenced to hang. The Freemasons renounced Dodd as well in a unanimous vote which expelled him from the Brotherhood in April of 1777. In June of that year before a huge crowd in Tyburn, William Dodd was hanged for committing the offense of forgery.

Of course, the tale of William Dodd doesn't end there. The events which transpired after the hanging remain in question as it was said that the Freemasons took Dodd's body to a house directly after the hanging where a not-quite-dead Dodd was revived and later smuggled to France. This account was allegedly substantiated by a letter written by Dodd to a friend a month after his hanging which recounted his resurrection and his current placement in France.

The flip-side of the story is also told, which is that the Freemason's carriage was unable to navigate the immense crowd who bore witness to Dodd's hanging and could not reach its destination before Dodd actually expired.

chapter 13

Demystifying Freemasonry

There are many mysteries associated with secret societies and Freemasonry is no exception to the rule. Of course, with mystery inevitably comes misconception and radical opinions based on theories ranging from mild to outrageous. While it is true that Masons do hold secret some aspects of the Craft, it is also true that their secrecy has more to do with privacy. Regardless, like any membership-driven organization, they have certain terms, symbols, and rituals that require explanation in context to the historic fraternal order.

Secret Society or Society of Secrets?

Anti-Masons have dredged up heaps of strident criticism out of the "secret society" moniker that continues to cling to Freemasonry. The very idea of a group of people who exchange ritual greetings, shake hands in a socially recognizable fashion, and hold gatherings in private behind closed doors, has been menacingly magical for centuries.

Over those centuries, opinionated, and often exploitive, individuals and groups would have everyone believe that there is *something going on in there.* In simplistic terms, these criticisms could also apply to board meetings, business conventions, pre-game football meetings, and quilting bees. So, what's with all the secrecy? Much of it lies in history and tradition. Even more of it is misconstrued and misdirected.

Secrecy on the Job

In the Middle Ages, when operative stonemasons came together to form guilds, there were many professional imperatives for establishing who was and who was not a qualified tradesman. Password greetings and specific handshakes identified craftsmen to one another, and to master masons who could employ them—in much the same fashion a union card serves in modern society. Semiskilled workers who knew just enough about the trade to be dangerous could be identified and either filtered out of the work force, or patiently trained to a journeyman level of ability.

From the perspective of safety in an inherently dangerous profession, and to prevent costly errors, there is no question that it served the best interests of journeyman level masons to keep the identifying signs of their craft jealously guarded.

Aside from providing employment opportunities, membership in Freemasonry also provided a form of social care and welfare. Masons in dire economic straits could apply for charity, and the families of deceased Masons could receive financial assistance. The temptation to cash in on these opportunities by non-Masons was obvious, and there was a practical necessity of verifying that applicants for charity were true members of the Craft. Record keeping was primitive at best, and the surest way of identifying a needy member of the Brotherhood was by testing his knowledge of closely guarded signals.

Masonic lodges have traditionally greeted roaming members of the fraternity with warmth and enthusiasm. While modern Masonic decorum suggests that traveling Freemasons instigate visits to lodges outside of their jurisdictions through prior contact and letters of introduction prepared by lodge secretaries, Masons in the past were free to visit lodges in other states, provinces, and countries at will. Here again, the knowledge of guarded passwords, hand signals, and Masonic ritual ensured host lodges that their hospitality was being extended to fellow brothers.

Suspicious Minds

There have also been decidedly sinister reasons for guarding the secrets of Masonic membership. Those reasons were triggered by a number of repressive and fanatical regimes throughout history that actively sought out and persecuted Freemasons. In this context, it's remarkably ironic that a fraternity based on equality, freedom of worship, the pursuit of knowledge and self awareness, and altruistic charity should find itself the target of suspicion in free societies. It was those very qualities that created distrust and cynicism toward Masonry in aristocracies and dictatorships that thrived on restricting freedom of thought, and demanded absolute obedience to their authority.

FACT

Adolf Hitler blamed the Freemasons and the Jews for Germany's involvement in both world wars. Benito Mussolini dissolved Italian Masonry in 1925, and Spanish dictator General Francisco Franco issued a decree in 1940 that suppressed Communism and Freemasonry.

In such climates, the maintenance of guarded identifying signals and words was an absolute necessity in order to protect one's life, property, and the safety of fellow members. It is worth mentioning that repression of

Freemasonry, and of most other forms of free thinking, continues in a number of countries today, including China, Vietnam, and Cuba.

Masonry Exposed

Virtually all of the "secrets" of Freemasonry have been revealed at one point or another in history. Exposés have been published from the 1700s to the present day, each promising to reveal more than the last. The Internet is full of sites dedicated to further exposing the so-called secret nature of Masonry. This has done very little practical harm to the fellowship of Freemasonry, and to the contrary, much of the publicity has actually proved to promote and illuminate the philosophies and intentions of the Freemasons.

In the western world, Freemasons make no secret of their affiliation with the fraternity. Masonic lodges are listed in telephone books and on the Internet, and their activities are publicized and actively promoted. Many Masonic lodges are "pillars" of their communities, and reflect amazing architectural and building expertise. Masonic pins, rings, tie clasps, and paraphernalia are freely available on Web sites and in stores worldwide. Freemasons are a highly visible force in their respective jurisdictions, and are invariably proud of their association with the fellowship.

The tradition of guarding handshakes, passwords, and signals of the degrees of Freemasonry continues to this day. Is this necessary in modern society? Probably not. But it does continue a long tradition of quickly identifying other Freemasons, and of maintaining a sense of camaraderie and fellowship. Realistically, it is about as harmful and secretive as the tradition of placing various symbols and graphic images on doors that identify restrooms.

Freemason Phraseology

Like many organizations, the Freemasons have certain terms and phrases that have specific meaning to the Brotherhood. Many of the terms are based in antiquity and are specific to the Masons as they appear in their tenets, constitutions, rituals, meetings, and legends. Others are general terms that are commonly used in public such as "third degree" and "on the level." As most sports have words that are particular to game play, so do the Masons have their own phraseology.

One of the most widely used Masonic phrases is "So mote it be," which is spoken at the beginning and end of every lodge meeting. Derived from the Anglo-Saxon word *motan* it means "to be allowed," or "so may it be." It can also mean "so be it," or when used in prayer, in deference to God as in "the will of God will be done." Even legendary English poet Geoffrey Chaucer used the phrase in his work to say "so may it be." In its most simplistic definition in the Brotherhood, it is basically used as an ancient form of the word "amen," a word that throughout the ages has been used, revered, and respected in its many spiritual incarnations.

To Masons, *so mote it be* is particularly significant as they are the final words that appear on the Regius poem, or Halliwell Manuscript. One of the most important documents of Freemasonry, it dates back to the late fourteenth century and includes, among other things, the legend of York and ancient governmental regulations of the Craft (see Chapter 2).

Terms of the Trade

Many terms that are used by Masons are not necessarily exclusive to the Brotherhood as they are often used by the general public. The phrase "on the level" or "meeting on the level," is another commonly used term among brothers. In context, its meaning to the Craft is that when Masons meet they meet as equals of all measure. The level by its very nature suggests balance, and for the brethren that translates to equality in regard to each individual's rights, duties, and privileges.

The word "hoodwinked" which is an often misconstrued practice in Masonic ritual, is simply the covering of an initiate's eyes. In mainstream conversation it's used in much the same manner, as a colloquial term meaning that someone is "pulling the wool over one's eyes."

Other terms such as "on the square" and "square deal" are also general phrases, but to Masons they bear obvious symmetry to their symbolism. The term "black ball," which is often used to signify someone of fallen reputation or one who has been excluded, applies to the Masonic voting process. The black and white balls used for voting have basically the same meaning. If a potential member is "blackballed," meaning he received a negative vote (literally a black ball), it indicates that his membership into the Brotherhood has been denied.

Sanctity of the Temple

Anti-Masons are usually quick to misconstrue literal meanings of archaic terms used in Freemasonry. The word "profane" in this instance bears explanation as Masonic use of the word is sometime seen as offensive when used in reference to non-Masons.

FACT

In the ancient form of the word *profane*, the Latin *pro* meaning "before," and *fanum* meaning "temple," translates to "outside the temple." It is basically an antonym for the word *sacred*.

When a Mason refers to an individual being profane or a group of individuals being "profanes," it is meant simply that those individuals are not Masons. That distinction means they are not allowed inside a Masonic Temple. It's a matter of semantics and interpretation, and in reality simply indicates nonmembers. Along the same lines, if Masons use the term "profane language," it is meant to indicate words that are not to be spoken within the sanctity of a temple. Perhaps part of the confusion is that the word *profane* is typically linked to profanity, which suggests vulgarity.

Religious Connotations

Freemasonry is often cited as being a religion, which is definitely not the case. Masons do believe in Deity, but the Brotherhood itself is not a religious organization. Several of the titles bestowed upon individuals who hold positions in the Craft and the various rites and degrees individuals earn do contain religious legends, symbolism, and terms like "worshipful" and "priest," and that is often a source of confusion to non-Masons.

In blue lodge, or Craft Masonry, the individual who is elected leader of a lodge is called the Worshipful Master. The term "worshipful" while religious in connotation is a title of respect that is not exclusive to Masonry, but is used much in the same way one would use the term "honorable" to address the mayor of a city.

ALERT!

Contrary to popular belief, a Mason who is serving as High Priest in a Royal Arch Chapter is not a man of the clergy. In reality, the title is more akin to his being a chairman or president of an organization.

Degrees relating to the Royal Arch of the York Rite have several ecclesiastical titles including High Priest, who is the presiding officer of the American Royal Arch Chapter. (In other countries, the term King is sometimes used or even first, second, and third Principal.) This continues in the hierarchy of the Royal Arch with the Grand High Priest and the General Grand High Priest. There is also an Excellent High Priest, Illustrious Master of a Council, and even Eminent Commander of the Commandery, though Masonry has no military force.

Secret Handshakes and Passwords

Much has been made in the anti-Masonic and conspiratorial worlds about Freemasons instituting secret passwords and handshakes. Taken out of context, a gesture, grip, or odd word spells doom for a society termed "secret." Of course, how secret can it be if everyone knows about it?

Freemasons take an oath that requires certain things be kept secret, among them the various metaphors of Masonry and certain modes of recognition. Much like any other group or individual there are certain personal incidents that one means to keep private. It is a matter of semantics, with privacy often misconstrued to mean secrecy. If an individual is denied membership to any organization, the reasons are typically withheld so as to avoid hurt feelings. The same goes for Masonry.

The handshakes and passwords Masons vow to keep secret are minor in the scheme of the world. Critics have in previous centuries charged that these modes of recognition were practicing cronyism in that Masons who were looking for work could be given preferential treatment if their employer was a Mason and they recognized one another by a word or gesture. In truth, a secret handshake among Freemasons is no different than a handshake between two teenagers who devise a greeting based on some hip hop gesture or lyric. Masons keep these modes of recognition to themselves out of respect for the Craft and as a show of true fraternal bonding.

QUESTION?

What are Masonic codebooks?

In ancient Masonry, most everything about the Craft including its rituals and legends was communicated orally. There are no codebooks in the literal sense, but there are ciphers, which by definition are secretly coded messages. Ciphers acted as hints one could use to elicit memory of a certain legend or rite.

Geometry

The art and science as of geometry is highly revered in Freemasonry. As a symbol it is one of the most common. The letter "G," which alternately stands for God or geometry, is often used in conjunction with the square and compass (see Chapter 14). As one of the Seven Liberal Arts and Sciences geometry is often said to be the most important. In antiquity its links to ancient masons and their trade is obvious, as the principles contained in geometry work hand in hand with construction and architecture.

Masonic symbolism, legends, rites, and rituals are replete with geometry. Squares, circles, triangles, angles, and tools used to create geometrical figures are heavily associated with the Craft. They are also most noticeably recognized by the public. In ancient texts and constitutions Freemasonry is often called geometry, connecting the science and art to the Brotherhood in relation to very similar principles they share. Literally meaning the "measurement of earth or land," one can correlate that brothers in much the same way seek to measure their own spiritual and educational progress.

The Divine Principle

There are two legendary individuals who play a strong role in geometry and in the Craft. Euclid, a Greek mathematician who is known as the "father of geometry," lived in Alexandria, Egypt, until his death in 325 B.C. Author of a series of thirteen textbooks called *Elements*, Euclid used integers and geometrical objects as a base for axiomatic methods which evolved into modern-day mathematics.

One of the legends associated with Euclid is symbolic of Egypt and how closely connected the nation became with a marriage of religion and science, taking into account all of the varied Gods and the combined knowledge attained in mathematics, geometry, physics, and astronomy. In ancient times science such as mathematics was considered sacred. The elegant lines and correlations of geometry and its existence in most things provides harmony between art and science and the entire world. As such it is very closely linked to Freemasonry in both its symbolic simplicity and complexity.

The forty-seventh problem of Euclid, also known as the Pythagorean Theorem, is one of the symbolic jewels of a Past Master. The problem, which was first published by Euclid but discovered much earlier by Pythagoras, is also prominently featured in the initiation and ritual of the third degree, Master Mason. Symbolically, the problem teaches a love of the arts and sciences.

As philosophical mathematicians, Pythagoreans believed in many things aside from their focus on axiomatic geometry, including transmigration of the soul (reincarnation) and sexual equality.

Knowledge Seekers

Like Euclid, Pythagoras has also had an impact on the Brotherhood. A Greek mathematician and philosopher of the sixth century B.C., Pythagoras is considered to be the "father of numbers," and a huge proponent of the belief that all things were in relation to mathematics and could be predicted using rhythmic patterns.

Pythagoreans believed that numbers were at the heart of all things in life. In 529 B.C. Pythagoras instituted a school at Crotona in Southern Italy which focused on Pythagorean teachings. Many of the school's disciplines were adopted by Freemasons millennia later. A seeker of knowledge and lover of wisdom, Pythagoras clearly had an impact on the educational and philosophical aspects of the Craft.

By the Numbers

Numbers play a significant part in the fascinating legends of the Craft, and in the allegorical lessons taught to the brethren. The most notable and recognizable to the average Mason are the numbers three and seven. The roles that numbers play are largely as memory association tools and learning techniques, teaching that certain numbers are connected with specific sets of ideas and legends.

Critics of Freemasonry have had a veritable field day with fanciful attempts at applying *numerology* to Masonry. Numerology by definition is the study of occult meanings of numbers, but there is nothing remotely occult or secretive in the numbers and their meanings as they are recognized by Freemasons.

The Number Three

The number three carries a staggering amount of references within Freemasonry. There are three degrees of Craft Masonry, three positions of the square and compass, three lighted Cardinal points, three sides to a perfect triangle, the three principle tenets of Freemasonry—the list goes on and on. Lest we forget, there are also the three theological virtues of the Craft: faith, hope, and charity, and the three tenets of brotherly love, relief, and truth.

The Number Seven

As Masonic historians claim, there are hundreds of references to the number seven in Freemasonry: The construction of Solomon's Temple took seven years; there are seven Liberal Arts and Sciences; Noah had seven days in which to build the ark before the flood came; the ark came to rest on Mount Ararat in the seventh month; Pythagorean symbols of the square and triangle and their combined sides, four and three, is seven. Again, the list goes on and on.

Conspiracy by the Numbers

The combining of numbers and ideas in Freemasonry, while undeniably an effective memory and teaching tool, has also provided a great deal of fodder for conspiracy theorists, and critics of Freemasonry. It really doesn't take much imagination to fiddle with number combinations that appear to take on the dimensions of a pattern, particularly when that pattern suits the agenda of the number fiddler.

Combined with the occult-like references of numerology, virtually anyone with a modicum of mathematical ability, a handheld calculator, and an agenda can juggle numbers into a frightening portent of doom and gloom. A few of the more common examples (along with a few of the patently ridiculous) are included here.

The Mark of the Beast

Freemasonry has been linked to the concept of world domination for years, and with a single misconstrued reference to Lucifer by Albert Pike, the Brotherhood is characterized as dealing with the devil (see Chapter 16). Believers in this conspiracy theory are of the opinion that the Freemasons not only wish to achieve world domination by secretly running the U.S. government, but that they also consort with Satan. These individuals find what they deem numerical proof of this conspiracy in Washington, D.C.

FACT

The number 666 is directly referred to in the Bible, in Revelation 13:18, as the mark of the beast, generally known as the anti-Christ, who it is prophesied will bring the world to ruin.

Within the geography of Washington lie Dupont Circle, Scott Circle, and Logan Circle. All of these streets have six major streets running into them, which some believe is a code for the number 666. The House of the Temple, which is the Supreme Council of the Southern Jurisdiction of the Scottish Rite, is bordered by "R" Street. The letter "R" is the eighteenth letter of the alphabet, and if you add six together three times you get eighteen. This theory persists among some conspiracists despite the fact that the physical address of the House of the Temple is on Sixteenth Street.

Unlucky Number Thirteen

Other than the demise of Jacques de Molay on October 13, 1307 (Friday the 13th), there is no other meaningful relationship to this number and Freemasonry. Conspiracists have attempted to link Friday the 13th with the Freemason world domination/Satanism theory by pointing out that the American flag has a significant thirteen stripes. These individuals have even gone so far as to claim that the fifty stars are in fact fifty pentagrams. These examples are just part of another list that continues on with no rational association to Freemasonry.

Till Death Do They Part?

For as long as organized Freemasonry has existed, so have anti-Masons and other sundry theorists who've criticized the Brotherhood for the practices and rituals it performs under an alleged blanket of secrecy. Critics often cite Masonry for what it terms their "blood oaths," which critics deem both archaic and offensive. To Masons, the oaths are entirely symbolic in relation to ancient legend, and there is certainly no actual blood involved in any rituals. The oaths taken by the brethren are serious to them, and refer only to penalties in regard to each individual's obligation to the Brotherhood. In its most simplistic form, the oaths represent a man's shame in breaking a promise.

Blood Oaths

It's fair to say that all the hysteria of the past and conspiracies of the present regarding blood oaths likely stem from the Legend of Hiram Abiff, which figures prominently in rituals and initiation ceremonies of Craft Masonry (see Chapter 2). In order to comprehend the symbolism of the alleged blood oaths, it is important to understand that part of the legend in context.

The death of King Solomon's Master Mason Hiram Abiff at the hands of Jubela, Jubelo, and Jubelum was particularly violent. Hiram's throat was slit by Jubela with a twenty-four-inch gauge, Jubelo attacked him with an architect's square, and Jubelum issued the final killing blow on the head with a common gavel. They then hid Hiram's body and returned later that night in order to bury it.

ALERT!

So called "blood oaths" and the penalties to which they refer originated in Medieval England's legal system. At one time these were real punishments that were carried out on individuals who opposed religious or political tyranny.

King Solomon himself was made aware the next day of the plot to murder Hiram and sent searchers in an attempt to find him. It was one of those searchers who heard the lamentations of the three perpetrators as a result of the heinous act they'd committed. First heard was Jubela who cried:

O that my throat had been cut across, my tongue torn out, and my body buried in the rough sands of the sea, at low water mark, where the tide ebbs and flows twice in twenty-four hours, ere I had been accessory to the death of so good a man as our Grand Master, Hiram Abiff!

Jubelo was the next to be heard:

O that my left breast had been torn open and my heart and vitals taken from thence and thrown over my left shoulder, carried into the valley of Jehosaphat, and there to become a prey to the wild beasts of the field and vultures of the air, ere I had conspired the death of so good a man as our Grand Master, Hiram Abiff!

And then Jubelum, who confessed:

O that my body had been severed in two in the midst, and divided to the north and south, my bowels burnt to ashes in the center, and the ashes scattered by the four winds of heaven, that there might not the least track or remembrance remain among men, or Masons, of so vile and perjured a wretch as I am; ah, Jubela and Jubelo, it was I that struck him harder than you both. It was I that gave him the fatal blow; it was I that killed him outright.

After being returned to face King Solomon, the three men professed their wishes to die, and as such they were executed in the manner each described in his own words. Jubela's throat was slashed, his tongue torn out, and his body buried in the sand. Jubelo's heart was removed and his innards tossed over his left shoulder for the vultures to devour, and Jubelum was indeed cut in half, his parts carried in separate directions and his bowels burnt to ash.

FACT

In the movie From Hell, which follows the so-called royal conspiracy theory that Jack the Ripper was a Freemason, two of the Ripper's victims had their hearts removed and their vitals tossed over their right shoulders.

Symbolic Death

When reading of the murder of Hiram Abiff, it's easy to see how one could misconstrue the term "blood oath" in relation to Masonic ritual. The bottom line is that the initiate's repeating of the words spoken by the three ruffians during his initiation ceremony is purely symbolic. While it is true that Masons do take their obligations seriously and that there should be some penalty for dispensing confidential information it is in no way literal. In Freemasonry there are only three actual penalties—reprimand, suspension of membership, or expulsion—for violating laws of the Craft. No one has ever been harmed during initiation proceedings or as a result of leaving the Brotherhood.

chapter 14

Masonic Symbolism

The Brotherhood is rich with symbolism that is at the same time historic and highly allegorical in nature. Many Masonic symbols have a host of interpretations associated with them, but in general many of the objects are in direct relation to Operative Masonry and the tools of the trade. Symbols are often characterized as drawings, shapes, colors, letters, or objects that represent something in particular. In Masonry, symbols run the gamut from actual tools and architectural details to religious and geometrical philosophies.

The Masonic Influence

Most people have seen a number of Masonic symbols in architecture, literature, and cinema, most likely without realizing they are symbols of the Craft. The square and compass are often deemed the most significant symbols of Freemasonry and are widely recognized. The all-seeing eye which graces American currency is highly visible and most certainly a source of eternal debate. Less known are the symbolic beehives, pillars, and lambskin aprons.

Symbols associated with the Craft are taken very seriously, as evidenced by their importance in various Masonic initiation rites and public ceremonies such as burials. When used in conjunction with the Volume of Sacred Law, the square and compass become highly significant, as they form the *Three Great Lights of Masonry*. The combined moral square, the virtuous compass, and the sacred volume as a conduit to God become a formidable and powerful symbol.

FACT

The square is one of the Three Great Lights of Masonry and a working tool for Fellowcraft Masons. It also serves as the official emblem of the Master Mason.

The conceptual triad of body, mind, and soul also relates to the Three Great Lights and the three-tiered structure of Masonry. The square as body, the compass as mind, and the Volume of Sacred Law as soul reinforces the symbolic nature of earth, heaven, and man's relation to Deity.

Many Masonic symbols are evolved from ancient practices, each bearing its own interpretation and associated allegory be it of a practical, spiritual, physical, or religious nature. The *point within a circle*, for example, has many varied representations derived from ancient times. Pillars, dating back to the time of Solomon's Temple provide plenty of speculation from architectural to the obvious phallic symbolism.

Tools of the Trade

Operative Masons made use of a wide variety of tools, each unique in their perfection, design, and purpose. Many of these tools, like the square, compass, plumb line, and level relate to geometry. Other tools, like the trowel, gavel, and apron are more practical. A variety of esoteric symbols such as the hourglass, scythe, and pot of incense are also prevalent within the Craft.

One example of a symbolic and ancient masonry tool now used in speculative Freemasonry is the trowel, one of the working tools of the Master Mason. In practice the trowel is used to spread cement, the binding agent which glues all parts of a structure together. As a symbol this represents the spreading of kindness and affection that unites brethren the world over.

The *gauge* and the *common gavel* are also familiar symbols of the Brotherhood carried over from ancient times. The twenty-four inch *gauge*, or rule, was used by masons to lay out their stonework, and has become a broad symbol representing all types of measure, both in the literal and figurative sense. The number twenty-four applies to the size of stones being cut, and also to the number of hours in a day. Masons are taught to divide a full day into thirds, with eight hours devoted to the service of God and the relief of others in distress, another third for one's work, and the last portion for rest.

The gavel symbolically given to the Master Mason is called Hiram, in homage to the architect of Solomon's Temple. Like Hiram, this gavel governs the Brotherhood and instills order in the lodge.

The common gavel, one of the working tools of the Entered Apprentice, was a tool used to break off corners of a squared block of building stone called *rough ashlar*. Symbolically it encourages individuals to rid themselves of the vices and impurities of life, preserve a positive disposition, and fit the body as a "living" stone for the spiritual temple.

Square and Compass

Though simple in its nature, the square is one of the most significant symbols in Freemasonry, one that retains many historic and allegorical meanings. The square represents morality and truthfulness. To act honestly is to act "on the square." To the operative Mason, the square has a plain surface and sides angled at ninety degrees, and its purpose is to test the sides of a stone for accuracy.

Historically, the square is highly revered in many ancient cultures and retains specific meaning. Squares often symbolize perfection and goodness. Egyptian architects used a perfect square as the base for their pyramids. Chinese cultures believed the square represented goodness and just behavior. It is said that there is nothing more true than a perfect square—its sides equal to one another and its angles sharp.

The compass, unlike the familiar magnetic directional compass used by mariners or aviators, is a V-shaped measuring device used by operative Masons to determine the proportions of all aspects of a building's design. Architects use the compass to ensure the stability, accuracy, and beauty of their designs. Like the square, the compass is one of the most important and prominent symbols of Freemasonry, and is meant to symbolize virtue as a measure of one's life and conduct. It also signifies restraint, skill, and knowledge.

Used in tandem, the square and compass are the most visible symbols of Freemasonry, ones that have appeared throughout history—especially ancient carvings and works of art—and are often prevalent in modern-day art, literature, and film. A common interpretation of the square and compass is that it represents the union of heaven and earth, the square symbolizing earth, and the compass, the arc of heaven.

FACT

In the 2001 film *From Hell*, starring Johnny Depp, the square and compass are prominently featured on Jack the Ripper's case of surgical instruments.

The heaven and earth symbolism is related to astronomy. In his study of the stars, ancient man quickly realized that the square was not well-suited for analysis of the heavens, but a circle would prove invaluable especially in determining specific points. The compass was ideal for astronomical measurement and a natural companion to the earthbound square. In time, the compass and its circular renderings came to symbolize the spiritual virtue of man. A circle without end signified eternity and the Divine, and gave reason for man to gaze upward and pay homage to the Supreme Being.

Plumb and Level

Both the plumb and the level were tools used by operative Masons to prove that surfaces were horizontally level or perfectly upright. The Latin word for lead is *plumbum*. A plumb line is a cord or line that has a lead ball attached to the bottom. With this, the mason can use gravity to his advantage and test vertical walls to ensure his work is upright. Symbolically this extends to a man in that he stand straight—like a solid wall—and will not crumble under strain or pressure. The plumb line represents uprightness and rectitude.

The level is a measure of balance, especially on a horizontal plane, and for the operative Mason, this was crucial in the laying of stone. For all things to be equal, everything must be level. It is a similar concept to the plumb line in regard to perfection and symmetry, only it relates to horizontal measure. In Masonry, the level represents equality and the balance of the brethren, with each brother issued equal rights, duties, and privileges.

Dressing the Part

At first glance it might be odd to think of men who aren't chefs walking around in white aprons, but when taking up the study of the symbolic apron one quickly learns of its rich history. In speculative Masonry its importance is immediately obvious to the Entered Apprentice and increases in significance when a brother rises to Master Mason. The apron is, in fact, the dress code of the brethren, as everyone in attendance at lodge gatherings is required to wear his apron.

The Historical Apron

The apron as a symbol has appeared in many cultures and sects throughout history. Some speculate that Adam and Eve originated the apron when they fashioned aprons out of leaves after their notorious fall from grace. The apron has symbolized truth, pride, honor, preference, and in the case of royalty, it signified authority. Aprons appear in ancient Egyptian imagery, as well as Greek, Roman, and Palestinian depictions, and even in the Jewish religious sect of Essenes from the second century B.C. Even Israelite clergy wore *ephods*, a type of girdle with an apron down the front.

Aprons used by operative Masons in the Middle Ages were typically made of animal skin and were quite large, held by a leather strap around the neck, tying around the waist, and covering the mason from his chest to his ankles. Knee-length versions were later introduced, but it is speculated that leather aprons such as these were worn by many stonemasons until the early 1800s.

ALERT!

According to some historians, the earliest representations depicting a Masonic apron appear in 1717 in an engraved portrait of Grand Master Anthony Sayer, and in 1723 in an illustration on Anderson's first *Book of Constitutions*.

The practice of decorating aprons was begun sometime around the 1730s, as Masonic symbols became decorative additives. This artistic convention is now part of the blue lodge degree ceremonies.

Aprons in Ritual

The apron is considered to be the badge of a Mason and one that is evident at each lodge meeting. In the first degree a newly initiated Entered Apprentice receives a pure white lambskin apron as his "badge of innocence." Now his permanent property, the apron is void of decoration which serves to remind him of the purity of life and rectitude of conduct necessary for his ascension. Over time, brothers may receive different types of aprons, but for the new brother this first apron is highly significant as it denotes his admission into a lodge and his first gift given him by the lodge.

The significance of the lambskin is two-fold. Lambs by their very nature have historically symbolized innocence and slaughter. Innocence to the Apprentice represents his birth into the Craft. The esoteric aspect of his innocence indicates that he is free of moral defect.

FACT

In a scene from the 1969 western *True Grit* starring John Wayne, Kim Darby's character views her deceased father in the funeral parlor and then tells her farmhand, "When you get home, you put him in a better coffin and you bury him in a Mason's apron."

Individuals awarded a Fellowcraft degree also receive a white lambskin apron, but theirs features a pair of sky-blue rosettes at the bottom. The apron of the Master Mason, which represents a position of authority, expands in decoration with the addition of a sky-blue edging and lining, and another rosette on either the fall or flap of the apron. Only officers or past lodge officers have aprons adorned with their official emblem, typically in white or silver and featured at the center of the apron.

The Letter "G"

The letter "G" is another greatly revered and highly visible symbol of Freemasonry. It's no secret that God and geometry are deeply embedded in the Craft, and as such, both share in the representation of the letter "G." Reference to God as the Grand Architect of the Universe or Grand Master of the Universe is also a common interpretation. Where the symbol originated remains unclear, and it should be said that the letter "G" most often appears in regard to American and Canadian Masonry but less frequently in Britain and European brethren.

One of the most sacred symbols of the Craft, the letter "G" in North American Masonry is often placed in the center of emblems such as the square and compass. It's also very common on Masonic rings and other jewelry.

The marriage of geometry and Freemasonry has been a long and prosperous one, as ancient masonry is intrinsically linked to architecture which involves geometrical aspects. Many experts have surmised that the letter "G" shows no strict evolution as a Masonic symbol; however, it is a commonly held belief that the "G" originally stood for geometry and slowly grew to represent God when the second, or Fellowcraft degree, was established in the eighteenth century. It is during that initiation rite that a candidate is first introduced to the Seven Liberal Arts and Sciences which includes geometry.

As a representation of God, the letter "G" serves as a reminder that all individual actions are seen by God, that Deity pervades nature and all men, and that life's blessings which emanate from God are disrupted when a man's actions are contrary to "Divine Will." The "G" in relation to Deity is no stranger to antiquity. In the Greek alphabet it is the *Tau*, and in Hebrew it is *Yod*.

The aspects of God and geometry give the letter "G" a powerful place in Masonic symbolism. Brothers of the Craft regard the universe as one of the grandest symbols; together with the aspect of Deity and the science of geometry a deep bond is formed. In a sense, they give an individual the virtue needed to build a temple of Divine thoughts for his soul.

Other Significant Symbols

As a Brother progresses through the degrees of the Craft, he is taught the deeper meanings of Masonic symbols which through the use of allegory serve to further enhance his education and spirituality. Many of these icons are common to ancient civilizations, and open to a wide range of interpretation. Symbols often relate to science, architecture, and theology or the spiritual ascension of mankind, while those of an esoteric nature, like the scythe and hourglass represent life and time.

FACT

The ladder is another common Masonic symbol which inherently represents advancement and ascension from a lower to a higher plane. Ladders have historically been used as symbols in many cultures and typically have seven rungs.

Tracing Boards

In simple terms, a *tracing board* is the modern-day equivalent of a slide show that highlights various pictures and symbology. During the early days of speculative Masonry symbols were drawn on the floor in chalk which could later be washed away. Eventually the system evolved into drawing images on floor cloths that could then be rolled up and reused. The floor cloths were eventually placed on easels, and by the eighteenth century were transferred to tracing boards.

Tracing boards are commonly used as a training tool during various degree initiation rites and contain pictures and emblems specific to each degree. The drawings shown on the boards are highly symbolic and rich in allegory and are meant to confer a sense of history to the initiate and his brethren.

Tracing boards are often confused with trestle boards, which were used by operative Masons to place building designs and blueprints.

Pillars

In the Craft, *pillars* encompass several different symbologies and ideologies. Pillars are, of course, deeply rooted in history as evidenced by most ancient civilizations. Greek, Roman, and Egyptian architecture features pillars with various designs and emblems, while at the same time serving as monuments for various religious and symbolic beliefs.

The *pillars on the porch* and their symbolism play a large role in the initiation ceremony of the Fellowcraft degree, but the allegory surrounding these two pillars is prevalent throughout the Craft. In the Bible the pillars are named Jachin and Boaz, and they stood at the entrance to the Temple of Solomon. A striking presence, they represent establishment and strength and by association further the concept that a man must have a balance of power and control in his life in order to find ultimate success.

ALERT!

According to some historians, the two pillars of Solomon's Temple symbolize the Pillar of Cloud and Pillar of Fire that guided the Israelites to the Promised Land.

Symbolically, Masonic lodges are supported by three great pillars denoting wisdom, strength, and beauty. The pillars further symbolize the lodge's three principal officers. The pillar of wisdom is the Worshipful Master, who as the lodge's teacher can offer instruction and fraternal stability. The Senior Warden is the pillar of strength who assists the Master in lodge details and supports the harmony of the brethren. The pillar of beauty is the Junior Warden, whose observance of the sun maintains the beauty of the day.

Vertical Lines and the Point Within a Circle

The *point within a circle* and the *two vertical lines* associated with it are symbols of Freemasonry that are open to many different interpretations, some practical and some esoteric. In some instances, for example, a closed circle with a point in the center is representative of Deity and man's relationship to God. In general, however, it's fair to say that these two symbols are geometric in origin. The point is simply a dot surrounded by a circle, and the vertical lines appear on either side of the circle in parallel formation.

One common interpretation relates Freemasonry's patron saints, St. John the Baptist and St. John the Evangelist to the calendar and two days which mark extreme seasonal shifts. It is said that John the Baptist represents summer solstice and John the Evangelist, winter solstice. In this instance, each is a vertical line on either side of a symbolic sun which rotates between them. In this interpretation the symbols represent control of one's conduct. Taking it one step further, it is also said that in this speculation that the two vertical lines refer to the zodiac signs of Cancer and Capricorn.

Another theory about the symbols relates back to the circumambulation that takes place during a degree initiation ceremony. The circle represents the circuit that an initiate makes around the lodge's altar which represents the point within the circle. Brethren standing on either side of the altar are then symbolic of the vertical lines.

FACT

Alchemy by definition is a process of transmutation through means of a seemingly magical power. In regard to that science, the point within the circle symbolizes the sun and philosophic gold.

The point within the circle was in ancient Egyptian times a representation of the sun God Ra and his eternal nature. The lines on either side of the circle are reminiscent of the *akhet* which in one translation means the horizon, and further the rising and setting of the sun. As such, the akhet symbolizes an ancient gate of the sun and the actions of rebirth and resurrection.

Still another allegorical connection dates back to ancient mystical times and the symbolism of the phallus as male regeneration. In megalithic sites such as Stonehenge, single stones were often erected in the center of circles. As a representation of virility it becomes almost a religious symbol, which in some cultures points to sun worship and the regenerative powers of the sun.

Beehives

At first glance, a beehive might seem an unusual symbol to associate with a secret society, but in truth it's highly emblematic. The *beehive* signifies industry, not in the traditional modern-day sense of manufacturing, but as devotion to a specific task or endeavor. Masonic definitions of the beehive imply that each individual is born into the world a rational and intelligent being and, as such, should be industrious and never be content to not offer aid to others if it is in their power to do so.

Many ancient and modern cultures held the bee in high regard. For the Egyptians, bees signified obedience and worship of a singular king. After his coronation, Napoleon adopted the bee as a symbol which stood for efficiency and productivity and also as an emblem of immortality and resurrection.

Industry is a virtue that is taught to all Masons, in particular the Master Mason, that the wages he earns to support his family can also be used to help another brother or that brother's family if they are in distress. The bee and hive analogies mirror that cause. Alone a bee can do very little, but once in the hive and part of a systemized industry it becomes infinitely easier to accomplish singular tasks or goals.

Volume of the Sacred Law

Considered to be the most prominent of the Three Great Lights of Masonry (the square and compass being the other two), is the *Volume of the Sacred Law*. It must be said that the oft-used term "bible" is a misnomer. Because members of the Craft practice many different religions, the sacred text of choice varies. For Christian Masons, it is indeed the Holy Bible, however initiates during degree ceremonies are allowed to choose which sacred text they wish to be laid upon the altar.

The Volume of the Sacred Law is crucial to the perfection of a lodge, as its teachings help rule and govern individual faith. No individual can become a member of the brethren without professing belief in the grand truths contained within the sacred text he has chosen. The Sacred Law represents truth, and when combined with the square (morality) and compass (virtue) they represent the search for ultimate truth within the sacred text.

The Anchor and the Ark

A pair of highly allegorical symbols are the *anchor* and the *ark*, which represent hope and a well-spent life. The anchor is a hope of glory and fulfillment of God's promises to the soul, a symbol of keeping one steadfast to faith despite temptation. The ark refers to the Ark of the Covenant, the sacred chest said to contain the Ten Commandments.

In Masonry terms, the anchor and the ark together are "emblematical of that divine ark which triumphantly bears us over this tempestuous sea of trouble; and that anchor which shall safely moor us in a peaceful harbour, where the wicked cease from troubling and the weary are at rest."

Esoteric Symbols

There are a number of esoteric symbols denoting different aspects of the Craft, several of which apply to the degree of Master Mason. The *pot of incense* is emblematic of purity of heart and is a symbolic sacrifice to Deity. The glowing heat of the incense mirrors the glow of gratitude in one's heart toward the author of existence and the blessings one enjoys.

FACT

In the 1960 film *Elmer Gantry*, Edward Andrews plays real estate agent George Babbitt. At one point in the film he says, "Do you realize that practically every American president was a Mason and a Protestant?" Further into the film he also says, "I'm in business! I'm a thirty-second degree Mason!"

The *hourglass* and the *scythe* allegorically represent time in regard to the human journey. As a measuring device, the hourglass contains a fixed amount of sand that ascends from the top to the bottom chamber in the span of an hour. As a Masonic symbol, it represents human life for the fact that one cannot comprehend the tiny particles that imperceptibly pass until at last the hour ends. Life is short, but should never be wasted, and when the end arrives, death escorts one to a dark resting place.

The scythe, a long, curved, single-edge blade, cuts through the brittle thread of life and launches one into eternity. If one escapes the evils of early life and eventually reaches old age, one is cut down by the scythe of time and sent to the land of his forefathers.

chapter 15

Conspiracy Theories

As long as historians have been document-
ing history, so have the conspiracy theorists
been parsing fact and fiction in the hopes of
uncovering the next whopper of a conspiracy.
It's an ironic symmetry at best, as both hope
to expose the truth of events while striving
for accuracy. Freemasons have been unable
to escape the waves of conspiracy if only by
association with various groups or historical
events and people from Mozart to the Bavarian Illuminati.

Sworn to Secrecy

Freemasons will never be able to shake the term "secret society." It is a legacy that has enveloped them since their inception, whether one decides they originated from ancient stonemasons building King Solomon's Temple or the Medieval operative tradesmen who built the great cathedrals of Europe. The fact that their ceremonies and rituals were held in secret and they profess certain beliefs and obedience to rules unavoidably classifies them as a secret organization. Unfortunately, that makes them fair game for all types of conspiracy theories and wild accusations ranging from political to religious intervention.

The true irony is perhaps that Freemasons as a fraternity have always been true to their charitable roots, and oftentimes the sheer good they accomplish, especially in modern society, is often overshadowed by public misinformation. The mysteries surrounding Freemasonry remain a constant source of debate no matter whether the subject is based in the group's antiquity, alleged involvement in a particular event, or modern-day proceedings. The devil is in that terminally gray area between truth and falsehood, and when it comes to conspiracies—including those with alleged Masonic involvement—it all comes down to what is speculated, what is assumed, and what is known.

If conspiracy theorists ruled the world then Freemasonry would, no doubt, become extinct very quickly. If what is presented both in literature and on the Internet is to be believed, then Freemasons are Satanists, Luciferians, assassins, a religious cult, KGB infiltrators, keepers of the Holy Grail, and the Illuminati, a powerful group of enlightened and highly secretive men who control all that goes on in the world. And those are just the high points. The truth of the matter is that Freemasons are simply a fraternal organization, rooted in symbolic history whose aim it is to better themselves spiritually and morally while at the same time work to improve society.

The Bavarian Illuminati

One of the grander conspiracies of the past, present, and most assuredly the future is the concept that a small group of powerful men ultimately rule the world. These men comprise what in the broadest term is known as the Illuminati, or enlightened ones. Many have, no doubt, heard the term before, as this group is often featured in film and in literature, often in shady circumstances and focused on some evil purpose.

The mere whisper of the word "secret" in relation to Freemasonry is enough for conspiracy theorists to speculate that the Brotherhood is an arm of the Illuminati or that, in fact, the Illuminati evolved from Freemasonry. In most cases, there exists a significant lack of evidence, with grand conspiracies or claims often based on literal or historical misinterpretations.

The Bavarian Illuminati wasn't the first group of organized "enlightened" individuals. The sixteenth century Alumbrados of Spain were a mystical sect of reformed Jesuits and Franciscans often cited as Illuminati. Also, the French Illuminés of Avignon, formed in 1770, later became the "Academy of True Masons."

Scholars, historians, and conspiracists alike have plenty of historical fodder from which to draw in regard to the Bavarian connection. There is, in fact, a slim association between Freemasons and the Bavarian Illuminati, and it is that connection that has by association given rise to Masons being mentioned as part of various secret Illuminati-like organizations including the Priory of Sion, the Bilderbergers, and the Trilateral Commission to name a few.

Birth of the Enlightened Ones

Adam Weishaupt was born in 1748 in the German town of Ingolstadt. Educated by Jesuits, he went on to become a professor of Canon Law at the University of Ingolstadt in 1775. Weishaupt immediately had trouble, being that his views were radical and offensive to the clergy. He condemned bigotry and intolerance and challenged clerical superstitions. He then assembled a group of bright young men, and set about creating a private party of opposition within the University. Meeting in secret, Weishaupt introduced his philosophies and liberalism to the group, which marked the beginning of the

Order of the Illuminati or "Enlightened Ones," commonly called the Bavarian Illuminati.

On May 1, 1776, Weishaupt and his collaborator German Freemason Baron Adolph von Knigge officially founded the Bavarian Illuminati whose heady aim it was to overthrow the Roman Catholic Church and all governments, and eventually rule the world. This was to be accomplished by way of secrecy and subterfuge with conspiracy mixed in for good measure. With only five original members the group came to have over 2,500 members many of whom were alleged to be Masons or former Masons. It must be said that at the time of the Illuminati's founding, Weishaupt was not a member of the Brotherhood and his possible initiation is in dispute.

Freemasons and World Domination

There is no evidence to suggest that Freemasons supported or created the Illuminati, but the structure of the radical free-thinking group is quite similar to Masonic structure. Illuminati members were divided into three classes, they offered obedience, and there were various officers and ascending degrees. Some speculate that the Illuminati had established relationships with various Masonic lodges in Bavaria, and that their enlightened membership over ten years reached to over four thousand.

FACT

In the 2001 movie *Lara Croft: Tomb Raider* starring Angelina Jolie, Lara must fight to keep the evil Illuminati from finding an ancient artifact that will give them the power to control the world.

The political climate at the time was one of guarded tolerance toward Freemasonry. Bavaria was a conservative state dominated by aristocracy and the Catholic Church. The growing publicity and controversy surrounding the Illuminati tipped the balance of favor against all secret societies. As one expert tells it, Baron von Knigge ultimately disagreed with the direction Weishaupt was pursuing and broke from the group.

One theory suggests that the Jesuits who were still powerful despite having been abolished, set out to destroy Weishaupt and his Enlightened Ones. A royal decree was issued in 1784 which banned all secret associations from Bavaria. At that point, the Bavarian Illuminati supposedly ceased activity. Weishaupt escaped prosecution, but his ultimate goals would become public, as his revolutionary-based papers were discovered and printed by the government. What became of Weishaupt is unclear, but his character and ideals are often alternately reviled and revered to the present day.

The French Revolution

The influence of Adam Weishaupt, the radical Bavarian Illuminati and, by association, the Freemasons, helped popularize the theory that Freemasonry played an integral part in fomenting the French Revolution of 1789. There is little doubt that Masonic philosophies of tolerance, equality for all men, and the performance of charitable service for the betterment of mankind ran counter to the haughty attitudes of the French aristocracy. However, the extreme social and economic decay in France that led up to the revolution was far too widespread to apply blame (or credit) to any single group, and in reality, Freemasons fell into both sides of the conflict.

Prior to the French Revolution there were over sixty lodges in Paris and 463 in the provinces, colonies, and foreign countries, all under the Grand Orient of France. The Grand Lodge of France had over 130 lodges in and around Paris. During the war, only three of the lodges in Paris remained open.

During the eighteenth century French Freemasonry was a mix of various individuals including clergy, aristocrats, military officers and the bourgeoisie, and none of them were motivated to elicit change in the social system. By and large, Freemasons had little interest in the political climate. There was, in fact, the growing belief that a country ruled by the "correct" person and not by a particular religion, and that belief fueled the revolutionary flames.

It is alleged that Napoleon was initiated as a Mason in 1798 to the Army *Philadelphe* Lodge, and that his four brothers were also members of the Craft. The majority of Napoleon's Grand Council of the Empire and his imperial officers were also said to be Freemasons. One expert notes that Freemasonry had no part in instigating the French Revolution but the Brotherhood did greatly suffer as a result, as the majority of the Masters of Paris lodges lost their lives.

Mozart's Magic Flute

One of the most fascinating gems of historical lore, and one of the oddest Freemason conspiracy tales, is found in a relatively tiny corner of the historical upheavals of the eighteenth century. This is the story of the composer, Wolfgang Amadeus Mozart, and one of the most highly regarded and controversial operas ever written—*The Magic Flute*. In order to understand how Mozart lived and died as a Mason it is important to understand the climate at the time.

During the mid-to late 1700s in Europe, the Age of Enlightenment was in full swing. The Dark Ages were being swept away forever, and many of the basic tenets of Freemasonry contributed enormously to the intelligent discussion of fresh ideas and philosophies that became pervasive in virtually every country. Europe was experiencing a huge shift in cultural climate, and the number of dramatic world events that occurred during this relatively short period of time is astounding.

FACT

The American Revolution shook the British Empire to its very foundations. In 1778, Benjamin Franklin (a noted Freemason) succeeded in convincing the French to declare war on Britain in support of the fledgling United States. A scant dozen years later, the French would experience their own national revolution.

Nobles and royalty alternately embraced and vilified Freemasonry. Writers, musicians, and philosophers of the day became active Freemasons, and their influences and accouterments spread into the upper crust of society. This intellectual awakening was brought into sharper contrast by the repression of such freethinking by paranoid aristocrats and clerics who felt serious threats to the world order of power and influence to which they had long been accustomed. As monarchies were replaced and shifted by revolution and natural succession, tolerance and encouragement of Freemasonry shifted along with them.

Masonic Enlightenment

In 1780, Joseph II became the sole ruler of the Austrian Empire (then known as the Holy Roman Empire) upon the death of his mother, Maria Theresa. While Maria Theresa maintained a more repressive approach to rule, Joseph was one of the "enlightened monarchs" who strongly advocated the emancipation of the peasantry, the spread of education, and a greater shift away from religious orders. He was also influenced philosophically by Austria's greatest military threat, Frederick the Great of Prussia, who was also a noted Mason.

Joseph was intellectually sympathetic to Freemasonry in Austria, but he was also pragmatic enough to maintain a level of caution. The memories of the Bavarian Illuminati and the attendant guilt-by-association of the Freemasons were still cause for suspicion, and in 1785, Joseph issued an edict limiting the number of Freemason lodges in the kingdom and compelling officers of the lodges to reveal themselves to the authorities.

While Joseph's political views were guarded toward Freemasonry, he was still a liberal and enthusiastic patron of the arts, and supported artists who were open and active Freemasons. The most notable of these was Wolfgang Amadeus Mozart.

A Masonic Muse

Born in the city of Salzburg in 1756, in what was then an independent jurisdiction of the Holy Roman Empire, and what is now Austria, Mozart's musical talents became apparent at a very early age. His father, Leopold, was a renowned musical master and Freemason, who encouraged and instructed young Mozart in violin and piano. With the flair of an entrepreneur and a bit of a huckster, Leopold recognized that his son's immense skill could be parlayed into a steady income by peddling those talents as a curiosity in the courts of Europe.

After a trip to the Sistine Chapel for a performance of Allegri's *Miserere,* Mozart transcribed the complete musical score of the jealously guarded piece entirely from memory.

Beginning at the tender age of seven, Mozart was exhibited by his father at the royal courts of France, England, Holland, Switzerland, and Italy. The pace of touring throughout Europe continued well into Mozart's twenties. In 1781, after a dramatic falling out with a major financial patron, Mozart settled in Vienna where he married, started a family, and continued to develop his musical career. Although Mozart never succeeded in obtaining a permanent paid post with any of the royal courts, his career was kept afloat by the patronage of the likes of Joseph II.

Mozart developed close ties with contemporary free thinkers and artists in Vienna, and eventually became great friends and a fellow Freemason with the composer Joseph Haydn at the same lodge. Haydn and Mozart held one another in the highest esteem, and Mozart is known to have written six string quartets in Haydn's honor.

Music for Brothers

With the death of Joseph II in 1790, Mozart's income began failing at an alarming rate. Leopold II, Joseph's brother and successor, failed to recognize Mozart's musical genius, and lucrative commissioned works slowed to a trickle. It was at this economic low point in Mozart's life that an interesting opportunity was presented to Mozart by fellow Freemason and good friend, Emmanuel Schikaneder.

With Leopold II's ascension to the monarchy, the status of Freemasonry was again on shaky ground, and the mood of suspicion engendered by the French Revolution and the Illuminati once again threatened the existence of the Brotherhood.

Emmanuel Schikaneder was a well-known character in Viennese musical circles, and an ardent Freemason who, as had Mozart, written a number of musical works specifically for Masonry. It is not known specifically if Schikaneder alone came up with the proposal to Mozart, or if it was done at the behest of the Brotherhood, but the concept was clever.

With Mozart's fame as a composer, and Schikaneder's abilities as a wordsmith, Schikaneder's proposal was to write an opera based on well-known fairy tales with the universal box office appeal of noble causes, heartless villainy, and the exotic backgrounds of ancient Egypt, with the eventual triumph of good over evil. Great music, great storytelling, all done with pageantry and undeniable Masonic principles and symbolism.

The obvious goals of such an endeavor were two-fold. To develop a hit show and generate income, and to subtly weave the positive aspects of Masonry into the production for all to see. The subtext of the opera involved many artifacts of Freemasonry, from trials of fire and water, earth and air, references to foundations and walls, several direct usages of the number three, and multiple uses of Masonic musical chords. The Egyptian backdrop is particularly telling, considering the profound Masonic influences of ancient Egypt.

A Grand Opening

To bring some perspective to the impact that an operatic production had on the audiences of eighteenth century Vienna, it's helpful to remember that entertainment opportunities were relatively limited in comparison to the virtually limitless amusements we have in modern society. Operas were hugely popular and open to audiences from across the economic and social spectrum. The best seats in the house were usually occupied by the aristocracy and the affluent, but cheaper seats and standing room were readily accessible to those with very limited funds. This could be compared to the hypothetical concept of seeing a major Broadway production of *Chicago* or *Cats* for a dollar.

The Magic Flute opened on September 30, 1791, in Vienna to limited public notice, but quickly found its audience and received much critical acclaim and dozens of enthusiastically received performances. While *The Magic Flute* would live on as a well-loved masterpiece, the attempt at creating an influential Masonic coda was generally lost on the public, and would soon be completely overshadowed by more serious repressions of Freemasonry as the monarchy changed.

After the release of *The Magic Flute*, Mozart received a commission to write a requiem for a Count Von Walsegg. It is said that the commission was delivered to Mozart by a mysterious and unidentified hooded stranger. As the story goes, after beginning the requiem Mozart fell to brooding about his own mortality, and eventually became convinced that the requiem he was writing for Von Walsegg was in reality being written for himself. Mozart's health began failing, and quickly deteriorated. He passed away on December 5, 1791, at the age of 35, just three short months after the opening of *The Magic Flute*.

Musical Conspiracy

The attending physician at Mozart's death failed to issue a death certificate identifying the cause of death, and no autopsy was performed. These oversights paved the way for a slew of rumors and theories. The first rumors had it that Mozart had been poisoned, which begged the obvious question—by whom?

One unsubstantiated and implausible set of theories laid blame directly at the feet of the Freemasons. This series held that the Freemasons were upset with Mozart for revealing too many Masonic secrets in *The Magic Flute*, and went on to claim that Mozart had created an anti-Masonic sub-subtext underlying the Masonic subtext of the opera. This was later embellished to include the mysterious hooded stranger as a Masonic messenger of doom. These theories completely ignored the fact that Mozart wrote only the *music* to *The Magic Flute*, but that oversight in conspiratorial theory mongering was later appended to include the notion that the Freemasons later murdered Emmanuel Schikaneder.

FACT

Mozart had a well-known professional competitor named Antonio Salieri, who was quickly thrown into the mix of conjecture. Later unsubstantiated rumors had it that Salieri confessed on his deathbed in 1825 to murdering Mozart.

The conspiracy theories surrounding Mozart's death make for great storytelling, but there isn't, and never has been, any historical proof that Mozart died of anything other than natural causes (most likely, rheumatic fever). In Masonic circles, Mozart is a revered Brother who contributed much artistically to the world, and to Freemasonry.

The Priory of Sion

The Priory of Sion is a fascinating study in both history and conspiracy, especially in regard to its alleged connection to Jesus Christ, Mary Magdalene, the Medieval Knights Templar, and ultimately to Freemasonry courtesy of secret documents and various associations in history. In regard to the Priory, there is no lack of conspiracy theories which splinter in all directions from the eleventh century to the present.

Its origins as a secret organization are most definitely in dispute, some saying the group was founded in the 1950s, others claiming it dates back to the time of the Crusades in 1099 A.D. Add to the mix a set of secret documents, connections to France's mystical Rennes-le-Chateau, and the alleged lineage of Mary Magdalene that became the Merovingian dynasty and one can see why the Priory is a subject rife with controversy.

The *Prieure de Sion*, or Priory of Sion, was founded in Annemasse, France, in 1956 by Pierre Plantard. With a membership of five men, the society claimed it was originated from the Ordre de Sion founded by Frenchman Godfroi de Bouillon in 1090. A leader during the Crusades, de Bouillon became the first ruler of the Kingdom of Jerusalem in 1099. It wasn't long after de Bouillon's death that the Knights Templar were officially recognized. Some experts have speculated that it was the *Prieure de Sion* who created the Knights Templar as their military and administrative order. The name *Prieure de Sion* was allegedly changed in 1188 to the Priory of Sion when its members and the Templars parted company.

QUESTION?

Why does the name Priory of Sion sound familiar?
The name Priory of Sion may ring a bell because it plays a large role in Dan Brown's bestselling book *The Da Vinci Code*, in which the Priory and its Grand Master are integral to the story line involving the Holy Grail.

The Priory of Sion was said to have been a secret society that during various eras was led by Grand Masters including Leonardo da Vinci, Isaac Newton, Victor Hugo, and Sandro Botticelli. The first Grand Master was Jean de Gisors, who served from 1188 to 1220. Plantard himself claimed he first served as secretary-general before serving as Grand Master of the Priory from 1981 to 1984. If indeed the Priory existed the list of previous Grand Masters includes aristocracy, occultists, alchemists, and Freemasons.

Secrets or Lies?

In 1975, a set of parchments was discovered in Paris's Bibliotheque Nationale, documents that came to be known as Les Dossiers Secrets. How the Dossiers came to the Paris library is unclear, but some speculate that it was through Plantard himself, in an effort to further his Priory's claim to antiquity. In order to understand the contents of the documents, which included genealogies and some type of Masonic charter, it's necessary to examine one of the legends associated with the discovery.

It is said that Plantard's Priory disbanded in 1957, but that he made an attempt to revive it several years later. In doing so he enlisted the help of French author Gerard de Sède and filmmaker and journalist Philippe de Chérisey to create documents that would substantiate the Priory's claim to Godfroi's original Priory of Sion.

Gerard de Sède published a book in 1967 based on Plantard's story. It later intrigued three British journalists Michael Baigent, Richard Leigh, and Henry Lincoln, who went on a decade-long research quest before writing *Holy Blood, Holy Grail*.

The documents are said to have originated at Rennes-le-Chateau in Languedoc, France, a mysterious church that has long been an intriguing study of scholars and researchers for its alleged links to the Holy Grail, the Ark of the Covenant, Noah's Ark, and the hidden treasures of Solomon's Temple. The parish priest of the Chateau was Berenger Saunière who allegedly discovered four parchments within a hollowed out Visigoth pillar.

The tale Plantard told his friend Gerard de Sède was that the documents Saunière had uncovered confirmed French lore that Jesus had in fact evaded death and lived in France with Mary Magdalene. Their lineage resulted in the Merovingian dynasty. The Holy Grail, as Plantard asserted, or *San Greal* in French, literally translates to "Holy Blood." The implication was, of course, that the blood of Christ flowed through the Merovingian lineage. When the dynasty eventually fell and the descendants went underground, the Priory of Sion were their protectors, along with their associates which included the Knights Templar and the Freemasons who among others were intimately involved with the Priory.

The Truth Is Out There

Whether or not Plantard's story is true or if he and his cohorts did or didn't create the documents of the Dossiers Secrets is an ongoing debate. As for another of Plantard's Masonic connections, there is an additional theory that links Plantard and the Dossiers Secrets to the Swiss Grand Loge Alpina. It is alleged that "Les descendants Merovingiens ou l'enigme du Razes Wisigoth," which was the first of the four documents, was published at the Swiss lodge. To date there is no proof of this claim, and the lodge itself has denied any involvement.

One theory suggests Plantard and his colleagues Gerard de Sède and Philippe de Chérisey eventually had a falling out and that Plantard made it known that two of Sède's published parchments were indeed fabricated by Chérisey. There are no firm answers to the mystery of the Priory of Sion, but many exceptional books have been written about the legendary organization's existence and possible connection to the Knights Templar, Freemasons, and other individuals, groups, and events in history.

chapter 16

Discovering the Truth

Albert Pike is a towering figure in Freemasonry and is held in the highest regard by the Masons who know of him, his history, and his legacy. Pike is worthy of a book unto himself, but often remains in the limelight for a single comment he made in regard to Lucifer. The Internet is rife with anti-Masonic conspiracies surrounding Pike's comment and linking it to Freemasonry. There is, however, documented proof that effectively nullifies those claims.

Albert Pike: A Masonic Legacy

In the simplest terms of association with Freemasonry, Albert Pike was the Sovereign Grand Commander of the Southern Supreme Council of the Scottish Rite from 1859 to 1891. Pike's story and its influence on Masonic history is colorful, controversial, and contradictory. It presents one of the most fascinating and remarkable legacies of Freemasonry. To understand and appreciate the legend, influence, and controversy surrounding Albert Pike, it's important to place the man and his background into historical perspective.

Although his attendance at Harvard is questionable, it is known that Albert Pike became a country school teacher and taught in several schools in Massachusetts.

Albert Pike was born in Boston, Massachusetts, December 28, 1809, into a relatively poor household. Pike proved to be a brilliant student in public schools, and, at the age of fifteen, passed admission exams into Harvard. Although some historians believe that Pike attended Harvard until his junior year, and was forced to drop out because of financial limitations, no known records of Pike's actual attendance exist. Others claim that Pike was unable to attend Harvard at all, citing the lack of evidence, and the unlikelihood of his ability to have produced the university's requirement of two year's tuition, paid in advance.

Westward Adventure

At the age of twenty-two, Pike struck out for the West, beginning a series of roughshod adventures that would continue for many years. In St. Louis, Missouri, Pike joined a trading expedition that took him to Santa Fe, which at that time was still part of Mexico. Legend has it that he completed most of the journey on foot after his horse escaped him. Pike continued trapping and trading, and eventually worked his way eastward through the Great Plains.

Pike settled in Arkansas in 1833 at the age of twenty-four, where he again taught school before becoming a reporter for Little Rock's *Arkansas Advocate.* He married Mary Ann Hamilton, and with the financial aid of her dowry, purchased the newspaper and became the sole owner. During this period, Pike studied the law, and became a member of the Arkansas Bar between 1835 and 1837.

The Cavalry Calls

When the Mexican-American War broke out in 1846, Pike's adventurous and patriotic side got the better of him, and he joined the cavalry. He was commissioned as a troop commander and fought successfully in the Battle of Buena Vista, the last major battle of the war.

FACT

The U.S. forces at Buena Vista were commanded by General Zachary Taylor, who would capitalize on his success in the battle to win the presidency in 1848. Colonel Jefferson Davis, who commanded the Mississippi Rifles and who would later become the president of the Confederacy during the Civil War, was also a primary participant.

Albert Pike revealed elements of his rebellious and opinionated nature with undocumented comments regarding the conduct of the Arkansas infantry during battle, which were taken as grounds for a duel by their commanding officer, Colonel John Roane. The duel proved bloodless, with both parties firing and missing. Roane would go on to become governor of Arkansas in 1848.

Legal Eagle

After the Mexican-American War, Albert Pike returned to law, practicing in New Orleans, Louisiana. In 1857, Pike returned to Arkansas, where he developed a measure of stature as an attorney and author of legal treatises. Pike's earlier trading experiences had given him a useful background in working with Indians, and during this time, he won a large monetary settlement for the Creek Indians from the federal government. During these years, Albert Pike had developed an interest in Freemasonry and became an active participant.

In 1859, Pike was elected as the Sovereign Grand Commander of the Southern Jurisdiction of the Scottish Rite, a post he would hold throughout the Civil War and continue until his death.

Battle of Pea Ridge

Although he was a staunch believer in Southern states' rights in the politically charged years leading up to the Civil War, Albert Pike argued against secession. When war finally broke out and Arkansas seceded in May of 1861, Pike trusted his Southern convictions, and joined the Confederate Army as a commissioned brigadier general. Pike was given command of the Indian territory under Confederate influence, and recruited several regiments of cavalry from among the tribes sympathetic to the South.

Pike led eight hundred Indian warriors in the Battle of Pea Ridge in Arkansas, who were later accused of mutilating and scalping Union soldiers. These accusations, along with threats of arrest for charges of mishandling funds and material led Pike to desert the army and go into hiding. Several months later, Pike was finally arrested.

The charges against Pike for the Battle of Pea Ridge were largely unsubstantiated, and his resignation from the Confederate Army was accepted in July, 1862. Pike then spent time in New York and Canada, until he received a formal pardon by President Andrew Johnson in 1865. He returned to Arkansas where he resumed his law practice and later served a one-year term as an associate justice of the Arkansas State Supreme Court.

Pike's Later Years

In 1870, Albert Pike moved to Washington, D.C., continued practicing law, and became an editor of *The Washington Patriot*. He would remain in Washington and serve as the Sovereign Grand Commander of the Scottish Rite's Southern Jurisdiction for the next twenty-one years of his life. Albert Pike passed away on April 2, 1891, and is interred at the House of the Temple, the headquarters of the Southern Jurisdiction's Scottish Rite in Washington, D.C.

While these events in Albert Pike's timeline are extraordinary by any standards, they are only the colorful highlights of a life devoted to the study of ancient religion, history, language, metaphysics, and most importantly— Masonic philosophy.

Albert Pike and Freemasonry

Much of Albert Pike's Masonic legacy derives from his intensive revision of the Scottish Rite degrees. Pike spent years adding substance and significance to the degrees, and the Southern Jurisdiction of the Scottish Rite uses the basic Albert Pike rituals to this day. Because of the relative Victorian ponderousness of Pike's writing, the modern Southern Jurisdiction of the Scottish Rite has updated much of the language of the degree rituals to make them more accessible.

Much more of Pike's legacy, and a great deal of unexpected notoriety for Freemasonry resulted from his seminal work, *Morals and Dogma*, which is considered a cornerstone of the Scottish Rite. A combination of virtually every historical Masonic document in Pike's extensive library, commingled with Pike's own interpretations and commentary, this massive 871-page tome is variously considered to be a philosophic masterpiece of unredoubtable genius, or a cumbersome conglomeration of arcane, indecipherable, and obscure mysticism.

Despite Albert Pike's rough and tumble early years, he was first and foremost a scholar and a philosopher with an enormous intellect and voracious curiosity about the meanings of life.

Pike scoured European and Eastern philosophies, teaching himself the languages of Sanskrit, Hebrew, and Greek, and painstakingly translated dozens of works, and thousands upon thousands of pages into English. Pike's perspective was geared to the pursuit of knowledge. He was a firm believer in absolute freedom of interpretation, and insisted that no single authority could bind any Freemason to any one idea. This comes as no great surprise, considering that Albert Pike quite literally taught *himself* everything he knew.

The Ghost of Lucifer

Out of *Morals and Dogma* comes a single juicy phrase that has for decades sent anti-Masons and religious literalists into cartwheels of pious accusations and righteous cries of Satanic influence on Albert Pike, and by association, all of Freemasonry. This phrase is:

"Lucifer, the Son of the Morning! Is it he who bears the Light, and with its splendors intolerable blinds feeble, sensual, or selfish Souls? Doubt it not!"

While Pike's reference is quite clear to students of Greek and Roman terminology, mythology, and philosophy, his detractors have transformed it into a veritable cottage industry of anti-Masonic rhetoric.

Lucifer and King James

Lucifer, as many Christians associate the name, has been held as the name of the angel cast down from Heaven; otherwise known as Satan. This conception is often attributed to the King James Version of the Bible, in Isaiah 14:12, which reads:

"How art thou fallen from heaven, O Lucifer, son of the morning! How art thou cut down to the ground, which didst weaken the nations!"

In this single reference to Lucifer in the King James Bible, the name Lucifer began its downward spiral into an infamous synonym for Satan. And for Pike and the Freemasons, it would prove highly controversial. In order to show just how significant the following discovery is to Freemasonry, it is necessary to show the progression of how it came to be.

Lucifer in Literature

The King James Bible was first published in 1611 in England when English poet John Milton was three years old. Milton, who would become a steadfast Puritan in his later years, grew up with the "new" Book, although its influence on him throughout his education, and in his career as a writer would be overshadowed by the influence of the Geneva Bible, the accepted bible of his generation.

In John Milton's epic 1667 poem, *Paradise Lost*, he cemented the relationship by calling the fallen angel Lucifer being cast from the heavens "Satan." Milton was unquestionably influenced by that verse in Isaiah, along with the verse from Revelation 12:9, which reads:

"And the great dragon was cast out, that old serpent, called the Devil, and Satan, which deceiveth the whole world: he was cast out into the earth, and his angels were cast out with him."

At first glance, one might easily see a questionable connection between the use of the term "Lucifer" in the Bible, Milton's version of Lucifer, and Albert Pike's reference to the same name. The explanation is a fascinating historical journey of discovery.

Several contemporary publications concerning Albert Pike, Freemasonry, and the Lucifer connection cite that the term "Lucifer" in Isaiah 14:12 came into being as a mistranslation in the Latin Vulgate of 425, and go on to cite the Latin Vulgate as the primary source for the compilation of the King James Version of the Bible. The implication here is that the use of the term "Lucifer" is a mistake of scholarship that made the leap from the Latin Vulgate directly into the King James Version nearly 1200 years later—a leap disputed by historical fact.

The Latin Vulgate of 425 A.D. was translated by St. Jerome by order of Pope Damascus I. It was the first Christian Bible that translated the Old Testament directly from Hebrew, rather than the Greek Septuagint.

The Puritan Influence

When King James I ascended to the throne in 1603, the Church of England was sharply divided between Church traditionalists and a radical movement within the Church, whose practitioners were disparagingly known as Puritans. The Puritan groups, who objected to the pompous ceremony and aristocratic nature of the Church of England, were developing strong public support for reform, and were simultaneously creating a potentially dangerous divide in the political climate of England.

A Diplomatic Opportunity

In an attempt to gain control over the threatening political disaster, James held a conference of religious leaders. While the conference would prove to be a failure, it did lead to a diplomatic opportunity for James to mollify both parties by his decision to fulfill one of the their few concordant concerns—to authorize an official English version of the Bible. This decision served two practical purposes for King James, neither of which were religiously altruistic.

The Puritans devoutly adhered to the Geneva Bible, produced in Geneva, Switzerland, by English expatriates in 1560. The Geneva Bible was barely tolerated by the Church, but was in common use among the general public.

QUESTION?

Why did the Church of England dislike the Geneva Bible?
Part of the appeal of the Geneva Bible was the proliferation of annotations and margin notes, many of which were sharply critical of the Church of England.

In 1568, the Church authorized a revision of the Great Bible, known as the Bishop's Bible. The Bishop's Bible, while directly based on the Great Bible and the Geneva Bible, was markedly less inflammatory without the anti-Church/anti-monarchy annotations and thus more palatable to Church authorities. The Bishop's Bible became the common Bible for use within the churches, but never gained the same level of popularity and trust as the Geneva Bible in home use.

By authorizing the development of the new King James Version of the Bible, James hoped to make the Geneva Bible obsolete by giving the Puritans a homegrown work of reverence. At the same time, he would produce a work with no derogatory marginal notes or annotations, which would please the Church authorities.

King James Version Directives

The opinion that the Latin Vulgate was the prime source for the King James Version is belied by historical documentation, and the political and religious influences of the time. Of the fifty-four religious scholars appointed for the task of developing the new Bible, forty-seven are known to have participated. Their instructions, some of which are listed here in their original numerical order as they would pertain to Isaiah and in their original language, are documented, and quite specific.

1. The ordinary Bible read in the Church, commonly called the Bishop's Bible, to be followed, and as little altered as the original will permit.
2. The names of the prophets and the holy writers, with the other names in the text, to be retained, as near as may be, accordingly as they are vulgarly used.
4. When any word hath divers significations, that to be kept which hath been most commonly used by the most eminent fathers, being agreeable to the propriety of the place and the analogies of faith.
6. No marginal notes at all to be affixed, but only for the explanation of the Hebrew or Greek words, which cannot, without some circumlocution, so briefly and fitly be expressed, in the text.
14. These translations to be used, when they agree better with the text than the Bishop's Bible: Tyndale's, Coverdale's, Matthew's [Rogers'], Whitchurch's [Cranmer's], Geneva.

That the forty-seven learned scholars diligently fulfilled their instructions in this enormous undertaking is unmistakable. With the availability of transcribed Greek and Hebrew texts, and the complete library of listed reference Bibles, the Latin Vulgate was ignored. The word "Lucifer" would find its way into the King James Version through a more indirect path.

A Brief Biblical History

The history of the English Bible and the relatively minor story of the impact a single word had on Freemasonry is harrowing. Over the course of a thousand years, the people who painstakingly translated and transcribed the Scriptures were not only scholars of altruistic integrity, they were quite literally risking their lives.

The Wycliffe Bible

The first complete English translation of the Bible was prompted by an Oxford Scholar named John Wycliffe during the late 1300s. With limited access to Hebrew and Greek texts, Wycliffe's Bibles were transcribed by hand and translated directly from Latin. After Wycliffe's death in 1384, King Henry IV declared English scripture to be heresy and copies of the Wycliffe Bibles were confiscated and destroyed. Pope Martin V ordered Wycliffe's bones dug up forty-two years after his death and had them burned.

The Coverdale Bible

With English scripture still forbidden in England, William Tyndale translated and published his 1534 translation of the New Testament in Belgium. His translation of the Old Testament was partially completed when he was imprisoned, strangled, and his body burned. His close associate, Miles Coverdale, published a completed translation of the Bible in 1537, using much of Tyndale's Hebrew and Greek translations.

FACT

Despite the publication of the King James Version of the Bible in 1611, the Geneva Bible remained a popular favorite in England for many years. It became known as "The Pilgrim's Bible" when the Puritans brought it to America at Plymouth in 1620.

The Geneva Bible

The Geneva Bible was produced by English expatriates in Geneva, Switzerland. The Geneva Bible of 1560 was unique in its format and text. It was the first English Bible to include the chapter and verse divisions that continue to this day. It was heavily annotated with margin and footnotes, and would serve as the first practical "study" Bible for English-speaking people.

The Bishop's Bible

The Bishop's Bible was a revision of the Great Bible of 1539, which was the first English Bible authorized for public use. Introduced as a rival to the popular Geneva Bible, it was considered ponderous and questionably accurate and failed to gather support outside of the confines of the Church.

Having even this brief history of the Bible's transition into English helps tremendously in putting the verse from Isaiah into context and providing a rational perspective on the endless accusations leveled against Albert Pike and Freemasonry. What follows are the various versions of Isaiah 14:12 beginning with the modern King James Version and descending in order to the Latin Vulgate.

King James Version (Modern)

How art thou fallen from heaven, O *Lucifer*, son of the morning! how art thou cut down to the ground, which didst weaken the nations!

King James Version (1611)

How art thou fallen from heauen, O *Lucifer*, sonne of the morning? how art thou cut downe to the ground, which didst weaken the nations?

The Bishop's Bible (1568)

Howe art thou fallen from heauen O *Lucifer*, thou faire mornyng chylde? Howe hast thou gotten a fall euen to the grounde, which didst weaken the nations?

The Geneva Bible (1560)

How art thou fallen from heauen, O *Lucifer*, sonne of the morning? and cutte downe to the grounde, which didest cast lottes vpon the nations?

The Coverdale Bible (1535)

How art thou fallen from heauen (o *Lucifer*) thou faire morninge childe? hast thou gotten a fall euen to the grounde, thou that (notwithstondinge) dyddest subdue the people?

The Wycliffe Bible (1395)

A! *Lucifer*, that risidist eerli, hou feldist thou doun fro heuene; thou that woundist folkis, feldist doun togidere in to erthe.

The Latin Vulgate (425)

Quomodo cecidisti de caelo *lucifer* qui mane oriebaris corruisti in terram qui vulnerabas gentes.

There has been some speculation that St. Jerome, when creating the Latin Vulgate, either purposely or mistakenly translated the Hebrew *helal* into the Latin *lucifer*. *Helal* means "day star" as does the Latin, lucifer. St. Jerome's translation is technically quite correct, and the evidence indicates that the word *lucifer* was not translated from Latin into English.

This evidence is demonstrated by 2 Peter 1:19 in the Latin Vulgate which also uses the Latin *lucifer*. In descending order from the King James Version to the Latin Vulgate are the various shapes 2 Peter 1:19 has taken over the years in various versions of the Bible.

King James Version (Modern)

We have also a more sure word of prophecy; whereunto ye do well that ye take heed, as unto a light that shineth in a dark place, until the day dawn, and the *day star* arise in your hearts.

King James Version (1611)

We haue also a more sure word of prophecie, whereunto yee doe well that ye take heede, as vnto a light that shineth in a darke place, vntill the day dawne, and the *day starre* arise in your hearts.

The Bishop's Bible (1568)

We haue also a ryght sure worde of prophesie, wherevnto yf ye take heede, as vnto a lyght that shyneth in a darke place, ye do well, vntyll the day dawne, and the *day starre* arise in your heartes.

The Geneva Bible (1560)

We haue also a most sure worde of the Prophets, to the which ye doe well that yee take heede, as vnto a light that shineth in a darke place, vntill the day dawne, and the *day starre* arise in your hearts.

The Coverdale Bible (1535)

We haue also a sure worde of prophecie, and ye do well that ye take hede thervnto, as vnto a lighte that shyneth in a darke place vntyll the daye dawne, and the *daye starre* aryse in youre hertes.

The Wycliffe Bible (1395)

And we han a saddere word of prophecie, to which ye yyuynge tent don wel, as to a lanterne that yyueth liyt in a derk place, til the dai bigynne to yyue liyt, and the *dai sterre* sprenge in youre hertis.

The Latin Vulgate (425)

Et habemus firmiorem propheticum sermonem cui bene facitis adtendentes quasi lucernae lucenti in caliginoso loco donec dies inlucescat et *lucifer* oriatur in cordibus vestris.

In the colloquial Latin of the Vulgate, Lucifer is the name of the morning (or day) star, Venus. Biblical scholars in a number of Bible revisions have corrected the translation, whether it be from the Latin, Greek, or Hebrew. In The New American Bible, sponsored by the American Catholic Diocese, Isaiah 14:12 reads:

"How have you fallen from the heavens, *O morning star*, son of the dawn! How are you cut down to the ground, you who mowed down the nations!"

Albert Pike's Intent

Albert Pike was a man of enormous intellect and knowledge. He was also a devout Christian who was fluent in Hebrew and Greek. He was unquestionably aware of the Christian misinterpretation and false connotations of the term "lucifer." He was also unquestionably aware of the less common associations of the word. Lucifer, Eosphorus, and Phosphorus are Latin and Greek for the same thing—the morning star.

Albert Pike was well-versed in Latin and Greek mythology and philosophy, and the ancient writings of Valerius Flaccus, Ovid, and Cicero. All of them were renowned intellectuals and scholars, and all of them referred to Lucifer, the morning star.

In London in 1827, John Walker created the first friction match using phosphorus as an ignition agent. An entrepreneur named Samuel Jones recreated these "phosphorus" matches, packaged them, and labeled them "Lucifers." He sold them for years, and the name stuck for decades.

Along with his brilliant intellect, Albert Pike had little patience for ignorance. Isaiah 14:12 is universally accepted by scholars as a taunt, ridiculing the Babylonian king (probably Nebuchadnezzar) who persecuted the Israelites. It has nothing to do with Satan, and "lucifer" is just a Latin word. All of this new documentation provides evidence that the accusations against Albert Pike and the Freemasons regarding an association with Lucifer are completely false.

The Hoax of Leo Taxil

Leo Taxil, a confessed hoaxer and accomplished liar, contributed enormously to the absurd notion that Freemasonry was a front for the practice of devil worship. Gifted with an elaborate imagination, and cursed with few scruples, Taxil made Albert Pike the target of his unbelievable stories, and the Catholic Church—including the Pope—bought the entire charade lock, stock, and barrel.

The Palladium

An accomplished con artist, Leo Taxil was born in France as Gabriel Antoine Jogand-Pages in 1854 and recreated himself in 1885 as a former Freemason and devout Catholic with a tale to tell. He began writing and publishing inventive exposés that detailed the fictitious "Palladium" of Freemasonry, a cultish group of Masonic men and women who engaged in sacrilege, sadism, Satanism, and sexual orgies.

These claims were further elaborated by claims that Albert Pike was the Supreme Pontiff of Universal Masonry and directed a number of Supreme Confederated Councils of the World. Taxil brought into the story an innocent heroine who escaped the evil Palladium and its equally depraved director, Albert Pike. The public devoured this nonsense, and Leo Taxil fed it to them for twelve years. The hierarchy of the Catholic Church was as gullible as the public, and went so far as to invite Taxil to a private audience with Pope Leo XII.

The Confession

On April 19, 1897, Taxil gleefully confessed his hoax to a crowded auditorium of reporters, Catholic clergy, and an assortment of intellectuals. His confession, his hoax, and virtually everything else about Leo Taxil were soundly denounced in the press, by the Church, and by the public. Through his publishing efforts and speaking engagements, Leo Taxil had accumulated a substantial cash reserve and slipped quietly into retirement.

chapter 17

Fact or Fiction?

Freemasons, like many other alleged secret societies, have been associated with more than a few intriguing theories brought to light by mainstream authors, anti-Masons, and conspiracy theorists. As is commonly the case with conspiracies, the actual facts of a matter take a backseat to grandiose tales of mystery, mayhem, and murder.

Masonry as a Cult

The question of whether or not Freemasonry is a "cult" can be facetiously answered with, "It depends on your definition of the word." The *American Heritage Dictionary* defines "cult" six different ways that make for an ideal analysis:

1. A religion or religious sect generally considered to be extremist or false.
2. A system or community of religious worship and ritual.
3. The formal means of expressing religious reverence; religious ceremony and ritual.
4. A usually nonscientific method or regimen claimed by its originator to have exclusive or exceptional power in curing a particular disease.
5. Obsessive, especially faddish, devotion to or veneration for a person, principle, or thing.
6. An exclusive group of persons sharing an esoteric, usually artistic or intellectual interest.

The first three definitions, all religious, are clearly off-target, being that Freemasonry has never been, and never claimed to be, a religion. Freemasons are never discouraged from pursuing their personal religious beliefs, and are free to worship the Supreme Being of their choosing.

As for the fourth definition, no medical claims or restrictions of any sort are inferred or expected in Freemasonry, and appendant bodies such as the Shriners do actively support medical facilities and medical care for children and for the needy.

Regarding "obsessive, especially faddish, devotion to or veneration for a person, principle, or thing," rational behavior and independent thinking is a highly valued element of Freemasonry. There is no single person who leads Freemasonry, and all Masons are encouraged to participate in leadership roles within the lodge, and within their communities. While Freemasons use symbolism and objects as instructional tools, members are permitted to apply their own interpretations and meanings. After several hundred years of organized existence, Freemasonry is most decidedly not a fad.

The last definition is the closest in description to the Freemasons, but even from the very beginnings of the Brotherhood, exclusivity was one of the many social and intellectual barriers that Masons most definitely did *not* subscribe to. Masonic membership is open to all men equally. Nor are there restrictions that bar a Mason from joining any other organization or group.

Also not fitting a dictionary definition of the term "cult," Freemasons are free to terminate their memberships at any time, with no repercussions. Masons are never compelled to remain affiliated with the Craft, and most significantly, no one is asked to join the organization. Becoming a Freemason is done entirely of one's own free will. The question of whether or not Freemasonry is a cult is most accurately answered with one word: "No."

Satanic Suspicions

Anti-Masons and conspiracy theorists are never at loss when it comes to linking individuals and organizations to the Dark Lord. Given that Freemasonry is sometimes perceived as being a religious cult, it's only natural they be accused of having Satanic beliefs. Part of the conflict is perhaps in the Freemasons' professed belief in a Supreme Being, which doesn't specify a particular Deity. However, Freemasons as a whole dedicate themselves to finding Divine Truth and Light and educating and elevating themselves both morally and spiritually. A devotion to brotherly love, relief, and truth would appear to be in conflict with a belief in Satan.

One of the issues that anti-Masons focus on when discussing Freemasonry is the *pentagram*, a symbol that has roots in geometry and antiquity and is often taken to be a Satanic symbol. The pentagram, a five-pointed star, has no historical link to Satanism and is not used as a ritual symbol or in any lectures or teachings within the Craft. It is, however, used as an ornament on seals and banners of Grand Lodges and by lodge Masters and Grand Masters on their collars of office.

The Pentagram

The pentagram is primarily of interest to the Craft in relation to geometry. Historically the symbol was widely used throughout Christianity, better known as the Star of Bethlehem or Star of the East. In Medieval times trade masons associated deep wisdom with the pentagram, which has been used as an architectural adornment for centuries. Another common source of confusion is the pentagram's somewhat tarnished reputation in Satanic and Wiccan rituals. In addition to being considered a sign of healing, it was also a charm that served as a powerful symbol used to repel evil in the form of witches, demons, and spirits.

FACT

The pentagram is Greek in origin. Freemasonry values the study of the Pythagoreans and to them the pentagram represented knowledge and health. In Masonic iconography it is emblematic of initiation.

The Satanic Streets of Washington, D.C.

In addition to the previously mentioned belief by some anti-Masons that the streets of Washington, D.C. are representative of the number 666, which is considered a numerical symbol of Satan, is another more amusing and persistent conspiracy. This conspiracy focuses on a map of Washington, D.C., and a pentagram that results when connecting five major sites, including the Capitol building. It is alleged that many of the individuals involved in building and designing the city and its streets were Freemasons seeking to intentionally instill Masonic symbols throughout America's capital city.

A study of Washington's Satanic streets was revealed in *The Secret Architecture of Our Nation's Capital: The Masons and the Building of Washington, D.C.* by astrology teacher David Ovason. In his book, Ovason focuses on Washington's architecture, symbols, builders, and planners, weaving a Masonic and astrological thread between them.

Albert Pike and the Ku Klux Klan

Albert Pike will always be a controversial historic figure, and he has long been a prime target for anti-Masonic critics. In addressing common allegations that Pike was involved with the first incarnation of the infamous Ku Klux Klan, it is imperative to address the facts as they are known, and let the chips and disputes fall where they may.

The allegation centers around the book *The Ku Klux Klan* written in 1905 by William Fleming, which cites Albert Pike as a leading figure of the group. Fleming's citation has alternately been criticized as factual, fabricated, or simply misinformed, and Fleming himself has been cast as either a competent scholar, a Klan apologist, or a historical revisionist.

Birth of the Klan

The original incarnation of the Ku Klux Klan began in Tennessee in 1866, about a year after the end of the Civil War. The KKK was begun by a tiny band of Southern Army officers who continued to oppose the Union victory and the ensuing dismantling of the Confederacy. The spirit of the Klan was fueled by resentment of business and political interests from the North who were cashing in on the economic opportunities of the reconstruction, and gained regional footholds and popular support that spread throughout the southern states.

ALERT!

The name Ku Klux Klan was probably derived from the Greek word *kuklos*, meaning "band," and patterned after the college fraternity Kuklos Adelphon (Band of Brothers) that was founded at the University of North Carolina in 1812 and dissolved during the Civil War.

The Klan also attracted a rougher membership that included radical insurgents, malcontents, and outright criminals. Toward the late 1860s, activities from various forms of the KKK degenerated into violent acts of domestic terrorism that triggered harsh reactions from civil and military authorities. Civil and social pressures rapidly reduced the attraction of the group, and their de facto leader, Nathan Bedford Forrest, officially disbanded the Klan in 1869. Although Forest had little actual control over any of the factionalized groups, the KKK of that era was effectively dissolved.

The Enigma of Pike

That Albert Pike was a Confederate officer, a racist, and a segregationist is undeniable. Pike was the product of a social structure in which separation of the races was completely accepted. That Pike was a freely cooperative contributor to Prince Hall Masonry, and a champion of separate African-American Masonic membership is also undeniable.

It is not inconceivable that Albert Pike could, on an intellectual level, have been sympathetic with the original ideals and attitudes of the Ku Klux Klan upon its inception. What is known is that the originators of the KKK, whoever they were, eventually disavowed the concept as they witnessed the group degenerate into uncontrollable and lawless bands of misfits.

The Ku Klux Klan of 1868 quickly became socially disagreeable and corrupt, and subsequent rebirths of the KKK proved to be even more ethically and morally loathsome. On every rational level, any attempt at linking Freemasonry with the Ku Klux Klan is ludicrous.

The All-Seeing Eye

There is a great amount of confusion associated with the all-seeing eye and the eye in the pyramid that one finds on the American one dollar bill, and that confusion has been a favorite of conspiracy theorists for decades. The all-seeing eye, often called the eye of providence, is indeed a Masonic emblem. It is a symbol with a long history, as it has often appeared in Egyptian and Hebrew cultures as a representation of Deity, observance, and universal care.

The all-seeing eye within an equilateral triangle which can either point up or down is also a historic representation of Deity. It's one that appears in Christendom as a symbol of the Holy Trinity, and is often found in Masonic art. The eye is sometimes present in Masonic rituals depending on the jurisdiction. It is meant to remind an initiate of the Supreme Being and the watchful eye that acts as judge over his words and actions. A pyramid, which to Masons is an obvious homage to builders past, is not commonly used in rituals. The all-seeing eye combined with a pyramid is rarely if ever used in the Craft. It is, however, often used within a triangle, and that is where the confusion lies.

In 1776, four men took on the job of designing an official seal for the United States. The group was comprised of Thomas Jefferson, Benjamin Franklin, John Adams, and artist Pierre Du Simitiere, who contributed most of the designs. Of the four, only Franklin was a Freemason. By 1780, still no official design had been accepted until a consultant for the second official committee, Francis Hopkinson, presented a design using an unfinished pyramid. The group of men responsible for this second design had nothing to do with the Brotherhood.

FACT

An unfinished pyramid combined with the all-seeing eye is an American symbol, one specifically related to the United States Seal. It had, in fact, been adopted by Congress for use fourteen years before the Brotherhood officially added the all-seeing eye to their symbolic repertoire.

One interpretation is that the eye on the United States seal is more emblematic of Deity intervening in the actions of mankind. The Masonic eye hearkens back to antiquity, favoring the eye as a representation of Deity observing and being quietly aware of mankind's undertakings. This would seem a reasonable symbolic interpretation.

Unfortunately, the all-seeing eye conspiracy persists, with theories linking Freemasons to the founding fathers and many claims surrounding the architecture and infrastructure of Washington, D.C. Other theories claim that the eye and pyramid are signs of Masons and the Bavarian Illuminati.

Fallen Idols

Freemasons are often the victims of all types of conspiracy theories from the subtle to the outrageous. Two such theories involve high profile individuals, a president and a pontiff, who for one reason or another found themselves linked to the Brotherhood by happenstance. There is, of course, no proof that Masons shot John F. Kennedy or that they caused the death of Pope John Paul I, but that hasn't stopped the conspiracies from taking on lives of their own.

Masons on the Grassy Knoll?

It is no surprise that when it comes to the assassination of American President John F. Kennedy there would be conspiracy theories in existence linking Freemasons to the infamous murder. If it seems a bit far-fetched, it is only because at this point there appears to have been standing room only at the grassy knoll. But still the claims persist in regard to the fallen president, and more than likely will until history itself ceases to be documented.

As with most conspiracy theories there are typically a few facts that are correct about an incident only to be tailored or twisted before mutating into a new theory. In regard to Kennedy and the Freemasons, some theories are mild accusations and others are incredibly intricate linking back to Masons everything from street names and longitude to keystones and numerology. Masonic connections have also been theorized regarding the coincidences between Kennedy's and President Abraham Lincoln's assassinations.

John F. Kennedy was not a Mason, but it is said there were a number of Masons present for various events surrounding the assassination. Vice President Lyndon Johnson, for example, was a Mason but he never progressed past Entered Apprentice.

The most common bit of confusion is part of an address that Kennedy himself gave on April 27, 1961. Spoken to a group of media publishers, the statement was misconstrued and, of course, taken up by those looking for a conspiratorial link to the Masons. Part of Kennedy's address read as follows:

The very word "secrecy" is repugnant in a free and open society; and we are as a people inherently and historically opposed to secret societies, to secret oaths and to secret proceedings. We decided long ago that the dangers of excessive and unwarranted concealment of pertinent facts far outweighed the dangers which are cited to justify it. Even today, there is little value in opposing the threat of a closed society by imitating its arbitrary restrictions.

Some individuals, anti-Masons in particular, thought Kennedy's words were meant as an attack on Freemasonry. In truth, Kennedy's references and the rest of his address were a sharp criticism of the Central Intelligence Agency and not any public "secret" organization, Masonic or otherwise.

Death of a Pontiff

It was 1978 when Albino Luciani became the new head of the Roman Catholic Church. Dubbed the "Smiling Pope," Luciani took on the name Pope John Paul I. His reign, however, was short-lived as a mere thirty-three days later the pope was found dead, the official cause cited as a heart attack. For most, the story of the pontiff ends there, but for the conspiracy theorists that is only the beginning.

Pope John Paul was immensely popular with the public as a man who would forgo many of the staunch formalities a pontiff endures. In many ways, he was a liberal and a reformer, and it was said that he was planning to revise several of the Church's banishments including their long-term stance on contraception and treatments in relation to fertility.

Where many rumors began was with the conflicting accounts of his demise in regard to where he died, the time of death, and who discovered him. The fact that no autopsy was performed added fuel to the conspiratorial embers. The pope's plans to set the Church in a new direction is something that many have focused on in regard to their theories, as it is said that over a hundred Freemasons ranging in positions from priests to cardinals stood to be ex-communicated. It has been speculated that the pope was on the verge of cleaning up perceived corruption within the Vatican.

The conspiracy linking the Masons to the death of Pope John Paul I was brought to light in a 1984 book by David Yallop entitled *In God's Name: An Investigation into the Murder of Pope John Paul I*, in which it is alleged that the pope was poisoned by digitalis and in an attempt to cover up for a group of cardinals—who were also Masons—who were intimately involved in fraudulent acts involving the Vatican Bank.

The Vatican countered by launching its own investigation into the pope's death which resulted in another book that came to the conclusion that the pope's ill health resulted in his early demise. Another report appeared to back this up, suggesting that the pope was ill earlier that evening and refused to seek medical attention. A rumor was also allegedly leaked or it was suggested by Cardinal Jean Villot that the pope had accidentally overmedicated himself.

The alleged trigger that sealed the Pope's fate was an investigation he launched in 1978, when Cardinal Villot was asked by the pope to look into operations of the Vatican Bank. As a result, the pope generated a list of names of various clergy, some supposedly Freemasons, who would be asked to resign or be transferred to lower positions. Cardinal Villot, who at the time was secretary of state for the Vatican, was alleged to be a Grand Master Mason and as such, his name was on the list.

FACT

In Francis Ford Coppola's 1990 film *The Godfather: Part III* starring Al Pacino and Andy Garcia, infamous Don Michael Corleone focuses on legitimizing his empire by associating with the Vatican Bank.

Though many suspicions arose as a result of Pope John Paul's death, and connections later were made to Italy's Masonic P2 lodge (see Chapter 12), the pope's official cause of death has never changed, and whether Freemasons were involved has never been proven.

The Conspiracy of Secrecy

Freemasons are often linked by various authors, anti-Masons, and conspiracy theorists to other secret organizations. The association in this case is perhaps three-fold, the first issue being that Freemasonry is fraternal and often termed a secret society. Secondly, Adam Weishaupt, the founder of the Bavarian Illuminati was allegedly a Mason (see Chapter 15). Third, the Priory of Sion, if it indeed existed in antiquity and modern times, is allegedly linked to Freemasonry and the Knights Templar.

Organizations deemed "secret" who are comprised of a relatively small membership of powerful individuals have been a favorite of conspiracists the world over. Toss in the terms "world domination" or "new world order," and one has a theoretical smorgasbord of never-ending speculation and suspicion. The truth of any Masonic connection to other secret and powerful groups such as the Illuminati has been the subject of controversy for decades, and includes organizations such as the Trilateral Commission, the Council of Foreign Relations, the Bilderbergers, and the Club of Rome to name a few.

Many books have been written about the link between Freemasons and Illuminati-like organizations, one of the chief subjects being the Trilateral Commission, which has long been a favorite subject of anti-Masons and conspiracy theorists who speculate that the commission either has control of the Freemasons or is controlled by them. Founded in 1973 at the behest of David Rockefeller, the Trilateral Commission is a private group of several hundred distinguished individuals from the world's three democratic industrial areas—the European Union, Japan, and North America, which includes Canada and the United States.

The Club of Rome, often accused of being a front for the Illuminati, was founded by Italian scholar and industrialist Dr. Aurello Peccei in 1968. The group consists of heads of state, scientists, economists, and businessmen from all over the world whose concerns are globally focused on the future of humanity and the systems of the world.

The commission meets annually in an effort to cooperatively work together with their fellow nations, and they also discuss topics and generate reports focusing on a variety of subjects relating to societal issues among other areas. Members of the group, which do not allow those in governmental positions, include leaders in the areas of business, media, and academia.

Freemasons have long been associated with exclusive and powerful secret societies such as the Trilateral Commission, and have through various conspiracy theories been accused of all measure of control and power over many individuals.

The Holy Grail

A common misconception of Freemasonry is that the Brotherhood is somehow connected to the Holy Grail, which is commonly said to be the sacred vessel used by Jesus during the last supper. There are many different tellings of the legend of the Holy Grail and even more theories surrounding the mystery of its purpose, location, and those protecting it. Hundreds of books have over the centuries been written about the Grail—all measure of fiction and nonfiction—by various historians, scholars, and mainstream authors.

The Holy Grail has played a role in many modern films, including *Indiana Jones and the Last Crusade, The Fisher King, Excalibur,* and even in the cult classic comedy *Monty Python and the Holy Grail.*

In regard to Freemasons and their link to the Grail there is no evidence to prove the Brotherhood had any involvement with the sacred artifact. Connections that have been made are primarily associated with the Knights Templar, and though the Knights are part of the York Rite of Freemasonry, they claim no links to the original Medieval crusaders.

Undetermined History

There are many legends surrounding the Holy Grail. One is the traditional story of Joseph of Arimathea who took the sacred vessel and later used it to collect Christ's blood as he hung from the cross. Joseph then took the Grail to Britain and the legend became a quest by King Arthur and his gallant knights. The speculation surrounding the Grail is forever evolving, with various experts surmising that the Grail is the Shroud of Turin, or that it was the lance of the Roman soldier who pierced Jesus. One of the more popular speculations is one that links Freemasonry to the legendary object, which in this case, is not an object at all, but a person.

Holy Blood, Holy Grail

One of the more recent quests undertaken by modern-day pursuers is that taken by Michael Baigent, Henry Lincoln, and Richard Leigh in their landmark international bestseller *Holy Blood, Holy Grail,* published in 1982. With a focus on the Knights Templar and the secret society known as the *Prieure de Sion,* or Priory of Sion, they present a different look at the history surrounding the Grail and an alternate explanation for what, or in this case, who, the Grail really is.

Holy Blood, Holy Grail introduces the notion that Jesus survived his crucifixion and lived his life in France with Mary Magdalene who was, in fact, the Holy Grail. Their descendants became the Merovingian dynasty which over the centuries was protected by the Priory of Sion whose undertaking it was to return the dynasty to the throne. In antiquity, the Priory created the Knights Templar as their military arm. Along with the Templars, the Freemasons were associated with the Priory.

With the romance of legends and the mystery of secrets associated with those legends, especially those born in ancient and Medieval times, it is easy to see why Freemasonry is often in the mix. When it comes to the Holy Grail, however, there is no evidence that proves the Brotherhood had or has any connection to the sacred object. Despite that fact, or perhaps because of it, the Masons will no doubt continue to be mentioned in both ancient and modern mysteries.

QUESTION?

Isn't some kind of treasure buried underneath Rosslyn Chapel?
Due to its rumored history with the Knights Templar and Freemasons, some experts have theorized that instructions on where the Grail is located or the Holy Grail itself could be hidden in vaults below the Rosslyn Chapel.

The Rosslyn Chapel

Located in Roslin, Midlothian, Scotland, is one of the most intriguingly beautiful churches in Europe, one that has been linked to amazing legends, individuals, and treasures including the Holy Grail, the Ark of the Covenant, Medieval Knights Templar, and the Freemasons. Over the centuries, Rosslyn Chapel has provided historians, scholars, writers, and all manner of individuals with a rich legacy filled with mystery and history. The Masonic architecture and wall carvings replete with Craft symbolism and legend provide many speculative connections to the Brotherhood.

Rosslyn Chapel was built and designed by Sir William St. Clair, the last St. Clair Prince of Orkney, whose noble lineage is descended from Norman knights and, it is said, the Knights Templar. Work on Rosslyn Chapel was started in 1440, it was officially founded six years later, and it took forty years to complete. The interior of the chapel is replete with symbolic carvings that represent a wide range of imagery from biblical to pagan.

The chapel is renowned for a pair of pillars, the Apprentice and the Master pillars which flank on either side a distinctly different Journeyman's pillar. The resemblance to the pillars in the Hiram Legend are obvious, as many have surmised that the Apprentice and Master pillars are symbolic of Jachin and Boaz, the two pillars at the entrance to Solomon's Temple. The Apprentice pillar, in fact, according to one legend, serves as the hiding place for the Holy Grail. Another theory suggests that the mummified head of Jesus is hidden inside.

Carved into the walls of the chapel are many other images relating to the Masonic legend of Hiram. One of the most famous carvings that is steadily debated is the "murdered apprentice," the appearance of which appears to have been altered. The original face of the carving had a beard and mustache, which at the time of Hiram, only masters were allowed to wear. The alteration of the carving would then make it the "murdered master," which is an interesting link to Freemasonry. The Hiramic legend the Craft so reveres wasn't part of the Craft until the eighteenth century, several hundred years after the Rosslyn Chapel was completed.

FACT

A musical cipher carved into the stone ceiling of the chapel eluded scholars for years. In September 2005, Scottish composer Stuart Mitchell was able to solve the cipher (which was hidden in mystical symbols) and reveal a Medieval melody.

Another famous theory focuses on stone carvings in the chapel of plants such as maize, which were native only to the Western Hemisphere. This is especially intriguing, given that the chapel was finished six years prior to Columbus having set sail. Combined with other evidence, it was surmised that the Knights Templar and Freemasons who were stationed at Rosslyn at the time had perhaps come and gone to North America before Columbus had ever reached the New World.

chapter 18

Jack the Ripper

Freemasonry and Jack the Ripper. It seems an unlikely pairing of fraternity and psychopathy and, in truth, it is a connection that never would have seen the light of day had it not been for the BBC and a writer by the name of Stephen Knight. The now infamous royal conspiracy, which implicates the Freemasons in the Jack the Ripper murders, created quite a stir when it was first revealed in the early seventies. Despite its refutations, it is arguably the most popular of all the Ripper theories.

Crime of the Century

Only a handful of high profile crimes from years past continue to incite debate in the minds of modern thinkers. Arguably at the top of that list is the case of nineteenth century serial killer Jack the Ripper. Over the centuries the question of the Ripper's identity has plagued the psyches of historians, scholars, writers, scientists, detectives, and both amateur sleuths and professional "Ripperologists."

The brutal murders which took place in the Whitechapel district of London in 1888 have served as fodder for hundreds of books, films, and ongoing criminalistic, profiling, and forensic studies, yet despite all attempts to solve the infamous crime—from logical conclusions to sensational insinuations—the Ripper's true identity and the impetus for his hideous crimes remain a mystery.

ALERT!

The 1979 movie *Murder by Decree*, starring Christopher Plummer as Sherlock Holmes and James Mason as Dr. Watson, is loosely based on Stephen Knight's book.

The royal conspiracy theory was first revealed during a BBC documentary and later detailed in Stephen Knight's 1976 book *Jack the Ripper: The Final Solution*. It must be said that this particular theory is one of many relating to the Ripper murders—it just happens that it is a highly publicized theory. It is also important to note that as much information as Knight's theory provides, there is also plenty of evidence to the contrary. However, regardless of one's opinion on the matter, it's a fascinating study, and given that the prime suspects in this theory are Freemasons, it warrants discussion.

Murder Most Horrid

From August 31, 1888, to November 9, 1888, five Whitechapel prostitutes were killed and subsequently mutilated and eviscerated. Such was the brutality of the crimes that photographs of the victims to this day are difficult to comprehend. Mary Ann "Polly" Nichols, Annie Chapman, Elizabeth Stride, Catherine Eddowes, and Mary Jane Kelly were the unfortunate victims of the notorious serial killer. While logical evaluation of the murders suggests these women were simply in the wrong place at the wrong time, there are a host of theories and published conspiracies that suggest their murders were premeditated.

Where Jack the Ripper is concerned, outrageous claims and theories constitute the majority of known information. There are very few facts that can be confirmed, with everything from the Ripper's methods to the official investigation records either disputed, missing, altered, or misinterpreted. In regard to a Masonic connection, as with myriad other theories, the "facts" are pure speculation.

A Man Called Sickert

In 1973, the BBC came up with an innovative plan to once and for all solve the Jack the Ripper case. The avenue for accomplishing this task was the acquisition of new information coupled with a dramatic presentation that was part theater and part documentary. With a lead they eventually received from a detective at Scotland Yard, the television researchers set about interviewing a man called Joseph Sickert, the son of renowned English artist Walter Sickert. The elder Sickert imparted to his son a story that was unbelievable in its sheer audacity, and the time had come for his son to bring the details to light. According to the younger Sickert, Walter Sickert apparently harbored some measure of guilt over the information and, as such, finally let loose of the details of this sordid tale prior to his death in 1942.

FACT

Walter Sickert was a German-born English impressionist painter who was influential during the Victorian era. As a young man, his mentor was celebrated artist James McNeill Whistler, and he later studied in France with Edgar Degas.

Through interviewing Joseph Sickert, police discovered a bizarre chain of events, which involved a secret marriage between an heir to the British throne and a commoner, their illegitimate child, and a hired nanny. It further involved the queen, the prime minister, the queen's physician, a quartet of prostitutes, and ultimately, the Freemasons, whose alleged involvement was further detailed by Stephen Knight in his book.

A Royal Blunder

What Sickert told the BBC began with Prince Albert Victor Edward ("Eddy" as he was known), the duke of Clarence and Avondale, who was grandson of Queen Victoria and second in line to the British throne after his father, who eventually became Edward VII. Walter Sickert was a friend of Prince Eddy's. According to Sickert, the twenty-four-year-old prince became enthralled with a "commoner" and Catholic woman named Annie Elizabeth Crook, who worked at a tobacconist's shop. It was alleged that they had married. Adding to the unthinkable was the fact that Annie bore the prince an illegitimate royal child named Alice Margaret.

Prince Eddy is a controversial figure in his own right. Many conspiracies surrounded his sexual orientation, his intellect, and his death. It is said he died of pneumonia in 1892, but some speculate he died from syphilis or was murdered by a morphine overdose. Another theory claims he was in an asylum on the Isle of Wight until the 1920s.

When this information made its way to Queen Victoria, she called upon Prime Minister and alleged Freemason Lord Salisbury to handle the details. The political climate of the day was tumultuous at best. If a scandalous affair or marriage between an heir to the British throne and an illiterate Catholic and their illegitimate heir were to become public, a revolution could start and the monarchy could fall.

In an effort to make the sordid affair disappear, authorities raided an apartment on Cleveland Street at which time the prince and Annie were separated and taken away. It was said that Alice Margaret escaped the chaos. At that point, the Queen's personal physician, Freemason William Gull, entered the picture. Gull's intervention required performing "experiments" on the hospitalized Annie Crook that would cause memory loss, epilepsy, and eventual insanity.

Nanny and a Confessor

Joseph Sickert's story continued, to tell of a woman called Mary Kelly, whom his father had found in a poorhouse. Kelly was brought to Annie Crook at the tobacconist's shop and she eventually became nanny to Annie and Prince Eddy's daughter Alice Margaret. As Sickert tells it, the general assumption was that the little girl was with Kelly when the Cleveland Street apartment was raided. Not knowing what to do with the girl, Kelly left her in the care of nuns and soon became a prostitute in the East End of London.

The danger of Mary Kelly's precarious situation was her knowledge of the prince's incriminating dalliance. Unable to keep such damaging information to herself, the former nanny allegedly revealed her secrets to three other prostitutes—Mary Ann "Polly" Nichols, Annie Chapman, and Elizabeth Stride. Together they threatened to blow the whistle on Prince Eddy by means of blackmail.

Again, William Gull was called into action by Lord Salisbury when the blackmail plot became known, and it was at this point that Gull solicited help from Prince Eddy's coachman, John Netley, and Sir Robert Anderson, who was to keep watch during the crimes. Gull's sinister plan was, of course, to eliminate the quartet of potential blackmailers. Not being of sound mind and body, he gave birth to the name Jack the Ripper.

ALERT!

As Sickert tells it, the fourth Ripper victim, Catherine Eddowes, was a case of mistaken identity. Apparently Eddowes, by coincidence, sometimes called herself Mary Kelly, as she lived with a man whose last name was Kelly. This misinformation resulted in Gull and his cohorts allegedly killing her by accident.

Jack Be Nimble

With the horrid crimes now committed, things didn't go smoothly for those involved. Walter Sickert told his son that barrister Montague Druitt was the alleged scapegoat of the Ripper murders, and suggested that he was even killed because of it. It was rumored that physician Sir William Gull ended up in an insane asylum, and he apparently passed away not long after the incidents at Whitechapel. Annie Crook, now insane, was said to have died in 1920, and John Netley, who eventually drowned, was allegedly mobbed during an attempt at running down Crook's daughter Alice Margaret with his cab.

Perhaps the strangest part of Joseph Sickert's retelling of his father's story is the fate of Alice Margaret. According to Sickert, she was indeed raised by nuns, but upon adulthood actually married Walter Sickert and had a child. That child was Joseph Sickert.

When the BBC researched Joseph Sickert's story, they discovered that there was indeed a woman who lived on Cleveland Street called Annie Crook. They also confirmed Sickert's allegation that she gave birth out of wedlock to a daughter.

Walter Sickert painted many unusual works during his adult life including the cryptic *Camden Town Murder* and *Jack the Ripper's Bedroom*. Joseph Sickert's understanding of his father's festering guilt was that his father felt responsible for having introduced Prince Eddy to Annie Crook. Guilt, and the constant pressure of maintaining silence, gave Sickert no alternative but to leave clues in his work.

A Knight in Whitechapel

The royal conspiracy, based on the story told to Joseph Sickert by his father, Walter, is arguably the most sensational of the Ripper conspiracy theories. This royal and Masonic conspiracy, however, didn't reach its apex of notoriety until 1976, with the publication of Stephen Knight's book, which brought Freemasonry and its alleged secret plot under close public scrutiny.

Stephen Knight was intrigued by Joseph Sickert's story and eventually convinced Sickert to grant him an interview for a local newspaper. It was during meetings with Sickert, whom Knight felt was telling the truth, that Knight decided to investigate the story and, much to Sickert's chagrin, compile a book. The upshot of Knight's book was that the third conspirator of the Ripper murders was not Sir Robert Anderson—it was Walter Sickert.

In his book, Knight basically follows the same story line as it was first introduced in the BBC's documentary. However, he goes on a number of tangents in an effort to weave the web surrounding Prince Eddy, Alice Crook, and a wide range of individuals—all of whose participation are based on assumption and conjecture. As it stands, there is no evidence linking any of the main players to one another in this horrific production.

FACT

In the 2001 film *From Hell,* the title of which was taken from one of the Ripper's letters, Johnny Depp as Detective Abberline fights a formidable foe in murderous Freemason William Gull and his conspiratorial brethren.

In order for Sickert's story to be true, a conspiracy most certainly must have occurred, and that is indeed Knight's claim, the grand schemers of his theory naturally being the Freemasons. This is an instance in history where the term "secret society" worked against the Brotherhood.

A Masonic Plot

Knight's focus on the Freemasons as the perpetrators of the killings relies heavily on the supposition of Masonic symbolism and ritual practices. Using this as his basis he makes many assumptions. Catherine Eddowes's body, for example, was found on September 30, 1888, in Mitre Square. Both the mitre and the square are tools used by trade masons. It was also known at the time that Masons met at the Mitre Tavern.

Knight also alleges that coachman John Netley was, in reality, killed as a result of being run over by his own cab at Clarence Gate. The connection there is that the Masons did this intentionally because Prince Eddy was the duke of Clarence.

It is also asserted that the murders were essentially covered up by Lord Salisbury and his Masonic brethren who served in the government or police departments. Because of their bonds as brothers, they may not have approved of Gull's decision to kill the women in such a manner, but they had an obligation to protect a fellow brother and Freemasonry in general.

Fourth victim Catherine Eddowes had a triangular flap of skin removed from either cheek, which Knight equates to the "two triangles which represent the altar top of the Holy Royal Arch."

In this royal conspiracy, it is alleged that Gull was able to lure the women (with the exception of third victim Elizabeth Stride) into a carriage, murder and mutilate them, and then dispose of their bodies in very specific and Masonically relevant places. It's not impossible for a madman, but logic dictates that it would seem improbable for a man of Gull's age and health to physically murder and reposition the bodies of his victims. At the time of the murders Gull was 72 and had recently suffered a heart attack and, it is said, a stroke. Killing someone in the manner in which these women were slain would take considerable strength. The bottom line is that there is no solid evidence that links William Gull to the crimes.

Hiramic Murder?

Another of Knight's claims involves the Legend of Hiram Abiff, in which he equates the way the three conspirators who committed Hiram's murder were executed to the way each of the five women were slain. While it is true that Masons do study this legend, it is strictly symbolic and not literal in the slightest measure. But it does serve to further Knight's theory. The three murderers, Jubela, Jubelo, and Jubelum, when lamenting over their heinous act, screamed out various deaths they wished exacted upon them.

One conspirator wanted his throat cut and his tongue ripped from him. Another wanted his breast torn open and his heart and vitals removed and tossed over his left shoulder. The third, and most gruesome, wished his body severed and taken as such to the north and the south, and his bowels burnt to ashes.

The Ripper victims had their throats cut, were mutilated, and eviscerated in various grotesque abominations. In the case of second victim Annie Chapman, who was killed on the eighth of September, her tongue was protruded between her teeth, and like the fourth victim Catherine Eddowes, her intestines were placed over her right shoulder. On November ninth, authorities found unimaginable horror when they discovered Mary Kelly, who was barely recognizable and, it's alleged, the fireplace had been used.

FACT

In addition to linking the mutilation of Mary Kelly with the Hiramic legend, Knight further connects it to an engraving by renowned artist and Freemason William Hogarth. He claims that "The Reward of Cruelty," the last in the series *Four Stages of Cruelty* bears an "uncanny resemblance" to Kelly's mutilation.

It stands to reason, that without solid evidence, anyone can make alleged evidence fit a theory. Whether the method of killing in these cases reflects Masonic ritual is anyone's guess, but lacking proof, it again can only be described as pure conjecture.

The Smoking Gun

At the time of the murders, Sir Charles Warren was head of the London Metropolitan Police. He also served as Worshipful Master of the premier research lodge, the Quatuor Coronati Lodge 2076, which was holding a meeting the night of Catherine Eddowes's murder. At the scene of the crime, a section of bloodstained apron belonging to Eddowes was recovered along with a curious alliteration. On the wall above where the bloody cloth was found a now infamous message was scrawled in chalk: "The Juwes are The men that Will not be Blamed for nothing."

When Sir Warren arrived at the scene he made the unpopular decision to have the message erased, fearing that the words would incite anti-Jewish riots in the area. Had Warren not been a Freemason, his action would perhaps have been overlooked, but according to various theories the spelling of "Juwes" is nothing short of conspiratorial.

Knight suggested that the misspelling of the word *Jews* refers to the Hiramic legend and the trio of conspirators—Jubela, Jubelo, and Jubelum—responsible for the slaying of Master Mason Hiram Abiff.

Knight asserts that each of the murders were carried out by Gull according to Masonic ritual. However, as any Mason will attest, the blood oaths in Masonic rituals are allegorical and purely symbolic. They also refute the word "Juwes" as it has never been mentioned in any ceremony or ritual of the Craft. As one expert points out as well, the story involving the three conspirators was no longer part of English Masonic rituals, having been stricken seventy years prior to the Ripper murders.

Murder as Art

Walter Sickert's alleged involvement in the Ripper murders remains a source of great intrigue, depending on the theory to which you subscribe. Stephen Knight brings Sickert into his book right from the start and while it's unknown if he actually committed the murders, he does play a significant role in the book. He introduces Prince Eddy to Annie Crook, he brings Mary Kelly to them, he bears witness to their alleged wedding, he aids Gull in identifying the women, and he left clues to the murders in his paintings.

Wasn't Walter Sickert accused of actually being Jack the Ripper?

Yes. In Patricia Cornwell's 2002 novel *Portrait of a Killer: Jack the Ripper—Case Closed*, she makes a compelling argument for Sickert being the Ripper. Her DNA testing has proven inconclusive, but she does meticulously detail her findings and speculation.

Knight essentially wove Sickert into his theory based on the fact that Sickert appeared to know so much about the case, but those skeptical of Knight's contentions have pointed out more than a few specific contradictions. It is said that Alice Margaret was born April 18, 1885, which, if true, makes someone other than Prince Eddy the father because he was in Germany at the time of conception. Knight also claims that the prince met Annie Crook at Walter Sickert's studio the same year as the Ripper murders—1888. Experts point out that in 1886, the building was demolished and a hospital erected the following year.

To Hell and Back

Two years after Knight's book was published, Joseph Sickert, in an article in the *Sunday Times of London*, recanted his story, claiming that it was a hoax and he'd made up the entire tale. In his defense, Knight of course responded by saying the younger Sickert was simply incensed by Knight's naming Walter Sickert as one of the killers.

Renowned Ripperologist Donald Rumbelow in 1975 wrote what many consider to be the Jack the Ripper bible. Originally printed as *The Complete Jack the Ripper*, it was later revised under the title *Jack the Ripper: The Complete Casebook*. In the latter, Rumbelow did some digging into the background of Annie Crook, discovering that she made the rounds at various workhouses later in life. Accompanying her was her daughter Alice Margaret and her grandmother and mother, who allegedly suffered from epilepsy. This added a new spin to the royal conspiracy which alleges that Annie became an epileptic as a result of William Gull's medical experimentation.

Another potential discrepancy is evident in Knight's royal conspiracy. Knight claims that a pair of brass rings were placed at the feet of second victim Annie Chapman, along with her jewelry and coins. This, perhaps, relates to the Rite of Destitution an initiate takes part in during the initiation rites of Entered Apprentice. However, official reports show that no such trinkets were found at the crime scene.

From One Theory to the Next

Donald Rumbelow also refuted other inconsistencies in Knight's Masonic conspiracy. The location of the Cleveland Street building where the prince and Annie Crook were taken from didn't exist at the time of the murders, as it was being torn down for renovation.

Rumbelow also sheds another perspective on the incident Knight tells of in which Lord Salisbury purchases one of Sickert's paintings for a large sum of "hush money." Sickert didn't use his own name when relaying this purchase to his son Joseph, telling him instead that it happened to an artist called Vallon. Rumbelow discovered that the painting, which still belongs to the Salisbury family, was indeed painted by Vallon and not Sickert.

Other experts on the subject have brought up additional pertinent facts. In regard to the alleged marriage between Prince Eddy and Annie Crook, the laws of Britain state that the reigning monarch can set aside any marriage, and that any member of the royal family who weds a Catholic cannot inherit the crown. Given that bit of insight, there really was no reason for any of the murders to have taken place even if the prince and the pauper had wed. Beyond that, it's doubtful that another royal scandal could have actually sunk the British crown.

Catch Me If You Can

Over the years, the royal conspiracy has been portrayed in a number of films and documentaries and it will, no doubt, continue to be a part of the Jack the Ripper legacy until the next sensational theory comes to the forefront. Was a Freemason really Jack the Ripper? If one subscribes to the royal conspiracy, then yes, the Ripper was a Freemason. It's also possible that Walter Sickert was the Ripper or any one of a dozen or more suspects who have been implicated in the murders.

FACT

Records show that Walter Sickert was married three times and that none of his wives were named Alice Margaret. It is said he had a number of lovers, and if indeed Alice Margaret was one of them it's conceivable their tryst resulted in a son, Joseph Sickert.

Victorian London in the late 1800s was a dire place if you were an individual of unfortunate means, especially living in the East End in Whitechapel. The sheer crush of humanity, filth, and starvation permeated by thick polluted air must have made it a frightening place, most certainly at night when all that was seen through the mist were glimpses of faces by the light of oil lamps.

Five women succumbed to the ultimate darkness at the hands of a madman. If that man was a Freemason and there was a cover-up by the Masons it has yet to be proven. As it stands, there is absolutely nothing that implicates the Brotherhood in the Whitechapel murders.

chapter 19

The Fraternal Family Tree

Freemasonry is not just a fraternity, it's an entity that encompasses a wide variety of concordant and appendant bodies such as the Scottish and York Rites, the Shriners, Daughters of the Eastern Star, Prince Hall Masonry, and several youth groups to name a few. All of these organizations are primarily charity based with many of them specific to various causes or endeavors. It's a huge and impressive family tree with generations of offspring that remain active the world over.

19

Appendant and Concordant Bodies

It's a common misconception that Freemasonry, as a fraternal organization, is highly exclusive. There are, in fact, a number of appendant and concordant bodies associated with the fraternity, many of them focused on charitable causes, and many whose members are men, women, and children of all ages.

Craft Masonry, its concordant bodies, and all of the appendant groups can be confusing, so what follows is a breakdown of the entire fraternal family tree and an overview of each division or organization. The two main concordant bodies of Freemasonry are the Scottish and York Rites, and more in-depth descriptions of those degrees are discussed in Chapter 7.

Craft Masonry

Craft Masonry, or blue lodge Masonry as it is commonly referred to in North America, is the starting point for all individuals joining the Brotherhood (see Chapter 6). This includes the three basic degrees of Freemasonry, Entered Apprentice, Fellowcraft, and Master Mason, which are granted by Grand Lodges and the lodges under their jurisdiction. Once an individual has completed these three degrees, he can opt to move on to one of the concordant bodies such as the York or Scottish Rite, in order to earn additional degrees. Chapter 7 discusses these degrees in detail, but in a nutshell, and for reference, they are as follows.

The first degree, Entered Apprentice, marks an initiate's birth into the Brotherhood. It is a preliminary degree that serves to introduce a brother to the teachings he will undertake in the higher degrees. The focus of this degree isn't so much the history of the Craft, instead it makes clear the internal structure of the fraternity.

ALERT!

All lodges or blue lodges are warranted and governed by Grand Lodges. Only these lodges have the jurisdiction to confer the main three degrees upon Masonic initiates.

Fellowcraft, the second degree of Masonry, represents an initiate's adulthood and imparts upon him further knowledge and history of the Craft, again in preparation for the higher degrees. In this degree an initiate learns more about the symbols and allegorical legends of Freemasonry from the legend of Hiram Abiff to the operative masons of the Medieval age. Fellowcraftsmen are to use these lessons to improve their reasoning and intellect and continue their spiritual and educational journey.

The third degree of Craft Masonry is Master Mason which is required if an individual seeks to move to other bodies of Freemasonry or serve as an officer in a Grand Lodge. This degree is the culmination of his teachings in the lesser degrees, and marks his journey through manhood, symbolizing his achieving physical and spiritual growth. Becoming a Master Mason is taken very seriously among the brethren, and the rituals undergone are heavily laden with allegory and symbolism that marks the crowning achievement in Craft Masonry.

Ancient and Accepted Scottish Rite

Many Masons wishing to earn additional degrees enter the Ancient and Accepted Scottish Rite, or Scottish Rite as it is commonly known, which is evolved from the French Rite of Perfection. This Masonic body confers up to thirty-two symbolic degrees and has an honorary thirty-third degree. Individuals who attain these degrees are known simply as Scottish Rite Masons. The degrees vary from one jurisdiction to another, but basically they are divided into four sections. The rites below are according to the American Southern Jurisdiction.

Lodge of Perfection

The Lodge of Perfection offers the fourth through fourteenth degrees, known as ineffable, or those degrees incapable of being expressed. The rituals focus on Solomon's Temple and Master Mason Hiram Abiff. The degrees are Secret Master, Perfect Master, Intimate Secretary, Provost and Judge, Intendant of the Building, Master Elect of the Nine, Master Elect of the Fifteen, Master Elect of the Twelve, Grand Master Architect, Royal Arch of Solomon (Master of the Ninth Arch), and Grand Elect and Sublime Mason.

FACT In America, the first Lodge of Perfection was created in Albany, New York, around 1767. The first Princes of Jerusalem came about in 1788 in Charleston, South Carolina. Also established in that city was the initial Sublime Council of Princes of the Royal Secret, in 1797.

Chapter of the Rose Croix

The second level of the Scottish Rite is the Chapter of the Rose Croix. Here an individual progresses through the fifteenth through eighteenth degrees. The degrees here focus on conviction and dedication, truth and fidelity, allegiance to God, and faith and tolerance. The available degrees are Knight of the East or Sword, Prince of Jerusalem, Knight of the East and West, and Knight of the Rose Croix.

Council of Kadosh

After completing the first two levels, a Mason can move on to the third level, the Council of Kadosh, which features the nineteenth through thirtieth degrees. These lessons are highly symbolic and allegorical and further a man's virtue and belief system. The degrees are Grand Pontiff, Master of the Symbolic Lodge (Master ad Vitam), Patriarch Noachite (Prussian Knight), Knight of the Royal Axe (Prince of Libanus), Chief of the Tabernacle, Prince of the Tabernacle, Knight of the Brazen Serpent, Prince of Mercy, Commander of the Temple, Knight of the Sun, Knight of St. Andrew, and Knight Kadosh.

Consistory

The final level of the Scottish Rite is the Consistory, which includes the thirty-first and thirty-second degrees. The Inspector Inquisitor Commander, the thirty-first degree, focuses on impartial justice and purity of intent, while the thirty-second degree, Sublime Prince of the Royal Secret, teaches elevation of morality and reason. The thirty-third degree, Inspector General, is honorary and it is a Consistory group of elected officers who bestows this honor on a worthy Mason at an annual Supreme Council gathering. The

Scottish Rite system is governed by a Supreme Council that is established in each jurisdiction or country.

Scottish Rite Headwear

Scottish Rite Masons of the higher degrees can be identified by the color of the caps they wear. In fact, the Supreme Council has specific rules about how and where a cap must be worn. For a Mason, it is not to be removed, as it is considered part of his apparel. Caps must be worn during flag presentations, for example. The cap is also in place during times of prayer, where the Mason's arms are crossed at an eighteen degree angle. Caps are usually worn at meetings, but not in other public places.

The variety of colored caps worn include:

- **A black cap,** which is worn by thirty-second degree Masons.
- **A red cap,** which is worn by a thirty-second degree Knight Commander of the Court of Honour.
- **A white cap,** which signifies a thirty-third degree Inspector General Honorary.
- **A purple cap,** which is worn by a thirty-third degree Sovereign Grand Inspector General and active member of the Supreme Council.
- **A light blue cap,** which signifies that the man wearing it has, for fifty years or more, been a Scottish Rite Mason.

Appendant of the Scottish Rite

The *Knights of St. Andrew*, an elite Masonic unit, are an appendant body of the Scottish Rite. The Knights are a service organization that aids the Consistory in providing various services including acting as greeters, helping lodge Tylers, escorting dignitaries or women for special events, and providing assistance to Scottish Rite degree work.

Founded by Pierre De Mets in 1966, the Knights also call committees together and are often participants in parades. Only thirty-second degree Scottish Rite Masons may apply to be a Knight of St. Andrew. They are often easily identifiable in their Scottish attire, and typically are accompanied at events by a bagpiper.

The York Rite

Steeped in European history, the York Rite literally gets its name from the city of York in England, and the legend of King Athelstan dating back to 926 A.D. (see Chapter 7). Replete with highly symbolic teachings, many of which relate to the Knights Templar and the Crusades, the York Rite contains three main branches. Each of these three bodies, the Royal Arch Chapter, the Council of Cryptic Masonry, and the Commanderies of the Knights Templar, offer additional degrees, and two of them—the Royal Arch and Templars—have appendant bodies.

The Royal Arch Chapter

Commonly called Royal Arch Masonry, this chapter offers Masons four additional degrees, including Mark Master, Past Master, Most Excellent Master, and Royal Arch. These degrees and some of their titles vary according to country, but in general, the degree of Holy Royal Arch is highly revered. The first three degrees focus on specific teachings in preparation for the Royal Arch degree. The Royal Arch Chapter is governed by Grand Chapters, the Cryptic Council by what are called Grand Councils, and the Knights Templar are overseen by Grand Commanderies.

The first three initiation rituals of the Royal Arch degrees continue a Mason's spiritual education through the allegorical Legend of Hiram Abiff, and the highly symbolic building of Solomon's Temple. The fourth degree focuses on a later history of the Jews.

The first degree of Mark Master is considered the oldest and arguably the most respected degree, as it teaches order, discipline, regularity, and the precision and punctuality required for successful labor. From there an individual moves on to Past Master (often called Virtual Past Master), and learns the value of obedience and principles of governing oneself. The Royal Arch degree is the pinnacle of Masonic symbolism and a culmination of the knowledge gained from the preceding degrees.

The Council of Cryptic Masonry

Cryptic Masonry, as it is presently known, was formerly called the Council of Royal and Select Master. As the second body of the York Rite, it offers the three degrees of Royal Master, Select Master, and Super Excellent Master. Individuals electing to engage in these degrees must have earned the three degrees of Craft Masonry and the Royal Arch degrees.

The ritual of these three degrees focuses on the legends surrounding a hidden vault or crypt beneath the Temple of Solomon. The Royal Master and Select Master degrees extend the lessons an initiate was introduced to during his Fellowcraft rituals. Super Excellent Master is actually an honorary rather than a Cryptic degree and it is explored as preparation for the Knights Templar first degree, Order of the Red Cross.

Commanderies of Knights Templar

The third body of the York Rite, Commanderies of Knights Templar, is unique to Freemasonry in that it is strictly a Christian order. Called Chivalric Masonry, this body encompasses a trio of orders including the Illustrious Order of the Red Cross, the Order of Malta, and the Order of the Temple.

The lessons taught to an initiate to the Illustrious Order of the Red Cross focus on the virtue of truth and how its use will set one free. The Order of Malta, also called the Knights of Malta, has a Catholic membership and is the oldest charitable organization. Their ritual focus parallels the story of Jesus Christ. The pinnacle of York Rite Masonry is the Order of the Temple, whose rituals and lessons surround Christ's death and ascension into heaven.

Appendants of the Royal Arch

There are several appendant bodies associated with the York Rite and specifically the Royal Arch Chapter. The Allied Masonic Degrees, Knight Masons, and Masonic Rosicrucians are invitational organizations, that is to say individuals must be recommended by a current member.

The Allied Masonic Degrees

In 1880 in England, an organization was formed to oversee a variety of degrees and orders that were without central authority. As a result, the Grand Council of the Allied Masonic Degrees was created to govern the *Allied Masonic Degrees* (AMD), invitational groups, or councils, comprised of twenty-seven members who are interested in Masonic research and scholarship. Each member must have completed the three degrees of Craft Masonry and the Royal Arch degrees.

FACT

In the United States, a group similar to the Grand Council of the Allied Masonic Degrees was formed in 1892, calling itself the Sovereign College of the Allied Masonic Degrees.

Allied Masons strive to enhance the Brotherhood by focusing on study and research. Each council is led by a Sovereign Master and his officers, in a structure similar to that of blue lodge Masonry. There are typically ten degrees controlled by the AMD, including St. Lawrence the Martyr, Secret Monitor, Royal Ark Mariner, Knight of Constantinople, Grand Tylers of Solomon, Excellent Master, Masters of Tyre, Architect, Grand Architect, and Superintendent.

Masonic Rosicrucianism

The Rosicrucian Society of the United States, or *Societas Rosicruciana in Civitatibus Foederatis,* was established in 1880 by three colleges chartered by the Society in Scotland. As an autonomous institution, it is in amity with other similar societies around the world including the English *Societas Rosicruciana in Anglia* and the *Scottish Rosicruciana in Scotia.*

Individuals invited into the Society are Master Masons and Christians, and the degrees, or grades, members progress through are Christian based. The Society is different in that these grades are not an extension of the normal degrees of Freemasonry. The governing body of the Rosicrucian Society is called the High Council, which is overseen by a Supreme Magus.

What is Rosicrucianism?
Rosicrucians are a seventeenth century secret society whose members were philosophers, scholars, and other freethinkers. Many of these individuals were students of alchemy and metaphysics. They are usually symbolically associated with the Rose Cross.

Members who are invited to join the Rosicrucian Society are highly regarded for their scholastic, research, or educational abilities. In some cases, those who perform an unusual type of service for the Brotherhood are also invited.

Knight Masons

The Grand Council of Knight Masons was formed in Ireland in 1923, and traces its origins into the antiquity of Masonry. Knight Masons is an honorary body of Royal Arch Masons, in which membership is offered by invitation only. Knight Masonry was introduced into the United States in 1936, and has expanded to over seventy Councils with about seven thousand members.

Appendants of the Knights Templar

There are several honorary and unique appendant bodies associated with the Knights Templar. As with the Royal Arch appendants, these orders, the Red Cross of Constantine, Knights of the York Cross of Honour, Holy Royal Arch Knights Templar Priests, and the York Rite College, are primarily invitation only and consist of varying degrees.

The Red Cross of Constantine

It is said that the highest honor a York Rite Mason can receive is the *Red Cross of Constantine,* which was established in England in 1865. Each body of the Red Cross is called a Conclave, the numbers of which are strictly monitored by their governing body, the United Sovereign Grand Imperial Council. Individuals wishing to join the Order must have two basic qualifications, the first being that he is a Christian and the second that he is a Mason who is currently in good standing. Masons who are invited to join have typically been dedicated high level performers in Masonic activities. They must be invited by a current knight of the Order and be voted in unanimously.

The degrees of the Red Cross traditionally follow Constantine the Great's conversion to Christianity and an alleged vision he saw of a heavenly cross. Knight, Priest, and Sovereign Prince are the three primary degrees of the Order. The Knight degrees offer three additional orders: Knight-Companion of the Red Cross of Constantine, Knight of the Holy Sepulchre, and Knight of St. John the Evangelist.

Knights of the York Cross of Honour

Individuals belonging to the *Knights of the York Cross Honour* are York Rite Masons who have overseen Blue Lodges, Chapters, Councils, and Commanderies. Like many of the other appendant bodies, initiates must be nominated by a current member and then voted on by the organization's governing body called a Priory.

Holy Royal Arch Knights Templar Priests

The order of the *Holy Royal Arch Knights Templar Priests* dates back to 1786 England, and possibly to the late 1600s. Membership into the honorary organization is by invitation, with admission based on an individual's performance as a Commander of a Commandery of Knights Templar, Past Master, or Royal Arch member. In the United States, the Grand College of America, Holy Royal Arch Knight Templar Priests was begun in 1931.

FACT

Only thirty-three active Knight Priests are allowed within each group, which is called a Tabernacle, and is presided over by a Very Eminent Preceptor. The organization consists of thirty-three degrees.

The York Rite College

The York Rite Sovereign College of North America was founded in 1957 in Detroit, Michigan, in an effort to create a new organization. Five months later, the first *York Rite College* was formed, and by 1970, Colleges had been established in fourteen states and one Canadian province. By 2002, 177 Colleges were in full swing in the United States, Canada, and the Philippines.

Individuals invited to join a York Rite College are those who are members in all of the York Rite bodies—Lodge, Chapter, Council, and Commandery. The goal of each College and its membership is to offer promotion and support of the York Rite. Collegians are often active in festivals, drill corps, reward ceremonies, Masonic charity functions, and many other events that promote unification and education of the York Rite.

Social Groups

The Masonic family includes a wide range of social groups whose focus runs the gamut from charitable work to the research and promotion of Masonic fellowship. Arguably the most recognized of these groups are the Shriners, who are well known for their philanthropy and their children's hospitals.

Ancient Arabic Nobles of the Mystic Shrine

Shriners are probably the most visible and best known body of Freemasonry. Begun as a New York social group in 1872, by Walter Fleming and William Florence, the Shriners were initially formed as a boisterous counterpart to the Masonic Lodges of the day. Despite their reputation for partying and their trademark red fezzes, the Shriners are highly revered for their remarkable philanthropy. Today there are twenty-two Shriners Hospitals devoted entirely to children's care.

The acronym for the Ancient Arabic Order of Nobles of the Mystic Shrine, A.A.O.N.M.S., is an anagram for "a Mason."

Shriners are easy to spot in the United States, their members often seen in parades, parties, sporting events, and all types of social activities and extravaganzas. The organization has almost two hundred chapters or Temples throughout the United States, Canada, Mexico, and the Republic of Panama, and a membership of over a half million. In the past, membership was limited to thirty-second degree Scottish Rite Masons or Knights Templar, but that has recently been changed so that any Master Mason can join.

Mystic Order of Veiled Prophets of the Enchanted Realm

Established in 1889 as a social club in New York, the group's first title was the "Fairchild Deviltry Committee," which would a year later become the Mystic Order of Veiled Prophets of the Enchanted Realm. Nicknamed the "Grotto," the club is open to Master Masons in order to provide a fraternal playground apart from the solemnity of the Masonic lodge. The Order claims four United States presidents as former members. Along with its cheerful approach, the attendant mission of the group focuses on charity.

Tall Cedars of Lebanon

The Tall Cedars of Lebanon was founded in 1902 as a Masonic-related order in Trenton, New Jersey. With the creed, "fun, frolic, and fellowship," the order actively participates in civic projects and charitable events. The Tall Cedar Foundation was established in 1951, and was instrumental in providing assistance to the Muscular Dystrophy Association. They continue to support the Jerry Lewis Labor Day Telethon with funds and volunteers, and sponsor grants to further the diagnosis and treatment of neuromuscular disorders.

Ancient Egyptian Order of Sciots

The Ancient Egyptian Order of Sciots was formed in 1905 in San Francisco as a West Coast alternative to the eastern United States Masonic social clubs. The order's slogan is, "Boost one another." In accord with the spirit of Freemasonry and the variety of Masonic social groups, Sciots strongly support charitable organizations.

High Twelve

Founded in Sioux City, Iowa, in 1921, High Twelve is comprised of groups of dedicated Masons who meet informally outside of the lodge at the lunch hour—thus the moniker "high twelve." All Master Masons are eligible for membership in over three hundred clubs worldwide. While the High Twelve is regarded as a social club with a "call off from labor to refreshment" theme, it also supports the activities of the Freemason lodge to which they are affiliated, and actively participates in charitable pursuits.

National Sojourners

National Sojourners is a national fraternal organization of Freemasons dedicated to the needs of military Masons, and the advocation of patriotic programs. Membership is open to Master Masons who have served, or are currently serving in the United States military as commissioned officers, senior noncommissioned officers, or warrant officers. Membership is also open to officers of equivalent rank who have served with foreign allies of the United States during times of war.

The National Sojourners was conceived as a response to the needs of Freemasons who, as a result of military service, were effectively cut off from their local lodges. Thrown together from various parts of the country in military locations throughout the world, National Sojourners offers those Masons a supportive fraternal option.

Other Social Groups

In addition to those listed, there are many other social groups who are part of the Masonic family. Some focus on charity and relief assistance, others on Masonic research, and others on helping out larger fraternal organizations. A few of those are:

- **American Lodge of Research.** A group comprised of Master Masons whose focus is the study of Masonic history.
- **Ancient Egyptian Order of Princesses of Sharemkhu.** An organization of women related to Shriners who focus on charitable and social activities.

- **Daughters of Mokanna.** A fraternal organization for women who are related to members of Prophets of the Enchanted Realm.
- **Masonic Service Association of the United States.** A federation of Grand Lodges founded in 1919 that conducts education and welfare programs. Members visit veterans who are hospitalized and assist in disaster relief.
- **Philalethes Society.** A research group comprised of Master Masons dedicated to Masonic philosophy and the worldwide exchange of information.
- **Royal Order of Jesters.** An invitation-only organization consisting of Shriners whose motto is "Mirth is King."

Women's Orders

Freemasonry isn't just for men. There are a variety of social orders for women who are equally dedicated to their organization and the charitable causes they support. Most require that the women are either related or married to Masons, and several of the groups include both men and women.

Order of the Eastern Star

Considered to be the world's largest organization whose members include both men and women, the Order of the Eastern Star boasts a membership of over a million individuals worldwide. It is said that the Order originated in France in 1703, at a time when so called "androgynous degrees" were conferred. In the United States, however, the Order was founded in 1850 by poet laureate of Freemasonry Dr. Robert Morris.

FACT

When Dr. Morris created the initiatory degrees of the Eastern Star his first initiates were his wife, daughters, and female neighbors, to whom he gave various modes of recognition so that Masons could recognize them.

Like Freemasonry, the Eastern Star Order is nonsectarian and non-denominational. The organization is involved in a variety of charities and offers support to the three youth organizations, Rainbow Girls, Job's Daughters, and the Order of DeMolay.

Order of the Amaranth

In the seventeenth century, Queen Christina of Sweden created the Order of the Amarantha for her royal court of ladies and honored knights. It is said the name Amarantha comes from the red amaranthus flower found in Portugal and Spain. Still in existence today in Sweden, the Royal and Social Order of the Amarantha still includes members of the Swedish Royal Family.

While the Order of the Amaranth takes its inspiration from the Swedish Order, it is entirely separate from the modern-day organization which was founded in New York in 1873. The Amaranth's membership is comprised of Master Masons and their female relatives. The Order's primary philanthropic work is the Amaranth Diabetes Foundation which was founded in 1979. Since then the Amaranth have donated over seven million dollars to the American Diabetes Association.

The Order has over forty Grand Courts in the United States, Canada, Australia, England, the Philippines, and Scotland, with subordinate Courts in Hawaii, Ireland, and New Zealand. All are governed by a Supreme Council.

White Shrine of Jerusalem

The Order of the White Shrine of Jerusalem is an organization whose membership comprises both men who are Master Masons in good standing, and women who are related or family. Founded by Charles D. Magee in 1894, the White Shrine has several spiritual qualifications. Like Freemasonry, members must profess a belief in a Supreme Being, and a belief in Christianity and the defense of it as a religion. White Shrine rituals are based on the birth, life, death, and resurrection of Jesus.

The "material objective" of White Shrine members is their charitable work in ministering to the needy. There are over several hundred shrines in the United States and Canada with members, or sojourners, numbering over thirty thousand.

Social Order of Beauceant

In 1892, the Twenty-Fifth Triennial Conclave for the Grand Encampment of the Knights Templar was held in Denver, Colorado. The Knight of the local Commandery quickly realized they needed help when they were asked to host the event, so their wives stepped up to the plate. At an official meeting, the wives decided on the name S.O.O.B. which stood for "Some of Our Business Society." After helping out at the Triennial, they decided to continue on as a group.

The Social Order is dedicated to the cultivation of loyalty to one another and to the Knights Templar. As such, they adopted the Knights official charity, the Commanderie's Knights Templar Eye Foundation in 1957, to which they have donated over $1.5 million.

When the 1913 Triennial arrived, and after years of providing support to the Knights, the members of the S.O.O.B. decided to expand and changed their name to the Social Order of the Beauceant. The organization now has over seven thousand members and over one hundred Assemblies in thirty-five states. Members of the Order, as wives and widows of Knights Templar, are the sole female fraternal group who are eligible as a result of their spouse's Commandery membership.

Daughters of the Nile

Founded in 1913, Daughters of the Nile is a philanthropic international nonprofit organization for women. Since their inception, their North American membership alone is over fifty thousand, with 149 Temples located throughout the United States and Canada. Women who belong to the organization are related or married to a Shriner, Master Mason, or Daughter of the Nile.

The Daughters work closely with the Shrine of North America, helping the infirm at over twenty Shriners Hospitals for Children in the United States. Through their Supreme Convalescent Endowment Fund and Convalescent

Relief Fund the organization annually contributes over 1.5 million dollars to hospitals specifically to provide for children in need. Since 1924, the Daughters have contributed monetary gifts of almost forty million dollars for children in Shriners Hospitals.

Ladies of the Oriental Shrine

Founded in 1903 in Wheeling, West Virginia, the Ladies of the Oriental Shrine is a women's organization dedicated to extending financial support and assistance to the Shriners Hospitals for Children, focusing on hospital funding, sewing, and various projects. Shrine members are related or married to Master Masons.

The Grand Council of the Shrine was established in 1914 and incorporated in 1954. The Grand High Priestess presides over the Grand Council, with the High Priestess overseeing local courts. The Order has almost a hundred Courts in North America, Hawaii, and Okinawa, Japan.

Youth Groups

There are several popular youth groups associated with Freemasonry, each with an emphasis on widening the education and spiritual potential of young men and women. The Order of the Rainbow Girls, Job's Daughters, and the Order of DeMolay all enjoy bonds to the Brotherhood and in doing so have nourished thousands of individuals for many decades and many more to come.

QUESTION?

What does the rainbow stand for?
The seven Rainbow colors are symbolic of each member's journey and the pot of gold that awaits. Red is for love, orange for religion, yellow stands for nature, green for immortality, blue emphasizes fidelity, indigo means patriotism, and violet focuses on service.

Order of the Rainbow Girls

Founded in 1922 by Christian minister and Mason William Mark Sexson, the International Order of the Rainbow Girls is a nonprofit service organization for girls ages eleven through twenty. Members, who do not have to be Christian, are comprised of young women whose families belong to Masonry or Daughters of the Eastern Star. It is also open to their friends.

The Rainbow Order is an independent fraternal organization governed by a Supreme Assembly. Their goal is to teach young women the virtues of faith, hope, and charity. The Order is active all over the United States, Canada, Australia, New Zealand, Aruba, Germany, Bolivia, Brazil, Italy, Japan, and the Philippines.

Job's Daughters

The International Order of Job's Daughters was founded by Ethel Wead Mick in 1920 in Omaha, Nebraska. Members of this Order must be related to a Master Mason, be between the ages of ten and twenty, and possess a belief in a Supreme Being. Their groups, known as Bethels, are located all over the United States, Canada, Brazil, Australia, and the Philippines. The young women involved in the organization are taught moral and spiritual lessons, patriotism, and respect in an effort to cultivate strong business and social skills. Job's Daughters is also a charitable group, devoting time and effort to the Hearing Impaired Kids Endowment Fund.

The Order of DeMolay

Freemason Frank Land founded the Order of DeMolay in Kansas City, Missouri, in 1919. Land's dedication to his organization has resulted in over one thousand established Chapters throughout the world. Open to young men from ages twelve to twenty-one who believe in a Supreme Being, DeMolay strives to teach civic awareness, leadership, and personal responsibility. The name DeMolay pays tribute to legendary Jacques DeMolay, Grand Master of the Knights Templar during the Crusades (see Chapter 2).

chapter 20

Freemasons in Culture

Freemasons have impacted culture in myriad ways. The charitable deeds they perform are widely recognized, and their contributions to society in all parts of the world are highly revered by all the individuals they've helped. Their cultural legacy is a mix of old and new, the old being a legendary figure in American Masonry, and the new paying homage to the impact Masons have had on film, television, and literature.

Prince Hall Masonry

In free societies, racial segregation and discrimination is manifestly condemned, but the fact remains that the early history of the United States is inherently infused with legal and socially accepted segregation that spans a timeline from the birth of the country to the Civil Rights Act of 1964. Culturally, Prince Hall Masonry stands as a unique testimony to the fundamental and universal concepts of Freemasonry. It is also a lasting tribute to the perseverance, integrity, and social consciousness of a single man.

Birth of a Prince

The story of Freemasonry and its attraction to a freed slave in eighteenth century America is compelling and remarkable. Prince Hall's birth and early life are the subject of some controversy, and there is little documentation to support the various theories. The best estimates of Prince Hall's date of birth put it between 1735 and 1738. The exact whereabouts are unknown. The most reliable sources indicate that Prince Hall was a slave belonging to William Hall, a Boston leather worker in the 1740s.

After twenty-one years of service to William Hall, documentation shows that Hall gave Prince Hall, now probably in his early to mid-thirties, his freedom on April 9, 1770. To put this into historical perspective, that date was nearly one month to the day after the infamous Boston Massacre. Upon gaining his freedom, Prince Hall married and supported himself in the leather craft, and would eventually open his own leather shop in Boston.

It is thought that Prince Hall approached the St. John's Masonic lodge in Boston in early 1775, but was turned away. He and fourteen other free black men subsequently approached a British Army lodge (Irish Lodge No. 441) attached to the 38th Foot Regiment, which was stationed on the outskirts of Boston.

Prince Hall and his fourteen comrades were initiated into the lodge on March 6, 1775. Just over a month after their initiation, on April 19, the first shot of the Revolutionary War was fired near Lexington, only a dozen miles from Boston. For British strategic reasons, the 38th Foot Regiment would soon withdraw from the area, but before doing so, British Army Sergeant John Batt, who had overseen the Masonic initiation of Hall and his group, issued a permit that allowed the newly inducted African-American Masons to join together and hold their own meetings. On July 3, 1775, Prince Hall's group officially formed African Lodge No. 1, which became the first African-American Masonic lodge in history.

FACT

Records indicate that there were fourteen Masonic lodges attached to British military units in the Boston vicinity in 1775. Nine of those lodges were chartered Irish lodges, four of them were Scottish lodges, and one was English.

Cultural Awareness

There has been much speculation that the Masonic induction of Prince Hall and his fourteen comrades may have been irregular, and that the permit issued by John Batt held no authoritative value. However, there is no question that this group of African-Americans actively pursued Freemasonry, and treated their initiation and membership with absolute sincerity and great respect.

Prince Hall is generally considered to have supported the American Revolution, but there is no record that he took up arms. There is, however, documentation in the form of a sales receipt written by Prince Hall on April 24, 1777, that he supplied the Boston Regiment of Artillery of the Revolutionary Army with five leather drumheads.

It is known that he was politically active in the support of African-American causes, calling on the City Fathers of Boston and the state legislature to provide schools and education for the children of the Boston area. Hall was one of eight petitioners to the Massachusetts legislature requesting the abolition of slavery in the state in 1777. Although this petition would fall on the deaf ears of then-current political expediency in the legislature, the cumulative effects of growing public antislavery sentiment would have a profound impact on the state, and eventually, the entire country.

The Massachusetts State Supreme Court issued a ruling in 1783, finding that the State Constitution of 1780, which contends in its opening article that, "All men are created free and equal," effectively barred slavery. Prince

Hall, in no small way, played an active part in making Massachusetts the first state in the country to abolish slavery.

Charting a Course

As a result of the chaotic conditions of the Revolutionary War, there are no known records of African Lodge No. 1 activities during the final years of the conflict. The lodge was still in existence, but still without a permanent charter. In June of 1784, Prince Hall sought to remedy this by writing to William Moody, the Most Worshipful Master of the Brotherly Love Lodge No. 55 in London, seeking his aid in securing a charter from the Grand Lodge of London (the "Moderns").

In his second letter to Moody, Prince Hall indicated that African Lodge No. 1 had been operating under a "permet" issued by John Rowe, the Grand Provincial Master of North America, which allowed the lodge to march on St. John's Day and bury their dead in Masonic tradition. Evidence of this "permet" is extremely sketchy, and John Rowe was not appointed Grand Provincial Master of North America until three years after African Lodge No. 1 was originally formed. Whether or not the lodge was operating under the original permit from John Batt or a new permit from John Rowe is unclear.

Prince Hall also indicated in the letter that he had been pushed by unknown entities to apply for a charter to the Grand Lodge of France, but chose not to pursue that course for undisclosed reasons. This coincides with the rift in Freemasonry of the two independently operating Grand Lodges in Great Britain, and the Grand Lodge of France (see Chapter 4). One can speculate that Prince Hall, by this statement, had effectively taken a position against the French Grand Lodge.

Prince Hall's plea to William Moody was successful and three months later, in September 1784, a charter was issued from the Grand Lodge of London to African Lodge No. 459, with Prince Hall designated as Grand Master.

A Grand Solution

In historical perspective, it's interesting to note that the United States Congress ratified the peace treaty with Great Britain on January 14, 1784, five months before Prince Hall's request for a charter. There were two

Provincial Lodges operating in what was now the State of Massachusetts, two Grand Lodges operating in Britain, and the Grand Lodge of France. It can be surmised that Prince Hall, despite the political affiliations of warfare and inter-Masonic disputes, considered the Grand Lodge of London to have stewardship over Freemason lodge charters.

During Prince Hall's tenure as Grand Master, he ardently continued his civil and social support of African-American causes in Massachusetts, while continuing his battle against slavery.

On numerous occasions, Prince Hall petitioned for the provision of schools and education to African-American children in the state. Although he met stubborn legislative resistance, Hall never backed down from his unrelenting campaign.

Although slavery had technically been abolished in Massachusetts, participation in the slave trade continued. Prince Hall played a pivotal role in the abolition of the practice after three African-American Boston residents were kidnapped and shipped to the island of Martinique, where they were sold into slavery. The incident became public knowledge, and Prince Hall, along with twenty-one fellow Masons, petitioned the legislature on February 27, 1788, expressing their outrage and demanding legal intervention. The next month, the state legislature declared the slave trade illegal, and went so far as to provide monetary compensation for kidnap victims.

Lifelong Legacy

African Lodge No. 459 continued operating under the warrant of the Grand Lodge of England and paid dues to the Charity Fund of the Grand Lodge until 1797, when communications on both continents were lost, ignored, or incomplete. Also in 1797, Lodge No. 459 granted a charter to a group of African-Americans in Rhode Island who had failed in their attempt to gain a charter from the Provincial Grand Lodge—primarily on segregationist grounds. A year later they granted yet another charter in Philadelphia, and the Prince Hall family of lodges began spreading. Prince Hall continued his tenure as Grand Master until his death on December 4, 1807.

Although the Prince Hall Lodges operated, and continue to operate in every respect as "regular" Masonic lodges, jurisdictional misunderstandings and poor communication over the next few decades resulted in an announcement by Lodge No. 459 in 1827, declaring independence "from any lodge to this day."

FACT

In 1994, the United Grand Lodge of England adopted a resolution formally recognizing the Prince Hall Grand Lodge of Massachusetts. Today Prince Hall Masonry has over 300,000 members in 4,500 lodges worldwide.

The cultural significance of Prince Hall Masonry is unique in the annals of Masonic history. Prince Hall rose from the degradation of enslavement to embrace the very foundations and ethical conduct of Freemasonry. His efforts on behalf of his racial heritage, and his persistence in sharing and spreading equality and knowledge in the face of intense social opposition is one of the most inspirational lessons in American history.

Masons in Literature

There are far too many books to mention which over the centuries have included references to Freemasonry, both subtle and blatant. Authors like John LeCarré, Ernest Hemingway, Arthur Conan Doyle, and Rudyard Kipling are among the hundreds who have brought Masonry into their writings. Kipling, in particular, made numerous references to the Craft in his writings and poetry.

In 1976, Stephen Knight's book *Jack the Ripper: The Final Solution* caused a stir with the alleged "royal conspiracy" theory. His second book, *The Brotherhood: The Secret World of the Freemasons,* continued his theoretical speculations about the fraternity. Knight's is among many controversial books which, like those speculating about any other historic subject, have been countered by a number of factual books.

One of the foremost organizations for Masonic information is the Livingston Masonic Library in New York City, which houses the world's largest collection of Masonic literature, artifacts, archives, and memorabilia. The library is open to both Masons and the public.

Several contemporary writers have again brought Freemasonry into the public eye with their bestselling books. Masons Christopher Knight and Robert Lomas have written several books, among them, *The Hiram Key: Pharaohs, Freemasons and the Discovery of the Secret Scrolls of Jesus*, in which they explore the origin of Masonry back to Egyptian times.

Dan Brown's 2003 bestseller *The Da Vinci Code* focuses on the Priory of Sion and alleged Holy Grail Mary Magdalene. The story revolves around a Harvard professor, cryptologist, and the murdered curator of the Louvre. It has been speculated that his sequel, *The Solomon Key*, will focus on American Freemasonry.

Freemasonry in Cinema

Many films have made references to Freemasonry over the decades, some merely including subtle shots of a square and compass, others launching into full-fledged conspiracy theories. Still others have many times included other secret societies such as the Illuminati, who in most cases, are the bad guys. Films like *From Hell*, *Murder by Decree*, *Tomb Raider*, *National Treasure*, and *The Godfather Part III*, have based much of their plot on alleged Masonic connections.

FACT

In the 1986 film *Peggy Sue Got Married*, starring Kathleen Turner and Nicolas Cage, Turner's character is transported to 1960s America. Lucky for her, a group of colorful lodge brothers, whose lodge was founded by a time traveler, have a ritual that can eventually send her back. Those scenes were filmed at the Masonic lodge in Petaluma, California.

From Hell and *Murder by Decree* were both based on Stephen Knight's book *Jack the Ripper: The Final Solution*, which highlighted the so-called royal conspiracy implicating the Freemasons, among others, in the legendary murders (see Chapter 18). The third installment of *The Godfather* is said to be loosely based on events surrounding the Italian P2 lodge and the scandal that rocked the Vatican (see Chapter 12).

The more recent film *National Treasure* finds Nicolas Cage's character Benjamin Franklin Gates in pursuit of a treasure trove—including scrolls from the Library of Alexandria—procured by the Knights Templar and secretly hidden by Freemasons, including the founding fathers of the United States. Adding to the mystery are the clues, which happen to be concealed, among other places, on the Declaration of Independence.

Small Screen Brotherhoods

Television has had its share of fictional fraternities, most presumably drawing influence from real fraternal organizations like the Masons, Shriners, Elks, and others. Many of the classic sitcoms had—for better or for worse—fictional fraternal links. *Dallas* had the Daughters of the Alamo, *Dobie Gillis* had the Benevolent Order of the Bison, and *Northern Exposure* featured the Sons of the Tundra.

On *Mama's Family*, starring Vicki Lawrence, Ken Berry's character Vinton Harper joined the Cobra Lodge which was under the guidance of the Grand Viper. They had a secret hissing cobra handshake, and anyone violating their oaths was hissed out of the lodge.

Other small screen fraternities include:

- *Married with Children.* Al Bundy was a member of the misogynist National Organization of Men Against Amazonian Masterhood.
- *The Honeymooners.* Ralph Kramden and his best pal Ed Norton were members of the Raccoons.
- *Laverne and Shirley.* Lenny and Squiggy were initiated into the Fraternal Order of the Bass.
- *The Drew Carey Show.* Drew's father was a member of the Wildebeests.
- *Cheers.* Cliff Clavin belonged to an alcohol-free lodge called the Knights of the Scimitar.
- *The Andy Griffith Show.* Andy and Barney were members of the Regal Order of the Golden Door to Good Fellowship. The Order's password was "Geronimo!"

The *Newhart* show had the fictional Beavers, which did nothing for Bob Newhart's character Dick Loudon, as it turned out that initiates had to sport a beaver tail attached to the seat of their pants!

Reminiscent of a Shriner was Tom Bosley's *Happy Days* character Howard Cunningham, who as Grand Poobah of the Leopard Lodge No. 462, was often sporting a leopard print fez.

Animated Brotherhoods

As most cartoon aficionados can attest, there have been more than a few animated portrayals of the fraternal kind, two of which are part of television history—*The Simpsons* and *The Flintstones*.

Homer the Stonecutter

In a 1995 episode of *The Simpsons* entitled *"Homer the Great,"* Masonry makes an appearance when Homer becomes a member of the Springfield chapter of the Sacred Order of the Stonecutters. His initiation ceremony is replete with symbols of Freemasonry including a square and compass, and an eye within a triangle. In true *Simpsons* fashion, the initiation closes with the following declaration:

The Sacred Order of the Stonecutters has, since ancient times, split the rocks of ignorance that obscures the light of knowledge and truth. Now let's all get drunk and play ping-pong.

During the course of his initiation, the brethren discover that Homer has the birthmark of the "Chosen One," which is a birthmark shaped like a pair of hammers. He is then appointed Grand Exalted Leader.

A millenia-old fraternity, a member either had to be the son of a Stonecutter or save the life of one. Part of Homer's symbolic initiation ritual was a "leap of faith" off a five-storey building (which was actually a leap off a stage). The trio of rituals that follow are "Crossing the Desert," the "Unblinking Eye," and the "Paddling of the Swollen Ass." And then there's the infamous Stonecutter's song, which pokes fun at conspiracy theories in which the Freemasons are blamed.

Who controls the British Crown?
Who keeps the metric system down?
We do. We do.
Who keeps Atlantis off the maps?
Who keeps the Martians under wraps?
We do. We do.
Who holds back the electric car?
Who makes Steve Guttenberg a star?
We do. We do.
Who robs cave fish of their sight?
Who rigs every Oscar night?
We do. We do.

The Loyal Order of Water Buffaloes

Fred Flintstone and Barney Rubble were no strangers to chaos, chicanery, and hilarity. Much of the latter was due to their membership in what was originally called the Loyal Order of Dinosaurs but which later became the Loyal Order of Water Buffaloes Lodge No. 26. From 1960 to 1966, *The Flintstones* had more lodge fun than they could stand, complete with a Grand Poobah, secret handshakes, a furry oversized horned hat, and a secret password.

FACT

The four main *Flintstone* characters were inspired by the Kramden and Norton duos of *The Honeymooners*. It's no coincidence that Fred and Barney were lodge members—Ralph and Ed were members of the Raccoons.

During the course of the show, Fred and Barney get roped into all kinds of lodge activities, including judging the Water Buffaloes' annual beauty pageant, a Poobah-ordered lodge meeting during Fred and Wilma's anniversary, and Fred and Barney feuding like the Hatfield's and McCoys over the Water Buffalo of the Year campaign. There's even an episode where Wilma and Betty sneak into the lodge after the men veto a motion to allow women! One of the more hilarious lodge screw-ups is Pebbles's birthday party, in which the caterer confuses the entertainment for her party with that of a Water Buffalo party.

A Legacy of Brotherhood

If Freemasonry has established a legacy for itself, which includes even these comic representations of its history, it is, no doubt, reflective of the strong ties its members have to one another. Never has a fraternal organization endured over centuries and remained true to its goals and objectives. In truth, like any other organization, there have been tumultuous times, eras of persecution, scandals, and a few bad seeds, but Masons remain true to themselves and the quest for spiritual and educational enlightenment that serves to benefit individuals and society.

Enveloped in history, mystery, symbolism, and controversy, the legacy of the Brotherhood continues. Of course no discussion of Freemasonry would be complete without the good, the bad, and the ugly, but when studying this alleged secret society, one finds that when events and action are understood in context, there is much to be learned and much to admire about an organization that has survived for centuries.

Appendix A
Recommended Reading

Baigent, Michael, Henry Lincoln, and Richard Leigh. *Holy Blood, Holy Grail.* Dell, reissue edition, 1983.

Brown, Dan. *The Da Vinci Code.* Doubleday, New York, a division of Random House, Inc. 2003.

Bullock, Stephen C. "The Revolutionary Transformation of American Freemasonry, 1752–1792." *William and Mary Quarterly* 37, 1990.

Claudy, Carl H. *Introduction to Freemasonry I: Entered Apprentice.* The Temple Publishers, Washington, D.C., 1931.

———. *Introduction to Freemasonry II: Fellowcraft.* The Temple Publishers, Washington, D.C., 1931.

———. *Introduction to Freemasonry III: Master Mason.* The Temple Publishers, Washington, D.C., 1931.

Clausen, Henry C. 33°, Sovereign Grand Commander. *Clausen's Commentaries on Morals and Dogma. Supreme Council, 33rd Degree, Ancient and Accepted Scottish Rite of Freemasonry, Southern Jurisdiction.* Washington, D.C., 1974, 1976.

Coil, Henry Wilson. *Coil's Masonic Encyclopedia.* Macoy Publishing & Masonic Supply Co., Inc., 1996.

Cornwell, Patricia. *Portrait of a Killer: Jack The Ripper—Case Closed.* Berkeley True Crime, 2003.

de Hoyos, Arturo, and S. Brent Morris. *Is It True What They Say about Freemasonry?* M. Evans and Company, Inc., New York, 2004.

Hunter, Frederick M. *The Regius Manuscript.* Research Lodge of Oregon, No. 198, Portland Oregon, 1952.

Jacob, Margaret C. *Living the Enlightenment: Freemasonry and Politics in Eighteenth-Century Europe.* Oxford University Press, New York, 1991.

Jeffers, Paul. *Freemasons: Inside the World's Oldest Secret Society.* Citadel Press Books, Kensington Publishing Corp, 2005.

Knight, Christopher, and Robert Lomas. *The Hiram Key.* Fair Winds Press, Gloucester, Massachusetts, 1996.

————. *The Book of Hiram: Freemasonry, Venus, and the Secret Key to the Life of Jesus.* Element, an imprint of HarperCollins Publishers, Hammersmith, London, 2003.

————. *Uriel's Machine.* Fair Winds Press, Gloucester, Massachusetts, 2001.

Knight, Stephen. *Jack the Ripper: The Final Solution.* David McKay Co., 1976.

————. *The Brotherhood: The Secret World of The Freemasons.* Dorset Press, 1986.

Lomas, Robert. *Freemasonry and the Birth of Modern Science.* Fairwinds Press, 2003.

Mackey, Albert Gallatin. *The History of Freemasonry; Its Legendary Origins.* Random House Value Publishing, 1966.

Mackey's Revised Encyclopedia of Freemasonry. The Masonic History Company, 1912.

MacNulty, Kirk. *Freemasonry: A Journey Through Ritual and Symbol.* Thames and Hudson, 1991.

Macoy, Robert. *A Dictionary of Freemasonry.* Gramercy Books, Random House Value Publishing, 2000.

Naudon, Paul. *The Secret History of Freemasonry: Its Origins and Connection to the Knights Templar.* Inner Traditions, Rochester, Vermont, 1991.

Newton, Joseph F. *The Builders.* The Supreme Council, 33rd Degree, A.A.S.R., Lexington Massachusetts, 1973.

Pike, Albert. *Morals and Dogma.* Kessinger Publishing, 2004.

Ridley, Jasper. *The Freemasons: A History of the World's Most Powerful Secret Society.* Arcade Publishing, Inc., New York. 1999, 2001.

Roberts, Allen E. *Freemasonry in American History.* Macoy Publishing and Masonic Supply Co., Inc., Richmond, Virginia, 1985.

Robinson, John J. *Born in Blood: The Lost Secrets of Freemasonry.* M. Evans and Company, Inc., New York, 1989.

Rumbelow, Donald. *The Complete Jack the Ripper.* Little Brown & Co., 1975.

Short, Martin. *Inside the Brotherhood: Further Secrets of the Freemasons.* Dorset Press, 1990.

Young, John K. *Sacred Sites of the Knights Templar.* Fair Winds Press, Gloucester, Massachusetts, 2003.

Appendix B
Glossary

Albert Pike:
The Sovereign Grand Commander of the Southern Supreme Council of the Scottish Rite from 1859 to 1891.

Ancient Arabic Nobles of the Mystic Shrine:
The most visible body of Freemasonry, commonly referred to as Shriners.

Blue Lodge:
One of the most commonly used terms in Freemasonry for lodges conferring the first three degrees. It is primarily used in the United States and Canada.

Cable Tow:
Also a measure of distance, it symbolically binds each Mason to all of his brethren. The tie is as strong and lengthy as an initiate and the abilities he brings to the Craft.

Chapter of the Rose Croix:
The second division of the Scottish Rite system that includes the fifteenth through eighteenth degrees.

Circumambulation:
In a lodge there is a central object or point (an altar), which the initiate must walk around. This ancient practice is meant to show that an initiate is prepared to embark on his fraternal journey.

Commanderies of Knights Templar:
Also called Chivalric Masonry, it includes three orders including the Illustrious Order of the Red Cross, the Order of Malta, and the Order of the Temple.

Compass:
One of the most important and prominent symbols of Freemasonry, it represents virtue as a measure of one's life and conduct. It also signifies restraint, skill, and knowledge.

Consistory Degrees:
The fourth and final division of the Scottish Rite system which includes the thirty-first and thirty-second degrees. The thirty-third degree, though part of the Consistory, is honorary.

Council of Kadosh:
The third division of the Scottish Rite system which includes the nineteenth through thirtieth degrees.

Council of Cryptic Masonry:
Often called Cryptic Masonry, it is the second body of the York Rite which confers three degrees including Royal Master, Select Master, and Super Excellent Master.

Craft, the:
A common term which simply refers to Freemasonry.

Degree:
A level of Freemasonry to which individuals can ascend.

Entered Apprentice:
The first degree of Craft Masonry where an initiate is introduced to the Craft. It symbolizes an individual's spiritual birth into the fraternity, and begins his quest for "light," or knowledge.

Fellowcraft:
The second degree of Craft Masonry which signifies an initiate's adult phase into the Craft where he seeks to acquire the knowledge and spiritual tools necessary to build character and improve society.

Four Cardinal Virtues:
Temperance, fortitude, prudence, and justice.

"G," the Letter:
Symbolically it stands for "geometry" or "God." It also commonly refers to God as the Grand Architect of the Universe or Grand Master of the Universe.

Grand Lodge:
The governing body which oversees all regular lodges under its jurisdiction.

Grand Lodge of England:
The first Grand Lodge formed in 1717, when four lodges united in England. It is generally accepted that this marked the start of organized Freemasonry.

Grand Master:
The highest ranking individual of a Grand Lodge. It is an elected position and one of great prestige within the Craft.

Hiram Abiff:
The architect and Master Mason who oversaw the building of the Temple of Solomon. His legend is referred to throughout Freemasonry.

Hoodwinked:
Initiates to the Craft are hoodwinked, or blindfolded, which represents the veil of silence and secrecy that surrounds the mysteries of Freemasonry.

Knights Templar:
A military and religious order of warrior monks founded in 1118 by French Knight Hughes de Payens. The Templars fought during the Crusades.

Lodge:
A two-fold term referring to both a group of Masons and the building in which they meet. Masonic buildings are often called temples.

Lodge of Perfection:
The first division of the Scottish Rite system which includes the fourth through fourteenth degrees. Usually referred to as "ineffable" degrees.

Master Mason:
The third degree of Craft Masonry which symbolically links a Mason's soul and his own inner nature and belief system.

Operative Masonry:
Operatives refers to stonemasons who were part of the actual trade.

Order of the Eastern Star:
The world's largest social organization whose members include both men and

women. Their order includes over a million individuals worldwide.

Pillars on the Porch:

Symbolically linked to Solomon's Temple, they stand at the entrance to the Temple. The left pillar is called Boaz, and the right is named Jachin.

Royal Arch Chapter:

Part of the York Rite, Royal Arch Masonry consists of four degrees, including Mark Master, Past Master, Most Excellent Master, and Royal Arch.

Scottish Rite:

A concordant body of Freemasonry, it offers thirty-three additional degrees. Also called the Ancient and Accepted Scottish Rite.

Speculative Masonry:

Speculative refers to Freemasons who were not part of the actual trade of masonry.

Square:

One of the most prominent symbols of Freemasonry, it represents morality and truthfulness.

Supreme Being:

The Masonic reference to Deity. Given that Masonry is nonsectarian, each Mason's Supreme Being may be different. The more commonly used term among the brethren is Grand Architect of the Universe.

Thirty-Third Degree Mason:

One who has completed the first three degrees of Craft Masonry and the thirty-two degrees of the Scottish Rite. The thirty-third degree is honorary and the candidate must be voted upon.

Three Great Lights of Masonry:

The square, compass, and Volume of the Sacred Law.

United Grand Lodge of England:

The union of two Grand Lodges in Britain in 1813. Today the Lodge is formally known as the United Grand Lodge of Free and Accepted Masons of England, and informally called the United Grand Lodge of England.

Volume of the Sacred Law:

The most prominent of the Three Great Lights. Members of the Craft practice many different religions, so the sacred text of choice varies. In general, it is the Holy Bible.

Working Tools:

Each degree of Masonry has certain symbolism associated with its level which represent the morals and forces necessary in building and rebuilding the nature of humankind.

Worshipful Master:

The highest ranking member of a lodge or blue lodge. Also called a Right Worshipful Master. He is elected and serves a one-year term.

York Rite:

A concordant body of Freemasonry originating from the English city of York. It offers additional degrees within its three bodies—the Royal Arch Chapter, Council of Cryptic Masonry, and Commanderies of Knights Templar.

Index

THE EVERYTHING SERIES!

BUSINESS & PERSONAL FINANCE

Everything® Budgeting Book
Everything® Business Planning Book
Everything® Coaching and Mentoring Book
Everything® Fundraising Book
Everything® Get Out of Debt Book
Everything® Grant Writing Book
Everything® Home-Based Business Book, 2nd Ed.
Everything® Homebuying Book, 2nd Ed.
Everything® Homeselling Book, 2nd Ed.
Everything® Investing Book, 2nd Ed.
Everything® Landlording Book
Everything® Leadership Book
Everything® Managing People Book
Everything® Negotiating Book
Everything® Online Business Book
Everything® Personal Finance Book
Everything® Personal Finance in Your 20s and 30s Book
Everything® Project Management Book
Everything® Real Estate Investing Book
Everything® Robert's Rules Book, $7.95
Everything® Selling Book
Everything® Start Your Own Business Book
Everything® Wills & Estate Planning Book

COMPUTERS

Everything® Online Auctions Book
Everything® Blogging Book

COOKING

Everything® Barbecue Cookbook
Everything® Bartender's Book, $9.95
Everything® Chinese Cookbook
Everything® Cocktail Parties and Drinks Book
Everything® College Cookbook
Everything® Cookbook
Everything® Cooking for Two Cookbook
Everything® Diabetes Cookbook
Everything® Easy Gourmet Cookbook
Everything® Fondue Cookbook
Everything® Gluten-Free Cookbook
Everything® Glycemic Index Cookbook
Everything® Grilling Cookbook

Everything® Healthy Meals in Minutes Cookbook
Everything® Holiday Cookbook
Everything® Indian Cookbook
Everything® Italian Cookbook
Everything® Low-Carb Cookbook
Everything® Low-Fat High-Flavor Cookbook
Everything® Low-Salt Cookbook
Everything® Meals for a Month Cookbook
Everything® Mediterranean Cookbook
Everything® Mexican Cookbook
Everything® One-Pot Cookbook
Everything® Pasta Cookbook
Everything® Quick Meals Cookbook
Everything® Slow Cooker Cookbook
Everything® Slow Cooking for a Crowd Cookbook
Everything® Soup Cookbook
Everything® Tex-Mex Cookbook
Everything® Thai Cookbook
Everything® Vegetarian Cookbook
Everything® Wild Game Cookbook
Everything® Wine Book, 2nd Ed.

CRAFT SERIES

Everything® Crafts—Baby Scrapbooking
Everything® Crafts—Bead Your Own Jewelry
Everything® Crafts—Create Your Own Greeting Cards
Everything® Crafts—Easy Projects
Everything® Crafts—Polymer Clay for Beginners
Everything® Crafts—Rubber Stamping Made Easy
Everything® Crafts—Wedding Decorations and Keepsakes

HEALTH

Everything® Alzheimer's Book
Everything® Diabetes Book
Everything® Health Guide to Adult Bipolar Disorder
Everything® Health Guide to Controlling Anxiety
Everything® Health Guide to Fibromyalgia
Everything® Hypnosis Book

Everything® Low Cholesterol Book
Everything® Massage Book
Everything® Menopause Book
Everything® Nutrition Book
Everything® Reflexology Book
Everything® Stress Management Book

HISTORY

Everything® American Government Book
Everything® American History Book
Everything® Civil War Book
Everything® Irish History & Heritage Book
Everything® Middle East Book

GAMES

Everything® 15-Minute Sudoku Book, $9.95
Everything® 30-Minute Sudoku Book, $9.95
Everything® Blackjack Strategy Book
Everything® Brain Strain Book, $9.95
Everything® Bridge Book
Everything® Card Games Book
Everything® Card Tricks Book, $9.95
Everything® Casino Gambling Book, 2nd Ed.
Everything® Chess Basics Book
Everything® Craps Strategy Book
Everything® Crossword and Puzzle Book
Everything® Crossword Challenge Book
Everything® Cryptograms Book, $9.95
Everything® Easy Crosswords Book
Everything® Easy Kakuro Book, $9.95
Everything® Games Book, 2nd Ed.
Everything® Giant Sudoku Book, $9.95
Everything® Kakuro Challenge Book, $9.95
Everything® Large-Print Crosswords Book
Everything® Lateral Thinking Puzzles Book, $9.95
Everything® Pencil Puzzles Book, $9.95
Everything® Poker Strategy Book
Everything® Pool & Billiards Book
Everything® Test Your IQ Book, $9.95
Everything® Texas Hold 'Em Book, $9.95
Everything® Travel Crosswords Book, $9.95
Everything® Word Games Challenge Book
Everything® Word Search Book

Bolded titles are new additions to the series.
All Everything® books are priced at $12.95 or $14.95, unless otherwise stated. Prices subject to change without notice.

HOBBIES

Everything® Candlemaking Book
Everything® Cartooning Book
Everything® Drawing Book
Everything® Family Tree Book, 2nd Ed.
Everything® Knitting Book
Everything® Knots Book
Everything® Photography Book
Everything® Quilting Book
Everything® Scrapbooking Book
Everything® Sewing Book
Everything® Woodworking Book

HOME IMPROVEMENT

Everything® Feng Shui Book
Everything® Feng Shui Decluttering Book, $9.95
Everything® Fix-It Book
Everything® Home Decorating Book
Everything® Homebuilding Book
Everything® Lawn Care Book
Everything® Organize Your Home Book

KIDS' BOOKS

All titles are $7.95
Everything® Kids' Animal Puzzle &
    Activity Book
Everything® Kids' Baseball Book, 4th Ed.
Everything® Kids' Bible Trivia Book
Everything® Kids' Bugs Book
Everything® Kids' Christmas Puzzle
    & Activity Book
Everything® Kids' Cookbook
Everything® Kids' Crazy Puzzles Book
Everything® Kids' Dinosaurs Book
**Everything® Kids' Gross Hidden Pictures
    Book**
Everything® Kids' Gross Jokes Book
Everything® Kids' Gross Mazes Book
Everything® Kids' Gross Puzzle and
    Activity Book
Everything® Kids' Halloween Puzzle
    & Activity Book
Everything® Kids' Hidden Pictures Book
Everything® Kids' Horses Book
Everything® Kids' Joke Book
Everything® Kids' Knock Knock Book
Everything® Kids' Math Puzzles Book
Everything® Kids' Mazes Book
Everything® Kids' Money Book
Everything® Kids' Nature Book

**Everything® Kids' Pirates Puzzle and
    Activity Book**
Everything® Kids' Puzzle Book
Everything® Kids' Riddles & Brain Teasers Book
Everything® Kids' Science Experiments Book
Everything® Kids' Sharks Book
Everything® Kids' Soccer Book
Everything® Kids' Travel Activity Book

KIDS' STORY BOOKS

Everything® Fairy Tales Book

LANGUAGE

Everything® Conversational Japanese Book
    (with CD), $19.95
Everything® French Grammar Book
Everything® French Phrase Book, $9.95
Everything® French Verb Book, $9.95
**Everything® German Practice Book with
    CD, $19.95**
Everything® Inglés Book
Everything® Learning French Book
Everything® Learning German Book
Everything® Learning Italian Book
Everything® Learning Latin Book
Everything® Learning Spanish Book
Everything® Sign Language Book
Everything® Spanish Grammar Book
Everything® Spanish Phrase Book, $9.95
Everything® Spanish Practice Book
    (with CD), $19.95
Everything® Spanish Verb Book, $9.95

MUSIC

Everything® Drums Book (with CD), $19.95
Everything® Guitar Book
**Everything® Guitar Chords Book with CD,
    $19.95**
Everything® Home Recording Book
Everything® Playing Piano and Keyboards
    Book
Everything® Reading Music Book (with CD),
    $19.95
Everything® Rock & Blues Guitar Book
    (with CD), $19.95
Everything® Songwriting Book

NEW AGE

Everything® Astrology Book, 2nd Ed.
Everything® Dreams Book, 2nd Ed.
Everything® Love Signs Book, $9.95

Everything® Numerology Book
Everything® Paganism Book
Everything® Palmistry Book
Everything® Psychic Book
Everything® Reiki Book
Everything® Tarot Book
Everything® Wicca and Witchcraft Book

PARENTING

Everything® Baby Names Book, 2nd Ed.
Everything® Baby Shower Book
Everything® Baby's First Food Book
Everything® Baby's First Year Book
Everything® Birthing Book
Everything® Breastfeeding Book
Everything® Father-to-Be Book
Everything® Father's First Year Book
Everything® Get Ready for Baby Book
Everything® Get Your Baby to Sleep Book,
    $9.95
Everything® Getting Pregnant Book
Everything® Homeschooling Book
Everything® Mother's First Year Book
Everything® Parent's Guide to Children
    and Divorce
Everything® Parent's Guide to Children
    with ADD/ADHD
Everything® Parent's Guide to Children
    with Asperger's Syndrome
Everything® Parent's Guide to Children
    with Autism
Everything® Parent's Guide to Children with
    Bipolar Disorder
Everything® Parent's Guide to Children
    with Dyslexia
Everything® Parent's Guide to Positive
    Discipline
Everything® Parent's Guide to Raising a
    Successful Child
**Everything® Parent's Guide to Raising
    Boys**
**Everything® Parent's Guide to Raising
    Siblings**
Everything® Parent's Guide to Tantrums
Everything® Parent's Guide to the Overweight
    Child
Everything® Parent's Guide to the Strong-
    Willed Child
Everything® Parenting a Teenager Book
Everything® Potty Training Book, $9.95
Everything® Pregnancy Book, 2nd Ed.

Bolded titles are new additions to the series.
All Everything® books are priced at $12.95 or $14.95, unless otherwise stated. Prices subject to change without notice.

Everything® Pregnancy Fitness Book
Everything® Pregnancy Nutrition Book
Everything® Pregnancy Organizer, $15.00
Everything® Toddler Book
Everything® Toddler Activities Book
Everything® Tween Book
Everything® Twins, Triplets, and More Book

PETS

Everything® Boxer Book
Everything® Cat Book, 2nd Ed.
Everything® Chihuahua Book
Everything® Dachshund Book
Everything® Dog Book
Everything® Dog Health Book
Everything® Dog Training and Tricks Book
Everything® German Shepherd Book
Everything® Golden Retriever Book
Everything® Horse Book
Everything® Horse Care Book
Everything® Horseback Riding Book
Everything® Labrador Retriever Book
Everything® Poodle Book
Everything® Pug Book
Everything® Puppy Book
Everything® Rottweiler Book
Everything® Small Dogs Book
Everything® Tropical Fish Book
Everything® Yorkshire Terrier Book

REFERENCE

Everything® Car Care Book
Everything® Classical Mythology Book
Everything® Computer Book
Everything® Divorce Book
Everything® Einstein Book
Everything® Etiquette Book, 2nd Ed.
Everything® Inventions and Patents Book
Everything® Mafia Book
Everything® Mary Magdalene Book
 Everything® Philosophy Book
Everything® Psychology Book
Everything® Shakespeare Book

RELIGION

Everything® Angels Book
Everything® Bible Book
Everything® Buddhism Book
Everything® Catholicism Book

Everything® Christianity Book
Everything® Freemasons Book
Everything® History of the Bible Book
Everything® Jewish History & Heritage Book
Everything® Judaism Book
Everything® Kabbalah Book
Everything® Koran Book
Everything® Prayer Book
Everything® Saints Book
Everything® Torah Book
Everything® Understanding Islam Book
Everything® World's Religions Book
Everything® Zen Book

SCHOOL & CAREERS

Everything® Alternative Careers Book
Everything® College Major Test Book
Everything® College Survival Book, 2nd Ed.
Everything® Cover Letter Book, 2nd Ed.
Everything® Get-a-Job Book
Everything® Guide to Being a Paralegal
Everything® Guide to Being a Real Estate Agent
Everything® Guide to Starting and Running a Restaurant
Everything® Job Interview Book
Everything® New Nurse Book
Everything® New Teacher Book
Everything® Paying for College Book
Everything® Practice Interview Book
Everything® Resume Book, 2nd Ed.
Everything® Study Book
Everything® Teacher's Organizer, $16.95

SELF-HELP

Everything® Dating Book, 2nd Ed.
Everything® Great Sex Book
Everything® Kama Sutra Book
Everything® Self-Esteem Book

SPORTS & FITNESS

Everything® Fishing Book
Everything® Golf Instruction Book
Everything® Pilates Book
Everything® Running Book
Everything® Total Fitness Book
Everything® Weight Training Book
Everything® Yoga Book

TRAVEL

Everything® Family Guide to Hawaii
Everything® Family Guide to Las Vegas, 2nd Ed.
Everything® Family Guide to New York City, 2nd Ed.
Everything® Family Guide to RV Travel & Campgrounds
Everything® Family Guide to the Walt Disney World Resort®, Universal Studios®, and Greater Orlando, 4th Ed.
Everything® Family Guide to Cruise Vacations
Everything® Family Guide to the Caribbean
Everything® Family Guide to Washington D.C., 2nd Ed.
Everything® Guide to New England
Everything® Travel Guide to the Disneyland Resort®, California Adventure®, Universal Studios®, and the Anaheim Area

WEDDINGS

Everything® Bachelorette Party Book, $9.95
Everything® Bridesmaid Book, $9.95
Everything® Elopement Book, $9.95
Everything® Father of the Bride Book, $9.95
Everything® Groom Book, $9.95
Everything® Mother of the Bride Book, $9.95
Everything® Outdoor Wedding Book
Everything® Wedding Book, 3rd Ed.
Everything® Wedding Checklist, $9.95
Everything® Wedding Etiquette Book, $9.95
Everything® Wedding Organizer, $15.00
Everything® Wedding Shower Book, $9.95
Everything® Wedding Vows Book, $9.95
Everything® Weddings on a Budget Book, $9.95

WRITING

Everything® Creative Writing Book
Everything® Get Published Book, 2nd Ed.
Everything® Grammar and Style Book
Everything® Guide to Writing a Book Proposal
Everything® Guide to Writing a Novel
Everything® Guide to Writing Children's Books
Everything® Guide to Writing Research Papers
Everything® Screenwriting Book
Everything® Writing Poetry Book
Everything® Writing Well Book